SAGE was founded in 1965 by Sara Miller McCune to support the dissemination of usable knowledge by publishing innovative and high-quality research and teaching content. Today, we publish over 900 journals, including those of more than 400 learned societies, more than 800 new books per year, and a growing range of library products including archives, data, case studies, reports, and video. SAGE remains majority-owned by our founder, and after Sara's lifetime will become owned by a charitable trust that secures our continued independence.

Los Angeles | London | New Delhi | Singapore | Washington DC | Melbourne

EVOLUTION
of
BANKING
SYSTEM
IN INDIA
since
1900

EVOLUTION
of
BANKING SYSTEM
IN INDIA
since
1900

O. P. CHAWLA

Los Angeles I London I New Delhi
Singapore I Washington DC I Melbourne

First published in 2019 by

 SAGE Publications India Pvt Ltd
B1/I-1 Mohan Cooperative Industrial Area
Mathura Road, New Delhi 110 044, India
www.sagepub.in

SAGE Publications Inc
2455 Teller Road
Thousand Oaks, California 91320, USA

SAGE Publications Ltd
1 Oliver's Yard, 55 City Road
London EC1Y 1SP, United Kingdom

SAGE Publications Asia-Pacific Pte Ltd
18 Cross Street #10-10/11/12
China Square Central
Singapore 048423

Published by Vivek Mehra for SAGE Publications India Pvt Ltd. Typeset in 10.5/13 pt Adobe Caslon Pro by Zaza Eunice, Hosur, Tamil Nadu, India.

Library of Congress Cataloging-in-Publication Data Available

ISBN: 978-93-532-8467-1 (HB)

SAGE Team: Rajesh Dey, Guneet Kaur, Arshita Saxena and Rajinder Kaur

In the memory of my wife

Santosh

who is no more

Contents

List of Tables

List of Statements in Annexures

List of Abbreviations

AIRCSC	All-India Rural Credit Survey Committee
ALM	Asset-Liability Management
ATMs	automated teller machines
BC	Business Correspondent
BCA	Banking Companies Act
BF	Business Facilitator
BIS	Bank for International Settlements
BPLR	benchmark prime lending rates
BRA	The Banking Regulation Act
BS	Balance sheet
BSR	Basic Statistical Returns
CA	capital adequacy
CAGR	compound annual growth rate
CASA	current and savings bank accounts
CASA–DEP	CASA Deposits–Total Deposits ratio
C-BSR	Committee on Banking Sector Reforms
C–D	Credit–Deposit
C-FAB	Committee to Consider Final Accounts of Banks
CFS	Committee on the Financial System
C–I	cost–income
CRAR	capital to risk-adjusted assets ratio
CRR	Cash Reserve Ratio
CSBS	Common Size Balance Sheet
DCP	District Credit Plan
DRI	Differential Rate of Interest Scheme
EPS	earnings per share

FDI	foreign direct investment
FIIs	foreign institutional investors
FRA	Financial Restructuring Authority
GNPAs	Gross non-performing advances
GOI	Government of India
I–C	Investment–credit
ICT	Information and Communication Technology
I–D	Investment–Deposit
IBA	Indian Banks' Association
IJSBs	Indian Joint Stock Banks
Imperial/Imperial Bank	Imperial Bank of India
LBS	Lead Bank Scheme
NEFT	national electronic fund transfer
NIBM	National Institute of Bank Management
NII	Net interest income
NIM	Net Interest Margin
NNPAs	Net non-performing advances
NPAs	non-performing advances
NRI	non-resident Indian
OP	Operating profit
PAT	profit after tax
PBT	profit before tax
PLA	Profit and Loss Account
PNB	Punjab National Bank
PrSBG	Private Sector Banks Group
PrSBs	private sector banks
PSBG	Public Sector Banks Group
PSBs	public sector banks
PSL	priority sector lending
RB	Rural banking
RBEC	Rural Banking Enquiry Committee
RBI	Reserve Bank of India
ROA	return on assets
ROE	return on equity

RRBs	Regional Rural Banks
RTGS	real time gross settlement
SBI	State Bank of India
SCBs	Scheduled Commercial Banks
SLR	Statutory Liquidity Ratio
SSI	small scale industries
ST	Statistical Tables Relating to Banks in India
TA	Total Assets
TP	Trend and Progress of Banking in India
TSCBs	Total Scheduled Commercial Banks
UCO	United Commercial Bank
WWI	World War I
WWII	World War II
YOY	year over year

Foreword

The banking industry is passing through some interesting times at the present moment. The level of non-performing assets, particularly those of the public sector banks (PSBs), has reached alarming proportions, threatening the stability of the financial sector. Even though the government has belatedly introduced the Insolvency Code to deal with this problem, it still remains to be seen whether the judicial delays arising out of the litigation of the promoters involved in such enterprises, who might be deprived of their ownership and management rights, would make this effort ineffectual. The initial few cases resolved through this process, even though delayed beyond their stipulated period, have given hopes that this process will not go the same way as the earlier efforts made by the government.

The attention of the media is naturally focused on these issues as well as on those concerning the turf battle between the government and the Reserve Bank of India (RBI) with regard to the autonomy and independence of RBI. In the process, the issues which have given rise to the present situation have been pushed to the background. Unless the root cause of the present problem is resolved, there is every possibility of the crises emerging from time to time, unsettling the stability of the financial system.

If one were to go through the history of the banking industry, it is possible to identify three distinct game changers. The first is the nationalization of the Imperial Bank of India in 1955 to form the State Bank of India (SBI). The second is the nationalization of major PSBs in two phases beginning with 1969. The third is the reform process initiated in 1991 leading to the opening of the doors of the banking industry to private players.

The nationalization of the Imperial Bank of India was very much on the cards since Independence and one could only wonder why the decision took such a long time. There were acrimonious discussions between RBI and the government, on the one hand, and with the management of the Imperial Bank of India on the other. The SBI legislation that finally emerged was indeed a remarkable document which, while recognizing the right of the government to intervene in public interest, also ensured that the business operations of the bank were left in the hands of the board and the management. The government dealt with the SBI not directly, but through the medium of RBI, and in due course, the SBI emerged as a strong bank, professionally managed with strong financial stability.

The SBI also fulfilled its public purpose of extending the branch network beyond the tier I cities and district headquarters, and initiated the process of making available banking services to a much larger group of people, instead of confining itself to the 'elite' as was prevailing at that time. Meeting the requirements of the farmers by extending credit to agriculture, which was the major purpose of nationalization, still remained a far cry. During this period, the government continued to focus on the cooperative sector as a medium of extending credit in the rural areas and the State Bank's role was limited to extending refinance to the cooperative system. While this ensured that the financial stability of the State Bank was in no way impaired as the loans to the cooperative sectors had the implicit guarantee of the state governments, thanks to the inefficiency of the cooperative movement, the needs of the farming community were hardly met and lending to the farmers continued to be dominated by the money lenders at usurious rates of interest.

One area in which the SBI achieved notable success was the extension of credit to the small and the medium enterprises as mandated by the government. The needs of this sector were, however, so large that the State Bank's attempts in this direction though significant were found to be grossly inadequate and this sector also continued to be funded by the informal sector.

The nationalization of the PSBs was mainly seen as a power play by the then minority government to usher in a more vigorous socialist era in the economy. Nevertheless, it also simultaneously served a sound economic purpose in reforming the industry, which was till then owned and managed by the business houses primarily for meeting their own business ends. The newly nationalized PSBs were expected to extend the branch network into remote areas, fulfil the financial needs of the farming community and also extend credit to the small and medium enterprises. There was, however, a paradigm shift by the government in the management of the newly nationalized public sector banks. While the SBI enjoyed a measure of internal autonomy with regard to its business operations, the government took a decision much to the discomfort of RBI, to manage the PSBs directly, and introduced a separate department in the central government consisting of a full set of bureaucrats for this purpose. The direct management of the PSBs was to result in the politicization of the banking industry. In due course of time, the SBI was also to be treated just like other PSBs under the direct control of the central government and RBI's oversight was limited to the periodical inspection of the banks to protect the interest of the depositors. The government set unrealistic targets with regard to the extension of credit to agriculture and small-scale enterprises, and the banking industry was ill equipped to meet the demands made on it and conduct the lending operations with any degree of professionalism. This resulted in massive non-performing assets in these sectors which were pushed under the carpet to maintain a modicum of stability.

The third game changer was opening the doors of the industry to the private players in 1991. This was also the time when, in line with what was happening in the rest of the world, the country's economic model went through a change. 'Liberalization' and 'globalization' became the catch phrases of the new model of development, and it was widely expected that the government would give up the control and ownership over the banking industry and allow it to run on professional lines. However, the government contented itself to merely opening the doors to new private players and did not disturb the nationalized sector. With the abolition of the Permit and License Raj, private players were allowed to set up industries without the approval of the government. In the initial years of the reform process, there was a rapid growth in the industrial development, and the banking industry kept pace with the growth by expanding their operations to private industrial entrepreneurs. Here again, as in the agriculture and small-scale sectors, banks, except the few like SBI and the new private players, lacked professional capabilities of ensuring adequate safeguards in their lending operations. In the emergence of some unscrupulous promoters, rashness and adventurism in pushing ahead for growth along with continued political interference added further to an already difficult situation. Thanks to the lax accounting standards, these bad debts were also pushed under the carpet. There was, however, no crisis of confidence, as given the ownership of the government, the public depositors believed rightly that their deposits carried the implicit guarantee of the government.

Since the year 2000, one of the major developments in the banking industry has been the introduction of mechanization on a large scale. The technological transformation of the industry in turn led to a massive expansion. In recent times, the digitization wave accelerated this process considerably. Although, with respect to technology, the banking industry is seemingly at par with the more developed economies, in practical terms, there is a huge gap in the depth of the financial sector in India. More particularly, while the equity market has shown an impressive growth, there is a total absence of the bond market, and banking continued to be the major ingredient of the financial sector unlike in the more developed economies. There exists a significant gap in the composition of the financial sector between India and the rest of the developed world. Much ground needs to be covered, and the banking industry and the financial sector are still in the process of transition. A lot of attention has been paid to financial inclusion and extending the range of banking activities to the remotest corners of the country, but despite several new initiatives, a viable solution still eludes the policymakers.

Chawla's book in chronicling the events in the evolution of the banking industry since 1900 would turn out to be a significant contribution in this respect. Chawla has been associated with banking and finance in India as a researcher and teacher. I knew him personally since the mid-1970s as a colleague at the National Institute of Bank Management (NIBM) and I had always a high regard for his intellectual capability and willingness to apply himself assiduously to the task. He subsequently became the director of the NIBM and performed his function with distinction.

This book, which he has brought out, is a monumental exercise, and the amount of research involved in writing this book and the huge amount of data which he has collected by digging into old records are truly impressive. I have been familiar with the books on the histories of SBI and RBI, but I had not come across a comprehensive history of the rest of the industry. There have, of course, been interesting autobiographical accounts of bankers narrating their experiences, but apart from this, I am not sure whether a comprehensive narration of the history of Indian banking exists.

Any study of history serves a dual purpose. One is to record the chronology of events as it took place for the benefit of posterity. But more importantly, the true purpose of history is to draw lessons from the past with a view to avoid the pitfalls and mistakes that have occurred from time to time in the past. I am sure that this book by Chawla would not only be of use to the students of banking and finance but also to the policymakers in shaping the future of the industry.

Narayanan Vaghul, Padma Bhushan (2009)
Former Chairman and Managing Director of ICICI Bank
and Bank of India

Preface

Raison d'être

Here, we intend to introduce the broad contours of this book. This book is a piece of research on 117 years, 1900–2016-17, of the evolution of Indian commercial banking. The literature on this subject, to our knowledge, has missed on analytical studies of the major Indian events of the 20th century and the early years of the 21st century that have significantly impacted the banking system to change the course of its history. Thus, it is a fact that, until Independence and the enactment of the Banking Companies Act in 1949, available data on the financials of this industry was very scanty. This is also a fact that the available financial data on Indian banking till the advent of the 21st century had not been collected and presented for analysis. This book seeks to fill these large gaps.

The book focuses on significant events and macro bank-financials which have influenced the path of development of the Indian commercial banking system the most since 1900 and before. There are three landmark set of events which have been analysed at length.

One set of events, which had its origin in the 1950s, was the shift by RBI to direct instruments of credit and monetary policy. This shift was so heavy that it transformed the banking industry into an over-regulated system with seriously adverse consequences for banking and the economy of the country. This policy mechanism lasted for over 30 years.

The second transformative event was the nationalization of the major segment of the banking system. Nationalization was the strategy to achieve dual revolutionary changes: one was to take the banks to the poorest in rural and tribal undeveloped parts of the country. Rural banking and priority sector lending changed the face of Indian banking forever, as these programmes linked the Indian banking system to what we have termed as the 'national purpose'. The second purpose was to break the nexus between banking industry and 'big business' and thus change the future path of the Indian economy forever.

The third transformation was the deregulation and liberalization of the banking system. Begun by RBI in the early 1980s by way of small solitary steps, the Government of India (GOI) converted reforms into a torrent of deregulatory measures in the early 1990s. It liberated the banking system from the over-regulatory regime.

It should be noted that this study is not a history of banking. It does not seek to encompass all events of this vast and complex subject spread over more than a century. The study also does not cover the microfinancials of the banking system which would include the study of individual banks, a herculean task, apart from the fact that relevant information on each bank would be hard, if not impossible, to come by.

Modus Operandi

A major task this piece of research had to accomplish was to search and collect the required bank data. All the relevant financial and related data were searched and collected from several institutional libraries. It was quite difficult to fill the gaping holes in the financials of the banking sector. The collected bank financial data, available in diverse forms and formats, was converted to uniform formats. An equally major task was to carry out an in-depth analyses of those financials using the methods of accounting, finance and financial analysis. A comprehensive assessment of nearly 120 years of the financial journey of Indian commercial banking has been covered in six chapters. Additionally, another chapter titled 'Epilogue' has been added after the sixth chapter.

The study is divided into the following six periods: (a) 1900–1946, (b) 1947–1949, (c) 1950–1968, (d) 1969–1990-91, (e) 1991-92–2010-11 and (f) 2011-12–2016-17. The choice of the periods is made almost automatically by significant and/or historical dividers. A description and analysis of main developments in the commercial banking system in each of the six periods is made. This covers major policy, structural, regulatory and legislative changes that had formed the background as well as the springboard of banks' working, followed by detailed analyses of the significant financials of the SCBs. These analyses, hopefully, bring out the relevant history, achievements and weaknesses of the banking system; in a nutshell, the study provides the essence of Indian banking developments during 117 years since 1900.

It may not be out of place to point out that, to our knowledge, such a magnitude of bank data for such a long period has not been put together before. It has been assembled and arranged on a uniform and consistent platform to yield an accurate, comparable and conceptually sound data bank for future researchers.

Principal Sources of Bank Data

It is appropriate to describe the 'Principal Sources of Bank Data' here. The purpose is to minimize the inconvenience to the reader of referring to the lengthy notes at the end of the chapters. Most of the primary data for the study have been sourced from two annual publications of RBI. Repeated references to these publications will have to be made, but the inconvenience to the reader will be minimized by describing them here. It will allow the reader to enjoy the flow of the argument of the book smoothly.

1. '*Statistical Tables Relating to Banks in India*' is very often the only source of the early financial history of Indian banking. It was published for the first time by the GOI in 1915 incorporating banking data for the year 1913 and a few preceding years. It is the

only and the richest source of bank data, drawn mainly from banks' self-drawn and non-prescribed financial statements from 1913 to 1947. This publication is principally focused on the aggregates of the Indian banking system, and, in later years, on some bank groups of this system. Most of the data relating to financials of Indian banks in this book have been taken from these *Statistical Tables*. *Statistical Tables* were published by the GOI from 1915 to 1938. This task was transferred to RBI from 1939. Since then, RBI continues to publish it annually.

The two sources, that is, GOI and RBI are described as below:

(a) *Statistical Tables Relating to Banks in India*, 1913–1938, Government of India, Department of Statistics/Commercial Intelligence and Statistics, Calcutta/New Delhi.

(b) *Statistical Tables Relating to Banks in India*, 1939 onwards, Reserve Bank of India, Mumbai.

In the book, this publication is referred to as **ST** along with the year to which it relates. For example, ST relating to the year 1913 will be referred to as *ST 1913*, although it was published in 1915.

Let me add a story. Wherefrom were the ST data for about a century collected? The only source was RBI's Central Office Library at Mumbai. My several visits to that library resulted in the location of a minefield of banking data since the origin of *ST* in 1913. I was able to locate the earliest published editions of ST and to take notes from them. Securing it all was a great pleasure. Several STs of later years had been consulted from the library of NIBM, Pune.

A fuller story of this publication from 1913, its contents and formats and changes therein, and steps taken to harmonize its data for use in this book, is told in the appendix at the end of the book.

2. Report on *Trend and Progress of Banking in India* was the second most important RBI publication for the book. The Banking Companies Act enacted in 1949, required RBI to submit the *Report on Trend and Progress of Banking in India*. The first such report was published for the year 1949 and since then has been published annually. While *ST* is mostly a compendium of

summarized financial statements and related financials of banks, *Trend and Progress* not only supplements the financial information in *STs* but also reviews the annual performance and developments in the banking industry.

Trend and Progress is referred to as **TP**, in the book with the year for which it has been published.

3. 'History of the Reserve Bank of India'

RBI's *History of the Reserve Bank of India* in four volumes to date contains significant information about the activities of RBI vis-à-vis the GOI and the banking system. This inside information is not available anywhere else. Its detailed narration of events has been used extensively at several places in the book. References to these volumes have been made as follows:

(a) **Volume 1:** *History of the Reserve Bank of India (1935–1951), Reserve Bank of India, Bombay, 1970.*

It is referred to as: **RBI History-1.**

(b) **Volume 2:** *The Reserve Bank of India, 1951–1967, G. Balachandran, Oxford University Press, New Delhi, 1998.*

It is referred to as: **RBI History-2.**

(c) **Volume 3:** *The Reserve Bank of India,* Volume 3, 1967–1981, Reserve Bank of India, Mumbai, 2005.

It is referred to as: **RBI History-3.**

(d) **Volume 4:** *The Reserve Bank of India,* Volume 4, 1981–1987, Academic Foundation, New Delhi, 2013.

It is referred to as: **RBI History-4.**

4. *Evolution of Banking in India, Chapter III,* pp. 76–141, *Report on Currency and Finance,* 2006–08, Volume I, Reserve Bank of India, Mumbai, 2008. It is referred to as **C&F-1.**

Acknowledgements

I greatly cherish the love and affection of my daughters Anita, Sunita and Veena, sons-in-law Rajeev, Sanjay and Rishikesh, and grandchildren Amolika, Saloni, Sonali, Nidhi and Neha, that has sustained me throughout this academic effort.

It is with great pleasure that I sincerely acknowledge the invaluable assistance by my close friends and well-wishers Messrs Rameshwar Kabra, Sunil Goyal and Manoj Singrodia. They willingly provided me with skilled support from time to time for entry, tabulation and computation of piles of bank data to prepare it for my analysis. I am very grateful to them.

Much of the required bank data and other information available in the RBI publications could be taken from the NIBM Library, Pune. But there were large gaps. The missing annual reports of *Statistical Tables Relating to Banks in India* and *Trend and Progress of Banking in India* were available in the central library of RBI, Mumbai. It was gratifying to find *Statistical Tables* of 1913, the first published number, and the following years at that library. I must specially thank Ms Aruna Joshi, the deputy librarian of that library, who was my direct contact and was most helpful. I also wish to thank Dr Rajib Lochan Sahoo, chief archivist of the Pune office of RBI, for his assistance in securing soft copies of several of these reports.

Finally, but most importantly, I am grateful to Shri N. Vaghul for writing the Foreword for my book.

1

Pre-Independence Period (1900–1946)
Evolution of Commercial Banking

Our story of Indian commercial banking begins with the coverage of its evolution in the pre-1947 20th century. Two Indian banks, Allahabad Bank and Punjab National Bank (PNB), were established in the 19th century. The launch of the Swadeshi movement propelled the establishment of seven more Indian joint stock banks (IJSBs) between 1906 and 1911. But this chapter makes a quick journey from Indian banking's unorganized and indigenous beginnings much earlier than the nineteenth century to its status as less disorganised and faster growing system by the end of 1946. On the way, it attempts to fill wide gaps in its evolution including financials, in pursuance of one of the main purposes of this research effort. In doing so, it also strengthens the roots of the early history of Indian banking and builds a bridge to the path of banking in independent India.

I. PRE-20TH-CENTURY ERA

1.1. Indigenous 'Banks'

It is well known that several types of institutions in an 'unorganized' banking sector had existed in India for several centuries.

> According to the Central Banking Enquiry Committee, 1931, money-lending activity in India could be traced back to the *Vedic* period, i.e., 2000 to 1400 BC .... [A member of] the Royal Commission on Indian Currency and Finance (1926) had observed 'it may be accepted that a system of banking that was eminently suited to India's then requirements was in force in that country many centuries before the science of banking became an accomplished fact in England.' An extensive network of Indian banking houses existed in the country connecting all cities/towns that were of commercial importance.[1]

In villages, landlords often operated as moneylenders both for production and consumption purposes.

Moving closer to the 20th century, the term 'bank' was used, for several decades, as an undefined omnibus term under whose umbrella fell many loan companies, indigenous bankers, nidhis and other moneylenders who used *hundis* and other financial instruments in their deposit-taking and lending operations. Their numbers were believed to be very large, but hardly any documented records were said to be available. With the passing of the Companies Act, many of these entities got themselves registered under this law, presumably to reap the benefits of limited liability.

According to the Indian Central Banking Enquiry Committee again, the banking system in India in 1930 comprised 1,258 banking institutions registered under the Indian Companies Act, 1913.[2] Table 1.5 shows that there were 88 ('A' and 'B' Classes) IJSBs in

1930. It may therefore be derived that there were 1,170 other 'banks' registered under the Companies Act in that year. Besides, there were other obviously much larger number of smaller 'banks' that did not register themselves.[3] There were, no doubt, an even larger number of 'unregistered' moneylenders operating in the villages. It can only mean that 'other banks' were a huge unknown number.

At the time of its establishment in 1934, the Reserve Bank of India (RBI, hereinafter) was required to make concrete proposals for the linking of the indigenous bankers and moneylenders with the organized money market. The intent was that the services of the indigenous bankers and moneylenders should, after the suitable adaptation of their methods, be utilized in any scheme for the provision of credit to the economy. But there was hardly any positive development in this respect. The bone of contention was that RBI, rightly, wanted indigenous bankers to shed their non-banking businesses as a prerequisite to the 'link-up'. But indigenous bankers were not agreeable to do so.[4]

1.2. Western-Style Banking

The Western-style banking based on joint-stock ownership was initiated in India by the English agency houses in the early 18th century. (Government) Bank of Bombay (some called it Bombay Bank) was the first such bank to be established in Bombay (now Mumbai) in 1720 by the East India Company. The government decided to close it down around the year 1770 because the bank could not repay its debts. Bank of Hindustan was the next bank to be set up in Calcutta (now Kolkata) in 1770. This bank was closed down in 1832. Another bank to be opened in this century, on the proposal of the then Governor Warren Hastings, named the General Bank of Bengal and Bahar (later, Bihar), too had a short life.

Two Indian banks which were established in the 19th century are as follows:

1. Allahabad Bank, the oldest joint-stock bank of the country, was founded on 24 April 1865 at Allahabad. It was the first Indian-owned bank.[5] In 1923, it was taken over by the P&O Banking Corporation and its head office was shifted to Calcutta on business considerations.
2. PNB was established by a group of Indians at Lahore in 1894.

1.3. Presidency Banks

The 19th century dawned with the establishment of the first 'Presidency bank' in 1806. *The Bank of Bengal,* Calcutta came into being on the back of the felt-need for modern banking services as trading operations of East India Company expanded, and for remittances by British army and civil personnel. This bank began with a capital of ₹5 million,[6] 20 per cent of which was subscribed by the government. One of the tasks of the bank was to discount treasury bills. The bank had the power to issue notes since 1823. This was followed by the establishment of the other two Presidency banks: the Bank of Bombay in 1840 with a capital of ₹5.2 million and 'the Bank of Madras' in 1843 with a capital of ₹3.0 million. All the three banks were thus partly owned by the government. These banks were known as Presidency banks as they were set up in the three presidency towns of Calcutta, Bombay and Madras (now Chennai). From the year 1876, the three Presidency banks were governed under a common Act. Under this law, certain types of businesses were prohibited and periodic inspection of banks was instituted. At the same time, the partial ownership of the government was terminated. But these banks continued to perform some of the central banking functions.[7]

G. Findlay Shirras wrote an Introductory Memorandum in *Statistical Tables 1915* (see Section II; hereinafter, ST will be used for *Statistical Tables*) in which he observed about Presidency banks, 'There are … the three Presidency banks which enjoy the prestige of antiquity, and, one might also say, of official dignity derived from acting as bankers to Government'.[8] But the statement of the State Bank of India (SBI) is more revealing:

> The Banks of Bengal, Bombay and Madras established in the 3 presidencies of British India were primarily British creations. They were occasioned both by the compulsions of imperial finance and the felt needs of European commerce in the East. The British naturally looked upon them as instruments of colonial power and bestowed on them privileges which were unknown to Indian banking till then.[9]

1.4. Exchange Banks

Statistical Tables 1913 stated that there were three exchange banks with deposits of ₹5.2 million in India in 1870, the earliest year for which a little banking data was available. Exchange banks were foreign banks in India engaged mainly in the financing of foreign trade of the country. These European banks, whose head offices were located outside India, were of two types: (a) those which did a considerable portion of their business in India, such as the National Bank of India (1863) and the Chartered Bank of India, Australia and China (1853); and (b) those which were mere agencies of large banking entities doing business all over Asia. Both types financed the country's internal trade also, especially for moving goods between port towns and the interior. At the close of the year 1946, there were 15 exchange banks in India operating through 77 branches and had ₹1,812.8 million of deposits (see Table 1.5).

II. PRE-INDEPENDENCE 20TH CENTURY

1.5. Swadeshi Movement: New Indian Banks

The 20th century dawned with the launch of the Swadeshi movement in 1906. It germinated from the nationalist movement which was taking hold in the country. Swadeshi provided an impetus to Indians to establish their national banks. Even banks were established one after another between 1906 and 1911, four of them in 1906 alone (see Table 1.3):

1. Canara Banking Corporation (later renamed as Corporation Bank)
2. Punjab & Sind Bank
3. Canara Bank
4. Bank of India
5. Indian Bank
6. Bank of Baroda
7. Central Bank of India

These banks, along with Allahabad Bank and PNB, came to be called IJSBs and were distinct from Presidency banks and exchange banks, in as much as they were registered under the Companies Act, were started by Indians, and had their head offices in India.

1.6. First Official Bank Data: ST 1913

Till around the beginning of the 1900s, the Government of India (GOI) did not have any reliable information about the banking system in the country and its working. Whatever little it had was not put out in the public domain. A banking crisis arose in September 1913 in northern and western India with the failure of People's Bank of India in Punjab. When the government found that a large number of banks had failed in 1913 and 1914, it ordered a statistical enquiry into bank failures. When the results became available, the government decided to publish them. The outcome was the *Statistical Tables Relating to Banks in India*' for the year 1913, published in 1915 (abbreviated as ST 1913, with the year to which it relates, not the year of its publication). The opening paragraph of the Introductory Memorandum of ST 1913 states:

> The object of the statistical tables appended to this memorandum is to show in detail the latest available statistics relating to banking, and the results of a statistical enquiry into bank failures in India in 1913 and 1914.
>
> The statistics relating to working of these banks have been furnished direct by the banks in India, except in the case of Exchange Banks, the returns of which have been obtained through His Majesty's Secretary of State for India.
>
> The statistics relating to bank failures in each province have been obtained from local authorities.[10]

It is educative to look at the first-ever data on banks in India given in Tables 1.1 and 1.2, as published in STs 1913, 1915 and 1917.

1.6.1. Bank Failures

Table 1.1 shows the month-wise bank failures for 12 months from November 1913 till November 1914. Dates of 10 bank failures were presumably not known. All the failed banks were IJSBs.

The extent of bank failures can be gauged with reference to the actual number of banks in existence. This is illustrated below for the year 1914:

1. Number of banks on 1 January 1914   = 41
2. Number of failed banks in 1914   = 42
3. Number of banks on 31 December 1914   = 42
4. Number of new banks set up in 1914 (derived) = 43

Table 1.1 *Bank Failures: 1913–1914*

Month/Year	Number of IJSBs Failed	Paid-up Capital (₹000)
November 1913	7	2,591
December	5	922
January 1914	2	121
February	3	159
March	8	7,708
April	3	66
May	1	18
June	4	227
July	4	355
August	1	4
September	4	903
October	4	144
November	1	32
Months unspecified	10	1,189
Total	57	14,439

Source: ST 1913, Table 5, p. 6.

Note: Subsequent editions of STs corrected the number of bank failures in 1914 from 45 in this Table, first to 43 and later to 42.

Thus, the number of failed banks in 1914 was more than the total number of banks in existence at the beginning of the year. Again, equally interestingly, new banks were being set up as fast as existing banks were failing. Could it be that new banks were being set up by the promoters of the failed banks, with ulterior motives?

1.6.2. Banks and their Deposits

Table 1.2 provides data on the number of banks and their deposits for six select years during the years 1870–1913.

Table 1.2 *Select Bank Data: 1870–1913*

	Presidency Banks		IJSBs		Exchange Banks		Total Banks	
Year	No. of Banks	Deposits (₹ in Lakhs)	No. of Banks	Deposits (₹ in Lakhs)	No. of Banks	Deposits (₹ in Lakhs)	No. of Banks	Deposits (₹ in Lakhs)
1870	3	1,183	2	14	3	52	8	1,249
1880	3	1,140	3	63	4	340	10	1,543
1890	3	1,836	5	271	5	754	13	2,861
1900	3	1,569	9	808	8	1,050	20	3,427
1910	3	3,654	16	2,566	11	2,479	30	8,699
1913	3	4,237	41	2,410	12	3,104	56	9,751

Sources: ST 1915, Tables 1–3, pp. 4–5; ST 1917, Table 3, p. 16.

Note: For the years 1870–1910, data for IJSBs is for large (ST 1913)/or principal (ST 1915) banks (capital of ₹500,000 and above).[11] For 1913, data is for banks with capital of ₹100,000 and above.[12]

1.6.3. The 21st-Century Banks: 1913

Table 1.3 shows those 12 banks (10 banks only, as we treat the three Presidency banks which existed in 1913 as one—Imperial Bank of India, into which these banks had merged in 1921, and which was nationalized in 1955 and given the name of State Bank of India still continues to exist. This list had risen to 42 largest Indian scheduled commercial banks (SCBs) in 1946 including Imperial Bank of India. Any of these banks which got merged into any other of these banks, like the three Presidency banks, is counted as 'continued to exist' at March-end 2011. Some of these banks did get merged into other banks in this list, so that this list had got reduced to 38 banks at the end of 2010–11. It would be interesting to view the movement of these banks in terms of size, that is, (a) balance sheet (BS) size or total assets (TA) and (b) number of branches, among contemporaries over the nearly 100 years, 1913/1946–2011. This will be attempted at the end

Table 1.3 *The 21st-Century Banks: 1913*

(First in the Series)

Bank (Listed in Order of Date of Establishment)	Date of Establishment	Total Deposits (₹ in crore)	Rank (In Terms of Deposits)
1. Imperial Bank of India (1921):			
Three Presidency banks		42.37	1
Bengal	2 June 1806		
Bombay	15 April 1840		
Madras	1 July 1843		
2. Allahabad Bank	17 April 1865	6.77	2
3. PNB	19 May 1894	1.33	4
4. Corporation Bank (Canara Banking Corporation)	26 May 1906	N.A.	–
5. Punjab & Sind Bank	4 June 1906	N.A.	–
6. Canara Bank	30 June 1906	N.A.	–
7. Bank of India	7 September 1906	2.23	3
8. Indian Bank	5 March 1907	N.A.	–
9. Bank of Baroda	20 July 1908	N.A.	–
10. Central Bank of India	21 December 1911	1.15	5

Sources: ST 1915, Table 13; ST 1947, Table 11.

N.A.=Not Available.

Note: The banks in this table are which have been combined into 10, of which deposit figures of only 5 were available.[13] These five banks are ranked on the basis of total deposits. Data of their TA and branches were not available in 1913.

of this and the following four chapters. These 5 tables at the end of 1946, 1949, 1968, 1990–91 and 2010–11 will tell the history of Indian banking and banks in a distinct fashion by depicting the ups and downs of these top banks which have traversed the turbulent landscape of 100 years. Comparative analysis of these banks is attempted in Chapter 6 (that would become the seventh table in the series). This will become part of the history of evolution of the Indian banking system.

1.7. Bank Categories

ST 1915 classified all banks into:

- Presidency banks
- European exchange banks
- IJSBs and
- Private and unincorporated bankers and moneylenders. (Statistics relating to this last class were generally not available.[14])

IJSBs were further classified as below:

1. They were initially divided into two categories by ST 1913 and ST 1915:
   a. ST 1913 referred to banks with capital of ₹500,000 and above as larger banks.
   b. ST 1915 sub-divided these banks into two classes, namely:
      o Class A: those with a capital of ₹500,000 and above, and
      o Class B: those with a capital of between ₹100,000 and less than ₹500,000.

   This classification continued until 1938, the last year for which ST 1938 was published by the GOI.
2. For the publication of the next ST, RBI decided to expand the coverage of banks by collecting statistics of smaller banks, that is,

banks with capital of less than ₹100,000 also in order 'to make the picture of Indian banking as complete as possible'.[15]

At the same time, RBI introduced the classification of banks into scheduled banks and non-scheduled banks. Section 2(e) of the RBI Act, 1934, defines a scheduled bank. It states that a 'scheduled bank' means a bank included in the 'Second Schedule' (of the Act). Section 42(6) of this Act reads that the Bank shall, by notification, direct the inclusion in the Second Schedule of any bank which carries on the business of banking in India and which

- has a capital of an aggregate value of not less than ₹500,000 and
- satisfies the Bank that its affairs are not being conducted in a manner detrimental to the interests of its depositors.

Banks which were not included in the Second Schedule by RBI, even though they had capital of ₹500,000 and above, came to be termed as non-scheduled banks.

3. Thereafter, all the IJSBs came to be re-classified as follows:
   - Class A1: Scheduled banks with capital of ₹500,000 and above and included in the Second Schedule;
   - Class A2: Non-scheduled banks with capital of ₹500,000 and above but not included in the Second Schedule;
   - Class B: Non-scheduled banks with capital of more than ₹100,000 and less than ₹500,000;
   - Class C: Non-scheduled banks with capital of more than ₹50,000 and up to ₹100,000; and
   - Class D: Non-scheduled banks with capital up to ₹50,000.

From the year 1936, Imperial Bank as well as exchange banks also came to be termed as scheduled banks.

1.8. IJSBs under Company Law

1.8.1. The Companies Act, 1850

The first formal legislative reference to banks had occurred when the Companies Act of 1850 was passed. This Act stipulated unlimited liability for banks. Ten years later, in 1860, the Indian law accepted the principle of limited liability following the introduction of this concept in Britain. This led to the establishment of an increased number of banks, many of them with majority shareholdings by Europeans. Allahabad Bank and PNB were two of them.

1.8.2. The Indian Companies Act, 1913

The 1850 Act was replaced by a comprehensive new company law in 1913. The Indian Companies Act, 1913, required that no company, association or partnership consisting of more than 10 persons shall be formed for the purpose of carrying on the business of banking unless it was registered as a company under this Act. The object of this requirement was that, as far as possible, the carrying on of the business of banking must be done by a company registered under this Act so that it will be subject to some legal requirements. The Act provided for such a company to submit a prescribed statement in the Third Schedule to the Act. It also empowered the local government to appoint inspectors to investigate into the affairs of a banking company. Apart from this, there were hardly any provisions special to banks. As a result of this enactment, the number of reporting banks increased from 30 in 1910 to 56 in 1913, 23 of them being smaller banks.

1.8.3. The Indian Companies (Amendment) Act, 1936

The next level of supervision over banks was reached when the Indian Companies (Amendment) Act, 1936, incorporated specific bank-related provisions in a new part of that Act. Besides defining a banking company, it included various provisions which were in accordance with the recommendations of the Indian Central Banking Enquiry Committee (1931). It prohibited banking companies from carrying on business other than that specified in the definition of banking. It put restrictions on the managing agency system in respect of banks. It provided for a minimum paid-up capital of ₹50,000 for banks. These provisions and others sought to reinforce the object of the legislature, viz., the business of banking should, as far as possible, be done by a company which will 'be subject to control and directions which were necessary in the interests of the general public who deposit their money'. Importantly, this Act also required banks to prepare their BS in a specified form as contained in the Third Schedule to the Companies Act; importantly again, this provision was made applicable to Imperial Bank also, a first in the history of Indian banking legislation.

The above amendments, combined with the provisions of the RBI Act which had come into force earlier in July 1935, placed banking law on a better footing.[16]

1.9. Three Global Upheavals

1. The 'World War I' (WWI; 1914–1918) began in July 1914. In the crisis situation created by the war in the months before as well as following its commencement, 45 banks failed in 1914 (revised later to 42; see Table 1.1). Bank failures continued and the number of failed banks in the next 4 years of the war was another 40. But new banks established in the same period were more than the failed ones.

    While the number of large reporting IJSBs was 18 in 1913, it fluctuated between 17 and 20 to finally close at 19 in 1918. As regards small reporting IJSBs, their number increased from 23 in 1913 to 28 in 1918.[17]

2. 'The Great Depression' (1929–1934) 'had an impact on the Indian banking industry with the number of failed banks rising sharply due to their loans going bad. The average size of capital of banks that failed was lower than the average size of the capital of reporting banks in categories A and B indicating that the banks that failed were small'.[18]

3. The effects of the World War II (WWII; 1939–1945) on Indian banking were far-reaching. India became a supply base for the Allied armies. Consequently, government expenditure on defence and supplies to the Allies led to a rapid expansion of currency. This led to the large income increase of some sections of the population.[19] This, in turn, led to the rapid increase in the number of scheduled banks from 56 at the end of 1939 to 62 at the end of 1942 and to 91 at the end of 1945 (excluding Burma); their bank deposits increased from ₹2,400 million at the end of 1939 to ₹4,450 million at the end of 1942 and to ₹9,530 million at the end of 1945.[20] Expansion of branch network of IJSBs was equally rapid. The scheduled banks (other than Imperial Bank and exchange banks) increased their branches from 677 in 1938 to 844 in 1940 and to 2,451 in 1945. The non-scheduled banks increased their branches from 650 in 1940 to 2,245 in 1945.[21] The rapid growth of the economy of the country during the war period warranted a rapid growth of banking. But

> [T]here was a pronounced tendency for opening banks with little intrinsic strength in the form of a sound capital structure and liquidity of assets; more serious was the rather indiscriminate opening of branches and employment of unsound methods to attract deposits. The motives behind several of the new banking ventures were not altogether legitimate or worthy.... There was again, in some cases, a desire on the part of industrial houses to have under their control sizeable banking and insurance establishments; this interlocking of interests between banks, insurance companies and industrial concerns was generally detrimental to the interests of bank depositors. There was moreover, in some cases, the dressing up of accounts to give a

misleading impression of the financial position of the banks. A number of banks also engaged in dubious devices to become eligible for inclusion in the Second Schedule.[22]

'One bank with a capital of less than ₹200,000 opened more than 75 branches. The banking system … was as freer than the free banking that prevailed in the US around the civil war.'[23]

In India of those days, even the minimum norms of banking were not enforceable. A total of 73 banks had failed in 1938. The number of bank failures during 1939–1945 was 482.[24]

1.10. Imperial Bank of India: 1921

WWI had impacted the business of the three Presidency banks very adversely. These banks began to fear their potential acquisition by the large London joint stock banks. This led them to discuss consolidation by amalgamating into a single entity. By early 1919, these banks had started discussions on the subject with the government. The Imperial Bank of India Act, 1920, was therefore passed to take them over, and Imperial Bank came into being on 27 January 1921.[25] Table 1.4 shows the three principal resources of the Presidency banks as on 31 December 1920 and of Imperial as on 31 December 1921.

1.10.1. Multiple Roles

Note the name 'Imperial'. The new creation under a special Act was given special privileges, special roles and special responsibilities. In return, the government came to exercise specific controls over the management of the bank. The new bank came to engage in nearly all types of commercial banking activities except foreign exchange dealings. It had undertaken an obligation to open 100 branches within five years of its establishment, which it fulfilled. Right from

Table 1.4 *Presidency Banks before Amalgamation and Imperial Bank after Inception*

Resources	Three Presidency Banks (31 December 1920)	Imperial Bank (31 December 1921)
1. Deposits (₹ in million)	863	726
2. Capital+reserves (₹ in million)	75	96
3. Branches (number)	72	80

Source: Report of the Banking Commission, Statement A.XI.1.

its inception, Imperial enjoyed the status of a quasi-central bank. It undertook banking operations and some overseas roles for the government, and managed its rupee debt. Imperial also functioned as a bankers' bank. Being the largest commercial bank of the country with the largest branch network which enjoyed a special relationship with the government, many banks voluntarily maintained balances with it and could obtain accommodation from it. The bank also managed clearing houses and provided remittance facilities between its branches to other banks. At the same time, there were limitations to its role as a bankers' bank, as it acted both as a competitor as well as a facilitator.[26]

By virtue of being the banker to the government, the bank was instrumental in assisting the money market. For instance, in times of large payments by the public to the government, the bank would receive large interest-free funds (termed 'float' in banking parlance) which it would use to lend in that market. For some period, thus, it performed the twin roles of a commercial bank and a quasi-central bank.[27]

These roles gave the Imperial Bank a special status and also some benefits and responsibilities. After the formation of Reserve Bank in 1935, some of those responsibilities were taken over by RBI.

Simultaneously, some of the powers granted to the GOI over Imperial under the Imperial Bank of India Act were also taken away. Even after that, Imperial continued to manage currency chests and treasuries at many centres, it continued to manage several quasi-public funds, and it continued to manage clearing houses and accept other banks' deposits where RBI did not have its offices. This enabled it to continue to get the benefit of large interest-free float.

Complaints were often made against Imperial in the legislature about its 'unfair competition' vis-à-vis other banks. Complaints were also sometimes made to the RBI against the high-handedness of local Imperial Bank agents. The response of Imperial was that it was a commercial concern and so long as it kept within the four walls of the law under which it was created, neither the government nor the legislature had any right to dictate its policy or the manner in which it should conduct its day-to-day business.[28]

1.10.2. Imperial and Corporate and Banking Legislations

When the first attempt at banking legislation was made by passing the Indian Companies (Amendment) Act, 1936, Imperial was left out of the purview of the applicable banking provisions barring a couple of exceptions.

In 1939, RBI submitted to the government proposals for a separate banking law to replace the banking-related provisions in the Companies Act and to bring the entire joint stock banking sector under the control of the RBI. When RBI's proposals were circulated among the public, Imperial Bank of India was among the critics who opposed the creation of a separate bank law. In April 1940, Imperial's Managing Director W. Lamond wrote to the governor of RBI his reactions to the proposed banking law. It is worth noting his argument in some detail. He observed, inter alia, 'To us it seems that inexperience, lack of business acumen and failure to appreciate the accepted canons of sound finance can never be remedied by legislation'. He was also of the opinion that as joint stock banking in India was still in its 'infancy', the interests of the banking system could best be served by 'leaving it as free as possible from legal restrictions'. Further, Lamond wrote, 'In other words, we share the view that banking practice should be allowed to develop on convention rather than on legislation.' His long argument 'concluded by reiterating that appropriate amendments to the Indian Companies Act would meet the case without the necessity for the introduction of an Indian Bank Act'.[29]

In March 1941, RBI advised the GOI that time was 'still not ripe for undertaking an elaborate new banking legislation'.[30]

But, in November 1944, when the Banking Companies Bill was introduced in the Legislative Assembly, RBI proposed to extend it to the Imperial Bank. The Imperial Bank again opposed it with long-drawn arguments. For example, regarding the proposal to impose restrictions on loans on the security of a bank's own shares to directors and firms or companies in which they were interested as partners or directors, Lamond observed that it would 'not be equitable' to preclude a company of undoubted standing from availing itself of clean accommodation from its bankers 'merely because the company and the bank had a common director'. On a section in the bill dealing with accounts and BS, Lamond observed,

> [I]t would appear that the intention is to require banks to disclose their contingency reserves which ... are required by most leading banks, the world over, as being in the nature of 'hidden' reserves'. You will, I think, agree that it is most desirable that banks should not only be permitted, but encouraged to maintain undisclosed reserves in keeping with the volume of their business from which to meet unforeseen contingencies such as losses caused by violent fluctuations in the securities markets, severe breaks in commodity prices, etc.

He concluded by drawing a reference to the opinions of the bank contained in its letter to the Reserve Bank in April 1940 and hoped that the governor would recommend the exclusion of the Imperial Bank from the scope of the enactment.[31]

Today's students of banking, fed on heavy doses of best practices of shunning conflicts of interest and ensuring transparency in bank dealings, particularly in accounting, would surely be amused by the advocacy of contrarian unfair practices in the 1940s by the top banks of the country.

RBI, later, wrote to the GOI in January 1945, (repeating arguments put forth by Imperial Bank in its above [29 December 1944] letter), '[W]e do not consider it necessary to press for an amendment to bring that Bank within the purview of the Banking Companies Bill'.[32] Read together with the advice of the RBI to the GOI in March 1941 on the need for a separate bank law shows up the extent to which RBI was influenced by the 'opinion' of Imperial. Also, of course, Imperial Bank enjoyed certain powers and privileges under the Imperial Bank of India Act which it did not want to lose.

Despite opposition of the Imperial and the recommendation of the RBI, the Select Committee of the Legislature in 1947 recommended that most of the important provisions of the proposed bill be made applicable to the Imperial Bank.[33]

There was a general belief in those years that the Imperial Bank favoured European business interests in the country and that small trade and industry had little access to it. These views had persisted even after the coming into being of RBI. The above matters and others reflected a certain stance of Imperial Bank in dealing with various institutions, other banks and its customers which was often translated into an attitude of superiority (of knowledge) and arrogance (of power) on the part of the bank.

1.11. Indian Central Banking Enquiry Committee: 1931

The Government of India had appointed the Indian Central Banking Enquiry Committee in 1929 to report on matters of development of banking with a view to its expansion in the country, its regulation with a view to protect the interests of the public, and banking education with a view to provide Indian personnel in adequate numbers and with necessary qualifications, to meet the increasing need for a sound and well managed national system of banking. The Committee submitted its report in 1931.[34]

Public attention had been drawn to the desirability of the statutory regulation of banks as early as 1913–1914 when the banking crisis of that year revealed some of the weaknesses of the banking system.[35]

The Central Banking Enquiry Committee went into the causes of bank failures and listed the following among the principal ones: combination of trading with banking, dishonest management, incompetence of directors, bad and speculative investments, unrestricted loans to directors and to concerns in which they were interested, injudicious advances, insufficient capital and low levels of liquidity.[36]

While dealing with the issue of banking regulation, the Committee observed,

[T]hat the banking institutions of a country served as repositories of cash resources of all classes of people and exercised a very powerful influence on their economic life; the business of banking, therefore, had come to be regarded as quasi-public in nature. Hence, the business of banking warranted legislation for safeguarding the interests of depositors on whose confidence rested the entire banking structure of a nation, and for ensuring and fostering the growth of banking on sound lines.[37]

The Committee report further stated,

> We are of the opinion that the existing provisions in the Indian Companies Act governing banking companies are inadequate. Several important matters having an important bearing on questions such as the initial organization of banks, their efficient management and stability, provisions for supervision and examination and publication of accounts, the safety of shareholders and depositors and the development of banking generally on sound lines, remain to be provided for.[38]

The Committee also 'opined, therefore, that the promulgation of a special Bank Act, comprising necessary provisions governing all banking institutions would be more convenient to the public as well as to the banks.'[39]

> The Report stated that one of the advantages of incorporation of banks under an Act of the Legislature was that it rendered possible for Government to prevent the growth of mushroom banks with insufficient capital, which, in the nature of things, would have a less extensive distribution of risks and would be less able to withstand shocks than banks of larger size.[40]

> After taking note of the statistics relating to banks in India and giving glaring instances of so-called banks, the Report had observed that 6 out of 16 banks that failed or went into liquidation in 1927 had practically no paid-up capital, and that the paid-up capital of one of those banks was only a small amount of ₹800. Therefore, the committee recommended that banking regulation should provide that a bank registered as per the legislation should not commence business until its paid-up capital was at least ₹50,000.[41]

1.12. Establishment of RBI: 1934

Efforts to establish a banking institution in India with some features of a central bank have a long history which can be traced back, it is said, to as early as 1773. The Hilton Young Commission, appointed in 1925, examined the matter of the need to set up a central or state bank. It strongly recommended the establishment of a central bank in its report submitted in July 1926. The bank was to be called 'RBI', and all central banking functions were to be entrusted to it. Following this, a proposal to set up RBI was unsuccessfully introduced in India's Legislative Assembly in January 1927. Between 1926 and 1933, several attempts were made within the legislature and outside to proceed with the establishment of the Reserve Bank, but these could not be taken to fruition owing to a few major differences. One of the matters at issue was whether the Bank should be government-owned or be a private shareholders' bank. (More of this, infra) another issue was whether elected members of the legislature should be represented on the Bank's Central Board.

Finally, the RBI Bill, 1933, was passed in the Legislative Assembly in a special session on 16 February 1934. The Bank was to be a shareholders' bank and in the hands of an independent authority to ensure its independence. The Bill received the assent of the Governor-General on 6 March 1934 and the provisions of the Act relating to the constitution of the Bank became operative from 1 January 1935.

The preamble to the RBI Act stated that

[I]t is expedient to constitute a Reserve Bank for India to regulate the issue of Bank notes and keeping of reserves with a view to securing monetary stability in India and generally to operate the currency and credit system of the country to its advantage.[42]

The provisions of the Act required the RBI to act as a banker's bank. As the central bank, the operations of the Bank with the money market were to be conducted largely through the medium of member banks. RBI took over the function of currency issue from the GOI and the power of credit control from the Imperial Bank of India.

It has been stated that the issue of bank failures and the need for catering to the requirements of agriculture were the two 'prime' reasons for the establishment of the Reserve Bank.[43] But a central bank, anywhere, could not have been established for these two 'prime' reasons. As in other countries, RBI too was established to perform the role of a central bank as enshrined in the preamble to the RBI Act. It is true that 'bank failures' was an important issue of concern in India since the 1910s. But the remedies to prevent bank failures lay in the central bank performing the important functions of bank licensing, supervision and regulation of banks. It is also true that, in terms of its Act, RBI was accorded a special responsibility to take steps to promote agricultural credit through the banking system. The Act provided for the establishment of an Agricultural Credit Department in the Bank with the object of advising the governments and lending institutions on matters pertaining to agricultural credit.[44] Developments in performing this role by RBI are described in some detail at several places.

Soon after its establishment, RBI began to use its limited legal powers to supervise and regulate the banking system. The enactment of the Indian Companies (Amendment) Act in 1936 helped RBI in addressing this important function. RBI also began to enlist banks in the Second Schedule to its Act on fulfilment of minimum conditions of soundness of a bank's finances and modes of its working. In lieu of the privilege of being granted the status of a Scheduled Bank, provisions of the RBI Act enabled RBI to require those banks to maintain with it prescribed cash reserves based on their demand and time liabilities. These provisions also enabled the RBI to prescribe the banks to submit weekly returns to enable it to watch over the compliance of the above requirements. RBI could also inspect these banks for the limited purpose of determining their eligibility for inclusion or retention in the Second Schedule. But it is to be noted that initially, under the RBI Act, the RBI had no powers, in the absence of a banking law, to include in or exclude from the Second Schedule banks on its own. This power was vested with the GOI. Also, RBI had no other powers to audit or inspect these banks.

Despite the absence of powers to rein in non-scheduled banks, RBI made efforts to keep itself in touch with these banks. It was receiving the BS and other financial data about these banks from the registrars of joint-stock companies. According to this source of information, about 1,421 companies which could be considered as non-scheduled banks were operating in British India at December-end 1938. Many of these companies claimed that they were not banks, as the deposits accepted by them were not permitted to be withdrawn by cheque, draft or order.[45] It was only after the passing of the Banking Companies Act (BCA) in 1949 that these powers were vested in the RBI.

1.12.1. State versus Private Ownership

It has been noted previously that for several years before its establishment, a debate had raged over the issue of whether the Bank should be established in the public sector or in the private sector. In 1939, the initiation of the matter of passing a separate act for banking companies in the legislature started the debate on this hot issue anew. It is intended to touch upon this matter here not only because it frequently occupied the mind space of the lawmakers as well as the media but also, more importantly, because we now know that this issue raised its head again and again in the developing story of the banking system post-Independence.

When the first RBI Bill was introduced in the legislature, there was a strong demand for the Bank to be established as a wholly State-owned bank. The Congress Party had then vigorously and successfully championed the principle of State ownership of the proposed Reserve Bank. But the Bill was not proceeded with, as the government wanted the Bank to be a private shareholders' bank. This controversy over the matter of State versus private ownership continued to plague the Bill. Hence, this issue was regarded as mainly responsible for the long delay in the setting up of the Bank. Later, in 1933, a special session of the legislature was called in which a revised RBI Bill was listed to be considered. It was proposed in the Bill to establish the Bank as a shareholders' institution and not as a State institution. It was one of the most extensively discussed issues during the passage of the 1933 Bill. The Congress Party which continued to champion State ownership of the Bank decided not to attend this session. The Bill was finally passed. The Bank was to be established as a private shareholders' bank.

The demand for public ownership of RBI was revived after the announcement in 1945 of the proposal for the nationalization of the Bank of England. This announcement had been preceded by a general trend towards nationalization of central banks in Europe and elsewhere a few years before the commencement of WWII. Denmark and New Zealand had taken the lead in nationalizing their respective central banks in 1936. The Bank of England was nationalized in March 1946. Following this, the debate on the subject heated up when, on 26 March 1946, the leader of the opposition in the Legislative Assembly asserted that nationalization should be the keynote of all economic development in India. He also commented, '[S]o long as "British imperial domination" continued in India, the Reserve Bank of India could not possibly be nationalized.'

After the installation of the interim government in September 1946, there was a strong demand again in the Legislative Assembly and a section of the media that government should nationalize industries, public utilities, banks, civil aviation, etc. The Finance Department, GOI, anticipating that, during the consideration of the Banking Companies Bill (which was on the anvil), members would pick up the theme of nationalization again, felt that it was time that the government decided their stance on this issue. RBI was therefore requested towards the end of 1946 to convey its views on the possible advantages and disadvantages of nationalization.

RBI asked its Research Department to examine this matter. Pending this examination, the Bank sent to the government its interim response. It made a detour of possible reasons for the agitation for nationalization, including 'that it was feared that in future the Bank would not prove sufficiently pliable and responsive to the wishes of the Government in power', then concluded, 'We feel that nationalisation would not lead to any increased efficiency in the running of the Bank, but rather that its processes would be slowed down and its efficiency impaired owing to the intrusion of extraneous factors.' RBI further advised that, in case any 'oblique' reference was made by the Select Committee on the Banking Companies Bill, 'Government's answer should be that it was premature to consider the matter until a permanent constitution for the country had been framed'. In the meantime, in a minute of dissent signed by five members appended to the Report of the Select Committee on the Bill, it was stated, '[W]e wish to add that all banks should be nationalised at an early date and that as a first step, the Reserve Bank and the Imperial Bank may be made State Banks.'[46]

The debate continued into the years 1947–1949, only to become shriller.

1.12.2. Bank Credit to Agricultural Sector

Under its statute, as noted earlier, RBI was accorded a special responsibility to take steps to promote agricultural credit through the banking system. The Agricultural Credit Department in the Bank was expected to maintain an expert staff to study all questions of agricultural credit and advise the Central and local governments, provincial cooperative banks and other lending organizations on matters pertaining to agricultural credit.[47] The above translated into predominantly an advisory and developmental role for RBI to support existing lending institutions, particularly the cooperative banking system, in enlarging the quantum of agricultural finance and improving its delivery to farmers. By Independence, RBI's efforts had resulted in the establishment of a cooperative structure comprising primary cooperatives at village level, central cooperative banks at the district level, and state cooperative banks at the State (apex) level.

Issues in the provision of agricultural credit to farmers had 'natural' linkages with the providers of this type of credit, that is, the moneylenders, the cooperative banking institutions and the commercial banks in rural India, and the facilitators of transactions between borrower–farmer and lender–provider of rural credit, that is, the Central and provincial governments and the RBI. But these linkages seem never to have become strong due to gaps in perception of the problems of the poor borrower and the proposed solutions by the providers and the facilitators. On the top of this was the confusion about the specific role of RBI. The efforts of all these agents of change were to replace the moneylender (who was also most often the landlord of the village)—which they never could.

The Swadeshi movement (1906) had given impetus to the cooperative credit movement. Official attention began to be paid to provision of rural credit; laws were passed in 1904 and 1912 to give legal recognition to cooperative credit institutions.[48] The Royal Commission on Indian Agriculture (1928) observed, '[I]f Cooperation fails, there will fail the last hope of rural India'. The Indian Central Banking Enquiry Committee (1931) had also advocated spread of the cooperative movement, stating that 'there is no better instrument for raising the level of the agriculturist of this country than the cooperative effort.'[49] Thus, since long before RBI came into being, 'great faith has been placed in India in the potentialities of the cooperative organizations to serve the credit needs of the country, especially of the rural sector'.[50] The 12 years between 1935, when the Bank started its operations, and 1946 were marked by about six years of WWII and 2–3 years of turmoil preceding partition of the country. The RBI and the central government remained embroiled in the huge financial issues arising from those major events, leaving not enough time for the RBI to do much beyond performing its advisory and developmental roles. Under pressure to lend, RBI had also begun to channel agricultural credit to farmers via financial accommodation to the cooperative credit system.

Still it has been observed in *RBI History-1*, the official history of the RBI, that only modest beginnings had been made in the early years of the Bank and that the activities of RBI in this sphere did not blossom until about the 1950s.[51]

1. Indeed, even to this day, the progress made has been negligible, and it is doubtful if there was at all any scope for progress.[52]
2. Even with regard to the cooperative sector, it is perhaps correct to say that the Bank was not very active.[53]
3. The cooperative sector remained largely critical of the RBI's out-look and policies with regard to it (this sector).
4. It was perhaps the Bank's role in the sphere of rural credit that formed the main target of criticism during these years (up to 1951).

1.13. Proposals for a Separate Banking Law: 1939–1946

The Indian Banking Enquiry Committee (1931) had recommended the need for enacting a separate banking law. Within a short time of the enactment of the Indian Companies (Amendment) Act of 1936, its limitations began to manifest themselves.

The definition of a banking company incorporated in the Act gave rise to administrative difficulties in determining whether a company was a banking company or not.... The failure of the Travancore National & Quilon Bank Ltd in 1938 and the subsequent banking crisis in South India drew pointed public attention to the desirability of enacting comprehensive legislation for the protection of the depositors.[54]

It was in this context that, in 1939, RBI submitted to the GOI a set of proposals for a separate banking law to replace and to improve upon the inadequate bank-related provisions in the Companies Act. RBI's proposals were also widely circulated in the country. The reactions were mixed. The exchange banks and non-scheduled banks, which were likely to be 'adversely' affected (in the sense that their working would be regulated) by RBI's proposals, opposed it. Some felt that there was no need for a separate bank legislation and that the Indian Companies Act, as amended in 1936 in respect of banking companies, met the needs adequately. Another group of critics consisted of institutions like Imperial Bank of India, to whom the whole idea of further restrictive legislation was an anathema. Their views were based on the usual counts of opposition to any regulatory measure including that it was unfair that sound banking institutions should be regulated in order to check the undesirable practices of a few small or dishonest banks. But there were also views that the proposed Bill was too limited in scope. Thus, *The Times of India* (23 January 1940) suggested that the Bill could be refashioned to extend its scope to provide improved facilities in rural credit.

Reviewing the mass of comments as a whole, the Governor (of RBI) wrote to the central government in March 1941 that opinion in the country was still not ripe for undertaking an elaborate new banking legislation.[55]

1.13.1. Interim Measures

Although, thus the proposal for a comprehensive banking law was shelved, the need for early legislation on several compelling issues did not go away. Interim measures amending the provisions in the chapter relating to banking companies in the Companies Act were taken in 1942 and 1944. Obviously, those were considered too important to be postponed indefinitely.

In 1942, a provision was inserted in Section 277F of the Companies Act to the effect that any company which uses as part of its name the word 'bank', 'banker' or 'banking' shall be deemed to be a banking company irrespective of whether the business of accepting deposits of money on current account or otherwise subject to withdrawal by cheque, draft, or order is or is not its principal business.[56]

Two other significant changes were one which laid down a new capital structure for banks and the other that prohibited the management of banks by managing agents.

1.13.2. The Origin of Opacity

Under a notification issued by the GOI on 16 January 1937, banks were permitted not to show on their BS bad and doubtful debts for which they had made provisions to the satisfaction of the auditors. In a revision petition filed later in the Bombay High Court, the full Bench of the Court held that the notification was 'ultra vires' as it contravened Section 131 of the Indian Companies Act. 'This well-recognized practice followed in India and other countries by banks in preparing their BS was given statutory validity by an amendment to the Companies Act passed in November 1943.'[57]

Meanwhile, the demand from several sources for a comprehensive banking legislation gathered more strength. For example, the *Eastern Economist*, in its issue of 25 June 1943, writing on the 'crying need … for a comprehensive legislation', observed, inter alia that 'some of the salient defects of our banking system as at present organised are under-capitalisation, over-trading and wasteful competitive branch banking.'[58] In June 1943 itself, RBI decided that it was desirable to review the issue of a separate banking law. Accordingly, early in 1944, RBI took up the consideration of various suggestions received from time to time for modification of the original proposals. However, the Bank itself (a) began to doubt the appropriateness of a detailed legislation in the context of conditions then prevailing in the country and (b) developed self-doubt as to its ability to administer that legislation, as it did not then possess a suitably trained staff. RBI, therefore, decided to proceed with its original proposals by which it would 'attempt to lay down only the foundation covering general principles, leaving the super-structure of detailed regulation to be built up later'.[59]

A revised draft of the bank bill incorporating some changes in the light of suggestions received was prepared in April 1944. A few significant proposals of the bill were as follows:

- Prohibition of a bank engaging in trading activities,
- Inclusion of gold in the category of liquid assets,
- Submission by banks of a monthly return of assets and liabilities,
- Restrictions on advances on the security of own shares or to directors and firms and companies in which they were interested as partners or directors,
- Inspection of banks by RBI on being directed by the central government.

Internal consultations within the Bank led to two additional modifications:

- A foreign bank opening a new branch in India should be required to obtain a licence from RBI.
- The percentage of approved liquid assets to be maintained could be reduced from 30 per cent to 25 per cent.

The revised proposals of the Bank were sent to the central government in June 1944. RBI also sent to the government a new pro forma bank BS which modified the existing BS (Form F) prescribed for all types of companies under the Indian Companies Act. The new bank bill was introduced in the Legislative Assembly in November 1944. Following are the two suggestions made in the debate that followed:

- The Imperial Bank of India Act should be repealed and the bank should be brought under the scope of the proposed bank bill.
- Banking should be nationalized/socialized.

The central government sent the bill for circulation among the banks and the general public. On review of the responses received, RBI further lowered the proportion of liquid assets to be maintained from 25 per cent to 20 per cent. At that stage, the issues concerning position of the exchange banks and the Imperial Bank had been raised in the legislature and outside:

- Exchange banks were hitherto not submitting the BS of their Indian operations under the Indian Companies Act. They were also not subject to most other provisions of the company law. These banks were, thus, in a privileged position in the matter of statutory requirements and opposed the proposed banking legislation. They were also not required to obtain a licence to carry on operations in India. Public opinion was increasingly critical of the preferential treatment accorded to foreign banks. In 1947, the Select Committee recognized the validity of the criticisms and recommended extension of the provision of licensing to all banks incorporated outside India.
- Like the exchange banks, the Imperial Bank was not governed by the banking-related provisions in the Indian Companies Act, having been incorporated under a separate Act. In 1944, RBI took up the matter of extension of the proposed banking legislation to the Imperial, without affecting any of the provisions of the Imperial Bank of India Act or the regulations made thereunder. Despite the opposition of the Imperial, the Select Committee in 1947 recommended that most of the important provisions of the bill be made applicable to the Imperial Bank.[60]

WWII ended in May 1945. The Governor, RBI, while addressing the shareholders of the Bank, in August 1945, observed that 'while the general banking picture continues to be healthy and encouraging, there are certain undesirable tendencies, which, if not checked in time, might react unfavourably on the country's banking structure'. In September 1945, the Bank recommended to the central government the promulgation of an ordinance to bring into immediate effect the provision in the banking bill regarding inspections; the ordinance was to be operative until the enactment of the banking bill.[61]

In October 1945, the Governor-General announced fresh elections and dissolved the Legislative Assembly, and the banking bill was allowed to lapse.[62] Consequent to this and in view of the urgent need to carry out inspection of banks, the Banking Companies (Inspection) Ordinance was promulgated in January 1946. Under this ordinance, the central government was empowered to direct the RBI to undertake an inspection of the books and accounts of any banking company incorporated under the Indian Companies Act and to make a report to the central government. Based on the report, the government could proceed to take specific actions against that banking company. RBI carried out the inspection of 41 banks under this Ordinance up to the end of June 1949. The affairs of some banks were found to be carried on so badly that the Bank recommended drastic actions such as prohibition of acceptance of deposits or removal from the Second Schedule.

The banking bill was re-introduced in a revised draft in the new Assembly in March 1946. The bill was referred to a Select Committee of the Legislative Assembly in the next month. But the Committee could not meet until November 1946. Meanwhile, another important regulatory enactment titled

Banking Companies (Restriction of Branches) Act was passed in November 1946 to restrict the indiscriminate opening and shifting of branches by banking companies. It provided that no banking company shall open any new branch, or change the location of an existing branch, without obtaining prior permission from the Reserve Bank.[63]

As a result, the pace of branch expansion slowed down. In 1947, the number of applications received for opening of new branches and changing the location of existing branches was 487; 117 of those were rejected.

All these legislative measures and some others were later to be brought together under the BCA.

III. THE FINANCIALS

The limited bank data available for this period may now be put together to assess strengths and weaknesses of the banking system and progress made by it till the end of 1946.

1.14. Limitations of Available Data

The Appendix at the end of the book describes the degree of unavailability and inadequacy of data in the STs of the whole period of this study. A few additional comments, specific to this chapter, are in order to understand in proper perspective the presented financial data and its analysis.

1. Before 1913, information even about the number of banks was hard to come by; possibly, it was limited to the existence of three Presidency banks, three exchange banks and nine IJSBs. All other financial institutions called by the nomenclature of banks or otherwise, were in the unorganized sector and the government of the day was more or less incognizant of them. The new annual publication, ST, began to publish more information from 1913. It

consisted of banks' aggregated capital, deposits and cash balances. In the initial years, even this information was of doubtful quality as it kept changing from year to year, as even the number of reporting banks kept on diverging.

2. The passage of Indian Companies (Amendment) Act, 1936, which required the banks to publish their financial statements, albeit in the same formats as applicable to trading and industrial companies, improved the data availability. RBI, in the late 1930s, began to ask banks to provide more information on their working. It also began to increase the coverage of smaller banks. Still, the information on the banks' financials remained grossly incomplete. Available information was limited to 3+ BS items mentioned above. Data about banks' operations and profit and loss account (PLA, hereinafter) was not available throughout this period.

3. It was difficult to vouch for the accuracy of available data. But it can be stated that the coverage of banks in the system had widened as years passed by. Data on bank branches was also available.

1.15. Analysis of Financials

Subject to these serious limitations, the analysis of all the available bank financials of the period 1913–1946, reinforced by Tables 1.5–1.7, is presented in this section to produce an 'assessment' of the banking system's growth. These three tables present a profile of the banking system which encompasses the following:

- Comparative growth of different bank groups
- Major business parameters and their interrelationships
- Status of Imperial Bank in the banking system
- An assessment of bank failures
- An attempt at estimating new banks opened in 34 years

Following this section, Section IV complements our analysis by providing data on the 'top 42 21st-century banks' at the end of 1946.

Table 1.5 Growth of Indian Banking: 1870–1946

(Deposits, ₹ in lakhs)

Year	IJSBs			Presidency Banks/ Imperial Bank			Exchange Banks			Total		
	No. of Banks	No. of BR	Deposits	No. of Banks	No. of BR	Deposits	No. of Banks	No. of BR	Deposits	No. of Banks	No. of BR	Deposits
1870	2	–	14 / 1%	3	–	1,183 / 95%	3	–	52 / 4%	8	–	1,249
1880	3	–	63 / 4%	3	–	1,140 / 74%	4	–	340 / 22%	10	–	1,543 / 24%
1890	5	–	271 / 10%	3	–	1,836 / 64%	5	–	754 / 26%	13	–	2,861 / 85%
1900	9	–	808 / 24%	3	–	1,569 / 46%	8	–	1,050 / 31%	20	–	3,427 / 20%
1910	16	–	2,566 / 30%	3	–	3,654 / 42%	11	–	2,479 / 29%	30	–	8,699 / 154%
1920	58	335 / 72%	7,348 / 31%	3	72 / 16%	8,629 / 37%	15	55 / 12%	7,481 / 32%	76	462	23,458 / 170%

(Continued)

Table 1.5 (Continued)

(Deposits, ₹ in lakhs)

Year	IJSBs			Presidency Banks/ Imperial Bank			Exchange Banks			Total		
	No. of Banks	No. of BR	Deposits	No. of Banks	No. of BR	Deposits	No. of Banks	No. of BR	Deposits	No. of Banks	No. of BR	Deposits
1930	88	485	6,765	1	189	8,397	18	88	6,811	107	762	21,973
		64%	31%		25%	38%		12%	31%		65%	-6%
1940	177	1,494	13,061	1	383	9,603	20	87	8,533	650	1964	31,197
	452	76%	42%		20%	31%		4%	27%		158%	42%
	629											
1946	339	4,853	73,411	1	443	27,167	15	77	18,128	706	5,373	118,706
	351	90%	62%		8%	23%		1%	15%		174%	281%
	690											

Sources: Report of the Banking Commission, GOI, Statements A.XI.1 and A.XI.2, pp. 739–745, 1970; ST 1946, for figures for exchange banks for 1946.

Notes: BR=Branches; data for 1946 is for India excluding Pakistan; data for IJSBs:
1. For years 1870–1910, those with capital of ₹500,000 and above.
2. For years 1920 and 1930, those with capital of ₹100,000 and above.
3. For years 1940 and 1946, all scheduled and non-scheduled banks, which included all class A1, A2, B, and C banks, and even class D banks which had a capital of ₹50,000 and less.
4. Data for number of banks in the years 1940 and 1946 is given separately for classes A+B and C+D banks, in that order.

Table 1.6 Additional Parameters of Growth of Indian Banking: 1913–1946 (Select Years)

(Amount: ₹ in millions)

Year	Bank/Bank Group	Capital Amount	Deposits Amount	Loans Amount	Loans Percentage of Deposits	Investments Amount	Investments Percentage of Deposits	Cash Amount	Cash Percentage of Deposits
1913	IJSBs	27	193	152	79	32	17	38	20
	Presidency banks	74	424	275	65	67	16	160	38
	Total	101	617	427	69	99	16	198	32
1936	IJSBs	154	1,036	568	55	44	04	163	16
	Imperial Bank	111	789	268	34	526	67	86	11
	Total	265	1,825	836	46	570	31	249	14
1940	IJSBs	185	1,305	674	52	478	37	295	23
	Imperial Bank	112	960	323	34	486	51	248	26
	Total	297	2,265	997	44	964	43	543	24
1946	IJSBs	568	7,341	3,699	50	3,141	43	1,492	20
	Imperial Bank	118	2,717	943	35	1,545	57	424	16
	Total	686	10,058	4,642	46	4,686	47	1,916	19

Sources: STs, various years.

Note: Data about loans and investments became available in STs on a regular basis from the year 1936 only.

Table 1.7 Bank Failures and New Banks: 1913–1946

Year [1]	No. of Bank Failures [2]	No. of Banks (Beginning of Year) [3]	No. of Banks (End of Year) [4]	No. of New Banks Established ([4]−[3])+[2]=[5]
1913	12	18	41	35
1914	42	41	42	43
1915	11	42	45	14
1916	13	45	48	16
1917	9	48	43	4
1918	7	43	47	11
1919	4	47	47	4
1920	3	47	48	4
1921	7	48	65	24
1922	15	65	68	18
1923	20	68	69	21
1924	18	69	70	19
1925	17	70	74	21
1926	14	74	75	15
1927	16	75	77	18
1928	13	77	74	10
1929	11	74	78	15
1930	12	78	88	22
1931	18	88	88	18
1932	24	88	86	22
1933	26	86	89	29
1934	30	89	105	46
1935	51	105	62	8
1936	88	62	112	138
1937	65	112	148	101
1938	73	148	161	86
1939	117	161	678	634
1940	107	678	629	58

(Continued)

Table 1.7 (Continued)

Year [1]	No. of Bank Failures [2]	No. of Banks (Beginning of Year) [3]	No. of Banks (End of Year) [4]	No. of New Banks Established ([4]−[3])+[2]=[5]
1941	94	629	455	(80)
1942	50	455	475	70
1943	59	475	546	130
1944	28	546	628	110
1945	27	628	721	120
1946	27	721	690	(4)
Total	1,128	6,100	6,772	1,800

Sources: Column 2 (year-wise bank failures): C&F-1, Annex III.1; columns 3 and 4 (year-wise number of banks): Report of Banking Commission, GOI, 1970, Statements A.XI.1 and A.XI.2, pp. 740–745; column 5: our workings.

Note: No. of failures in 1913 are for the last two months of the year only.

1.15.1. Size of Banking Industry: Banks, Branches and Deposits

Table 1.5 shows the growing size of the commercial banking system over available select years from 1870 to 1946. It is shown for the three categories of banks, viz., IJSBs, Presidency banks/Imperial Bank and exchange banks, in terms of change in number of these banks, number of branches and amount of deposits. Data for branches became available only after the year 1915.

One can notice a rather mundane increase in deposits of Presidency banks and later Imperial Bank. Imperial Bank was required, after its formation in 1921, to add 100 branches to its network within five years, which it did; despite that, its deposits declined. One can also notice that deposits (including government deposits) of Presidency banks/Imperial Bank exceeded those of IJSBs in all the select years from 1870 to 1930. In fact, their deposits exceeded those of the latter till 1933 (₹805.7 million against ₹764.2 million). But in 1934, for the first time, the deposits of IJSBs (₹818.8 million) just went past those of Imperial Bank (₹818.0 million). Thereafter, the gap between the two classes of banks grew wider and wider.

Exchange banks had grown in terms of amount of deposits through this period. But their market share in deposits showed declines from 1930 onwards. The number of these banks had declined in 1946 compared to their number in 1940. Market share in number of branches declined from 12 per cent in 1930 to 4 per cent in 1940 and to 1 per cent in 1946.

It may be noted that the number of branches of the banking system had recorded significant growth of 158 per cent over the 10-year period 1930–1940. Their growth was spectacular at 174 per cent over the war period of 1940–1946. But the contributions of the three bank groups to this growth are worth noting too. The market shares of IJSBs, Imperial and exchange banks in terms of number of branches in 1930 were 64, 25 and 12 per cent, respectively. In 1940, their corresponding shares were 74, 20 and 4; in 1946, these shares had further changed to 90, 8 and 1, respectively. Thus, while the market share of IJSBs had gone up substantially, market shares of Imperial and exchange banks had declined.

The obvious explanation for IJSBs speeding ahead fast in terms of market share in deposits as well as number of branches in 1940 and 1946 is that many new banks, scheduled and non-scheduled, were being established and their coverage of geography was expanding fast in this period. Compare the number of IJSBs in 1930 with their numbers in 1940, the early WWII year, and 1946, the first post-war year. The number of these banks was 88 in 1930 and 629 and 690 in 1940 and 1946, respectively. Their breakup into scheduled banks (appearing first in Table 1.5) and non-scheduled banks (appearing second) in 1940 was 177 and 452; the corresponding numbers in 1946 were 339 and 351. Thus, while the number of scheduled banks had increased by 91 per cent, the number of non-scheduled banks had shrunk by 22 per cent.

The review of fast growth of the banking system, particularly of IJSBs, during the WWII period showed that the cheap money conditions created by the war generated large money with the public which went into the banks as deposits. Many new banks were established and existing banks expanded, and a large number of new branches were opened to mobilize those deposits. It turned out later that this growth was rather brittle; it got trimmed in the post-war years.

1.15.2. Bank Assets/Deposit Liabilities: Relationships

Available bank data on deposits, cash, investments and loans portfolios for select years of two bank groups, Presidency banks/Imperial Bank and IJSBs, are provided on comparative basis in Table 1.6.

Table 1.6, together with Table 1.5, allows us to secure new insights into the comparative deployment of funds by the two bank groups. As shown in Table 1.5, the number of IJSBs and their branches had been rising very fast and were at 690 banks against 1 Imperial Bank, and 4853 branches to 443 in 1946. It may be added, though, that a large number of branches of Imperial were located in presidency and other large towns, whereas a large number of branches of the IJSBs which belonged to A, B, C and D classes were small and were located in all sizes of towns. Hence, the fast-growing sizes of bank parameters of IJSBs, shown in Tables 1.5 and 1.6, which too outpaced those of Imperial Bank, could be explained, inter alia, by the comparative numbers and sizes of the banks and branches of the two bank classes.

The comparative significant relationships of different bank parameters, viz., credit–deposit (C–D), investment–deposit (I–D) and cash–deposit ratios, attempted in Table 1.6 may now be viewed:

1. The (C–D) ratio of IJSBs was higher than that of Presidency banks/Imperial Bank in all the 4 years, the difference being 14 percentage points or more.
2. While the (I–D) ratio of the two groups was almost identical in 1913, it was higher for presidency/Imperial group over the IJSBs in the other three years, particularly in 1936.

   The cash–deposit ratio of both the bank groups was high (on current standards, of course) throughout the years.
3. It is clear from the simple analysis above that, comparatively, presidency/Imperial group was conservative in the management of its funds; more so when it is assumed that while Imperial would have had mostly a European, high net-worth clientele, IJSBs would have had small, higher-risk borrowers.

So far as cash portfolio is concerned, it is a non-income-earning asset required to meet liquidity requirements. Hence, the efforts of any bank would be to maintain minimum cash balances for operational purposes. A higher cash–deposit ratio would imply a more conservative approach. A high cash–deposit ratio in this period could also be explained by virtually non-existence of a money market, smaller number of bank offices/branches located at substantial distances from each other, and weak infrastructure in terms of means of communication and transport. Also, those were the years when a large number of bank failures had occurred. But these factors would apply more to IJSBs. Given the location of Imperial's infrastructure, the high cash–deposit ratios of this bank again hints at its conservative approach to BS management.

1.15.3. Market Share of Imperial Bank in Business Parameters

Given the above analysis, it seems appropriate to work out the market share of Imperial, the leader of the banking industry, in the two most significant parameters in Table 1.6.

- Deposits: Imperial's market share (percentages) in total deposits was 69 in 1913 (Presidency banks), 43 in 1936, 42 in 1940 and 27 in 1946—declining.
- Loans: Its share was 64, 32, 32, and 20 in 1913, 1936, 1940 and 1946 respectively—declining.

Thus, Imperial's market share in the major parameters of the BS had declined over the 34-year period. As expected and, as can be seen from Table 1.6, its share in the investment portfolio of the industry was very high; it seemed that Imperial was risk-averse and played safe by keeping its funds invested in gilts. However, Imperial, being by far the largest bank, continued to dominate the Indian banking system.

1.15.4. Bank Failures and Establishment of New Banks: 1913–1946

Bank failures are one event which did not miss a single year of the 34-year period 1913–1946. As noted supra, the high incidence of bank failures was the reason why the fledgling banking system came to the active notice of the GOI in 1913. Table 1.1 had tabulated the number of bank failures which occurred every month from November 1913 to the end of 1914. Table 1.7 brings together interesting data on bank failures, number of banks at the beginning and at the end of each year, and new banks set up each year (derived from columns 2, 3 and 4 of Table 1.7) during the 34-year period.

1.15.4.1. Features of Table 1.7

1. On an average, annual bank failures were 33 and annual new banks established were 53 in the 34-year period.

    On a visual examination of the changes in the two parameters over the period, the whole period was divided into the 22-year period 1913–1934 and the 12-year period 1935–1946. For 1913–1934, it did not require a calculation of statistical correlation between movements of the bank failures and new banks established to identify a high positive correlation between the two parameters; it could be judged even by the naked eye. Thus, the number of failures in the 22-year period was 330 (average 15) and number of new banks established were 449 (20). In most of the 22 years, the two figures moved so closely that one could suspect that the businessmen-promoters behind bank failures and establishment of new banks were probably the same identities and this was being done with a 'purpose'.

As against this, the number of failures during 1935–1946 was 798 (average 66) and number of new banks established were 1,351 (113). This period covered the 'depression years' and WWII. The unorganized banking system had got 'freer than free'.

2. One can notice that the number of bank failures in 1913–1914, which had sent alarm bells ringing in the government corridors, in relation to the number of banks existing at the beginning of those years, was high. In fact, in 1914, the number of bank failures (42) was higher than the number of banks at the beginning of that year. This feature was replicated in 1936: 88 failures against 62 opening number of banks.

3. New banks established in 1941 and 1946 yield us negative figures. These figures cannot be less than zero. This result is obviously another proof, if all it was needed, that the figures published in those years could be inaccurate.

1.15.4.2. Causes of Bank Failures

Banks failed due to different causes. Some banks that failed had combined trading functions with banking functions. Several failed banks had a low capital base. For instance, average capital of failed banks in 1913 was ₹290,000 as against the average capital of ₹1,200,000 for class 'A' banks. These banks had also maintained low liquidity. Some big banks such as Indian Specie Bank and a British bank, with a paid-up capital of ₹7,560,000 also failed due to its involvement in silver speculation.[64] In retrospect, bank failures in India were attributed by scholars and committees, in a large measure, to individual imprudence and mismanagement, fraudulent manipulation by directors and managers, and incompetence and inexperience. Even exchange banks failed during the war mainly due to the problems relating to their parent companies and countries.[65]

Various committees that had gone into the causes of bank failures had recommended the setting up of a central bank. It was felt that the establishment of a central bank would result in better governance as such an institution would enforce a system of supervision and regulation over all banks in the system including weak, non-scheduled banks.[66] Hence, the issue of bank failures was one of the reasons that hastened the establishment of RBI.[67] But RBI was being managed with inadequate powers to supervise banks in the 10 odd years of its existence in the pre-Independence period; it was only after the enactment of BCA in 1949 that RBI secured its powers of supervision and regulation to be able to start mending the banking system.

IV. THE 21ST-CENTURY BANKS: 1946

Table 1.8 presents the status of 42 Indian SCBs which existed in 1946 and which had continued to exist at March-end 2011. This table is the second in the series of seven statements.

As shown in Table 1.8, at the end of 1946 and on the eve of Independence, the top five banks, in terms of size (TA), were Imperial, PNB, Bank of India, Central Bank of India and UCO Bank. One version reads, 'In addition to the Imperial Bank, there were five big banks, each holding public deposits aggregating ₹100 crore and more, viz., Central Bank of India Ltd, Punjab National

Table 1.8 *The 21st-Century Banks: 1946*

(Second in the Series)

Serial No.	Banks (Listed in Order of Date of Establishment)	Date of Establishment	TA ₹ in crore	Rank	No. of Branches Number	Rank
1	SBI (Imperial Bank of India)	2 June 1806	294.39	1	443	1
		15 April 1840				
		1 July 1843				
2	Allahabad Bank	17 April 1865	30.76	7	75	5
3	PNB	19 May 1894	77.81	2	279	3
4	City Union Bank (Kumbakonam Bank)	31 October 1904	0.49	36	10	31
5	Corporation Bank	26 May 1906	3.00	25	31	17
6	Punjab & Sind Bank	4 June 1906	3.56	24	10	31
7	Canara Bank	30 June 1906	6.45	16	47	8
8	Bank of India	7 September 1906	69.82	3	32	15
9	Indian Bank	5 March 1907	24.73	8	66	7
10	Bank of Baroda	20 July 1908	35.44	6	35	14
11	Central Bank of India	21 December 1911	42.54	4	361	2
12	State Bank of Mysore (Bank of Mysore)	19 May 1913	14.41	9	31	17
13	Dena Bank (Devkaran Nanjee Banking Company)	28 March 1914	10.46	12	47	8
14	Karur Vysya Bank	22 June 1916	0.69	33	15	26
15	State Bank of Patiala (Patiala State Bank)	14 November 1917	5.23	20	27	21
16	United Bank of India (Bengal Central Bank)	16 March 1918	12.82	11	31	17
17	Union Bank of India	11 November 1919	6.19	18	4	40
18	State Bank of Indore	23 March 1920	5.23	20	6	37
19	Catholic Syrian Bank	26 November 1920	0.93	30	12	29

Serial No.	Banks (Listed in Order of Date of Establishment)	Date of Establishment	TA ₹ in crore	Rank	No. of Branches Number	Rank
20	Tamilnad Mercantile Bank (Nadar Bank)	11 May 1921	0.38	38	27	21
21	Nainital Bank (Figures for September 1946)	31 July 1922	0.53	35	5	38
22	Andhra Bank	20 November 1923	4.07	23	39	11
23	Karnataka Bank	18 December 1924	0.60	34	8	36
24	Syndicate Bank (Canara Industrial & Banking Syndicate)	20 October 1925	4.26	22	89*	4
25	Lakshmi Vilas Bank	3 November 1926	0.39	37	10	31
26	Dhanlaxmi Bank	7 November 1927	0.28	41	3	41
27	South Indian Bank	25 January 1929	1.55	29	14	27
28	Vysya Bank	29 March 1930	0.73	32	16	25
29	Federal Bank (Travancore Federal Bank)	28 April 1931	0.03	42	2	42
30	Vijaya Bank	2 May 1931	0.33	40	13	28
31	Bank of Maharashtra	16 September 1935	2.07	27	17	24
32	Indian Overseas Bank	20 November 1936	8.67	14	43	10
33	New Bank of India	21 December 1936	8.31	15	39	11
34	Jammu & Kashmir Bank	1 October 1938	2.89	26	12	29
35	State Bank of Hyderabad (Hyderabad State Bank)	8 August 1941	12.94	10	32	15
36	United Commercial Bank (UCO Bank)	6 January 1943	41.97	5	69	6
37	State Bank of Bikaner & Jaipur (Bank of Jaipur)	8 February 1943	9.30	13	37	13

(Continued)

Table 1.8 (Concluded)

Serial No.	Banks (Listed in Order of Date of Establishment)	Date of Establishment	TA ₹ in crore	Rank	No. of Branches Number	Rank
38	Bank of Rajasthan (figures for 1947)	7 May 1943	0.77	31	9	35
39	Ratnakar Bank	14 June 1943	0.38	38	5	38
40	Oriental Bank of Commerce	19 December 1943	1.70	28	30	20
41	State Bank of Bikaner & Jaipur (Bank of Bikaner)	20 December 1944	6.37	17	24	23
42	State Bank of Travancore (Travancore Bank)	12 September 1945	5.35	19	10	31
Total			759	–	2,115	–

Sources: ST 1947, pp. 10–43; ST 1948, pp. 22–71.

Note: *31 out of 81 branches were 'pigmy' rural branches.

Bank Ltd, Bank of India Ltd, Bank of Baroda Ltd and United Commercial Bank Ltd.'[68] But, according to our version above sourced from STs, while those five banks were at the top, even their BS sizes (not to mention their deposits) were lower than ₹100 crore each. In fact, they ranged between ₹77.81 and 35.44 crore. In terms of the number of branches, the top five banks were Imperial Bank, Central Bank, PNB, Syndicate Bank and Allahabad Bank. Federal Bank was the last bank (42nd) in size, in terms of both TA and number of branches.

From a little that we can make out of the genetics of these banks in the Table 1.8, it is probable that many of them had been started by certain communities as against those established by business groups or promoter families. And these 'community banks' have survived.

V. SUMMARY: INITIAL PHASE OF AN EVOLVING SYSTEM

The Western-style banking based on joint stock ownership was initiated in India in the early 18th century. The few banks which were started could not succeed and had closed down. In its modern form, Indian banking was born in the 19th century when Presidency banks came into being between 1806 and 1843. These banks were the creation of the British Raj primarily for the use of the Britons. These banks were followed by the establishment of Allahabad Bank and PNB, both formed by Indians. The launch of the Swadeshi movement in 1906 saw the establishment of seven more Indian-owned banks one after another. The failure of a large number of banks during 1913–1914 drew the attention of the GOI to widespread ignorance of the working of the banking industry in the government echelons. It resulted in the launch of a country-wide survey to collect data on bank failures, apart from basic data on banks. The outcome was the publication of the first ST 1913. From then on, the government and its legislature became more and more involved about the working of the banking system. This growing interest by the State during the 34 years, beginning from 1913, manifested itself in the following:

1. Ordered an enquiry into bank failures and publication of the first bank data in ST 1913.
2. Enactment of various editions and amendments of the Companies Act, and bringing all banks under the jurisdiction of the Companies Act, 1913.
3. Actions by the government directly and through the medium of several committees and commissions to examine new and different issues concerning the banking system.

4. Amalgamation of Presidency banks to form Imperial Bank of India.
5. National legislature's increasing involvement in debating banks' role in dispensing rural credit, advocating social control and nationalization of banks and repeatedly reviewing Imperial Bank.
6. Debates for setting up a central bank for the country, on its role and functions, and about its ownership.
7. Developments in the banking system through the travails of WWI, the Great Depression and WWII, which spanned one-half of the period 1913–1946.
8. Long, arduous and incomplete journey to enact a separate law for banking companies.

All these and other developments produced a profile of the commercial banking system by the end of 1946 which bore significantly new contours from the ones that existed in the beginning of the 1900s. The banking system had expanded with time as the economy grew, particularly in the closing years of this period. The RBI slowly and steadily extended its hold on the banking system and had begun to lay the foundation of a system of bank supervision and regulation. Still, in the mid-1940s, the banking system grew at a hectic but uncontrolled pace. Underlying this haphazard growth was a degree of weakness and fragility of the banking system which was reflected in its weak financial picture. At the head of the system were some strong banks, but below it were still a large number of small and weak banks. At the end of this period, it was still an unsteady, fast growing, weak banking system built on inadequate capital bases, unhealthy bank practices and unskilled professionals. The efforts of the Indian polity to promote the institutionalization of banking system by enacting a banking law and to nationalize RBI in order to harmonize more smoothly the fiscal policy of GOI and monetary policy of RBI had not succeeded owing to the opposition of Imperial Bank and intransigence of RBI and the GOI, all being the instruments of the British Raj.

Notes

(Kindly refer to the Principal Sources of Bank Data under Preface for understanding the abbreviated but simpler use of notes below and in the following chapters.)

1. C&F-1, 74.
2. Ibid., Table 3.4, para 3.20, 79.
3. Ibid., para 3.21, 79.
4. RBI History-1, 199–200, 488, 843.
5. C&F-1, 76; Shahi, *Banking in India*, 69.
6. Millions/billions have been used at some places as per the author's discretion.
7. C&F-1, largely based on para 3.7, 75–76.
8. ST 1915, 1.
9. SBI, *Evolution of the State Bank of India*, vol. 3, 19. References to this publication, *hereinafter*, are stated as *SBI History-3*.
10. ST 1913, 1.
11. ST 1913, Table 3, 5; ST 1915, Table 3, 16.
12. As the words paid-up capital and reserves (at some places in STs abbreviated to capital and reserves appear together repeatedly, they are abbreviated to capital here and hereinafter).
13. To avoid confusion, one needs to clearly distinguish among three terms, viz., deposits, total deposits, and aggregate deposits.
    Note the use of the term 'deposits' in Table 1.2 and the term 'total deposits' in Table 1.3. In fact, both the terms are used inter-changeably. A bank's prescribed financial statements use the term 'deposits', whereas publications of RBI and other publications write 'total deposits' also. RBI collects data from banks for various purposes in various forms, in which it collects the figure of 'aggregate deposits'. This is the third term for deposits. 'Aggregate deposits' means demand deposits (current account deposits plus savings deposits) plus term (fixed) deposits. Deposits (or, total deposits) are a wider term which means aggregate deposits plus inter-bank deposits and contingency accounts, if any.
14. ST 1913, 1.
15. ST 1939–1940, Prefatory Note, iii.
16. Krishnan, *History and Scope of Banking Legislation in India*, 374–382; TP, 1949, 4–5.
17. ST 1916, 15–17.
18. C&F-1, 79.
19. Ibid., 83.
20. RBI History-1, vol. 1, 438.
21. C&F-1, Table 3.8, 63; ST, 1946, x.
22. RBI History-1, vol. 1, 436.
23. C&F-1, 84.

24. Ibid., Annex III.1, 139.
25. SBI History-3, 19–20, 34.
26. RBI History-1, 63–65.
27. Ibid., 64–65.
28. SBI History-3, 289, 291.
29. Ibid., 294, 295, 297.
30. Ibid., 297.
31. Ibid., 298.
32. Ibid., 298.
33. Read Section I of the chapter for details.
34. Krishnan, *History and Scope of Banking Legislation in India*, 375.
35. TP 1949, 3.
36. Ibid., 4.
37. Krishnan, based on GOI, *Report of the Indian Central Banking Enquiry Committee*, 375.
38. Ibid., para 671, 376.
39. Ibid. paras 672–673, 376.
40. Ibid., para 694, 377.
41. Ibid.
42. Read the Reserve Bank of India Act, 1934.
43. C&F-1, 80.
44. RBI History-1, 112–114.
45. C&F-1, 82.
46. Above discussion on bank nationalization is based on history of this subject in RBI History-1, 39, 83–84, 506–509.
47. Ibid., 112–114.
48. Ibid., 68; C&F-1, 77.
49. RBI History-1, 68.
50. Ibid.
51. Ibid., 199.
52. Ibid., 200.
53. Ibid., 471.
54. TP 1949, 5.
55. This paragraph, including some words and sentences (italicized), is substantially based on RBI History-1, 451–454.
56. Ibid.
57. ST 1942–1943, ix.
58. RBI History-1, 458–459.
59. Ibid., 460.
60. Ibid., 460–464. Developments narrated from 22 (last paragraph) to 24 (up to this point) are based on this reference.
61. Ibid., 718–719.

62. Ibid., 466.
63. ST 1945, p. x.
64. Tandon, quoted in C&F-1, 77.
65. C&F-1, 77–78.
66. GOI, *Report of the Indian Central Banking Enquiry Committee*, C&F-1, 80.
67. C&F-1, 80.
68. Ibid., 84.

2

The Transient Years (1947–1949)

A Bruised Banking System
Continues to Decline

I. A DISRUPTIVE CHANGE OVER

15 August 1947 brought new India both the elixir of Independence and the pain of Partition. The three-year period of 1947–1949 (i.e., seven-and-a-half months of 1947 before Independence and four-and-a half months of 1947 after Independence, and 1948 and 1949), was among the most politically volatile and hurtful periods between 1947 and 2011:

1. The end of WWII did not transit to a peaceful era in the Indian sub-continent. Soon the process of transition from the colonial *British Raj* to an independent India had begun.
2. The momentous change over in 1947 was marred by the disruptive partition of the single country into two nations.
3. The two transitions, following one another, caused not just a huge politico-religious upheaval; it affected the Indian economy severely.

It reshaped the Indian economy, in terms of both the agricultural landscape and the industrial sector whose raw materials were partitioned to Pakistan. However, the process of reconstruction of the Indian economy began soon thereafter.

4. The third transitional event was the integration of 538 princely states into the new India. This process began soon after 15 August 1947 and was virtually over by 1949. A few remaining states were integrated in 1950. That was a big achievement for the country. India then became a much larger country; its geography had been transformed.

5. Absorption of three transitions following one after another in a period of a little over two years was exceptional for an inexperienced leadership.

6. This three-year period was indeed a hugely transient period for the country. Obviously, it was dominated by big political developments. With these political developments as the background, this was also an equally huge transient period for the Indian economy and its banking system.

7. Built on wholly inadequate capital bases and unhealthy practices before Independence and still weakening economy after Independence, the weak banking system continued to record declines in its performance. Amid these developments, it was indeed creditable that RBI was nationalized and a BCA was put on the anvil.

Like the part of 1947 before the Partition, part of the year after the Partition was a very difficult one for the country.[1] Inflationary conditions had persisted since the time of WWII. Industrial production was hampered by virtual non-availability of capital goods, difficulties of transport, frequent strikes and other causes. The food position was causing grave anxiety. The Annual Report of RBI for the year stated:

> The most urgent and serious problem that will claim the attention of the two States as soon as they settle down to the real job of governance is that of the all-pervading corruption that is destroying

the vitals of public life generally and the administrative machine in particular.[2]

At the same time, processes for reconstruction of the economy had begun. The Planning Advisory Board appointed by the interim government in 1946 in its report in early 1947 had recommended the establishment of a whole time non-political Planning Commission.

The year 1948 is considered as one of comparative peace on the political front and free from communal disturbances. But the economic conditions facing the populace were still deteriorating and the general price level was still rising, as shortages of food and industrial raw materials persisted. A major policy development was the formulation of Industrial Policy in April 1948, which laid down the relative roles of public and private sectors in various segments of industry, as also the role of State regulation and control of certain industries. The socialistic streak of the party in power was already beginning to show. As a result, serious apprehensions were created in the minds of the captains of industry regarding the role of the private sector. This uncertainty was bound to affect future industrial development adversely.

The last year of this period, that is, 1949 (the major part of the financial year 1949–50) continued with the previous year's story in terms of deteriorating economic conditions. Prices continued to rise. A major event of the year was the devaluation in September of the currencies of countries in a large part of the world in terms of the US dollar. India too devalued its rupee in concert with the pound sterling. The policy cycle of control-decontrol-control of food supplies continued with no clear impact. Implementation of the Industrial Policy announced in the previous year was to begin by enacting necessary laws. Over the year, helped by an improvement of the transport situation and better labour-management relations, production in the industrial and agricultural sectors was on the whole maintained well.

One can conclude from the above brief description that each of these years was marked by big political events which severely impacted the economy. The central and the provincial governments were all the time grappling with the emerging economic issues. Economic policies were still at the formulation stage. In the last year of this period, a stable socio-economic-political scenario was beginning to emerge.

II. THE FAST-CHANGING BANKING SCENE

2.1. The Inheritance

Four-and-a half months of 1947 inherited an unorganized and weak banking system. WWII had simultaneously expanded it and weakened it. Non-scheduled banks remained outside the purview of RBI; even their exact number was not known. Ever since some records became available in 1913, not a single year had passed without bank failures. In fact, the number of bank failures had increased since mid-1930s into the 1940s. It had been said then that the Indian banking system 'was freer than the free banking that prevailed in the US around the civil war'.[3] Although RBI was already in existence for more than 12 years, it hardly had any powers to supervise and regulate the banking system; those powers lay with the GOI. RBI's repeated efforts since 1939 to get a banking company law passed had not succeeded.

At the end of 1947, only two banks—Imperial Bank and Central Bank of India—had TA and total deposits of more than ₹100 crore; another two 'big' banks—Bank of India and Punjab National Bank—had TA/total deposits of more than ₹50 crore; and another two 'big' banks—UCO Bank and Bank of Baroda—had TA/total deposits of ₹47/35 crore and ₹36/33 crore, respectively. The geographic location of both scheduled as well as non-scheduled banks in the country at the end of 1947 was quite uneven. More than one-half of the scheduled banks were based in West Bengal, Madras and Bombay, in that order. One-Third of the non-scheduled banks, 186 out of 555, were head-quartered in Madras, distantly followed by West Bengal and Bombay. Total number of branches of all joint stock banks (foreign banks and non-scheduled banks included) in the Indian Union (Pakistan excluded) had declined from 4,855 at the beginning to 4,819 at the end of 1947. Branches of Indian SCBs had declined from 2,881 in 1947 to 2,851 in 1948 and to 2,728 in 1949. Branches of non-scheduled banks had declined from 2,028 to 1,832. The tendency towards a rapid expansion of branch network, particularly of smaller and non-scheduled banks during WWII and later, had lost its momentum in the year 1947.[4]

2.2. The Post-Partition Change

The disturbances that followed the partition of the country completely dislocated the banking system in the affected areas, particularly Punjab and Bengal. In 1947, 38 banks had failed, of which 17 were in West Bengal alone. The next year was even worse as 45 banks, including some relatively larger ones, closed down. A number of offices of Indian banks in Pakistan were closed permanently. The government took measures to mitigate the severity of the dislocation, inter alia, by passing emergency ordinances.

Many banks with their registered offices in East Punjab (India) and Delhi found that while most of their assets were in West Punjab (Pakistan), most of their deposit liabilities had been transferred to their branches in India, especially East Punjab and Delhi. As a result, and particularly because of the difficulties of access to their records and assets in West Punjab, some of these banks found it difficult to meet their depositors' demands. To facilitate the smooth working of these banks as well as to alleviate distress of depositors, mostly refugees, the grant of temporary facilities was thought desirable.

Hence, the government promulgated two ordinances in September 1947. A period of moratorium was announced to meet the minimum demands of funds of bank depositors. RBI was empowered to grant necessary advances to the banks to enable them to meet these demands. To ameliorate certain other financial difficulties of banks, the government, by another ordinance in December 1947, temporarily amended the Negotiable Instruments Act, 1881, and the Indian Limitation Act, 1908.

The banking system that seemed to be bearing the strains and stresses of the partition fairly well was faced with new problems around mid-1948 resulting from a severe contraction of banking resources. This was mainly a part of the wider post-war economic adjustments. But, for some banks, these problems developed into a crisis as a consequence of both indiscriminate expansion as well as disregard of the accepted norms of commercial banking. Some scheduled and non-scheduled banks suspended payments in September–October 1948. As the post-war recovery in bank advances continued and as cash ratios were maintained at the levels of the previous years, the impact of increased funds requirement fell on the investment portfolios of banks which faced a considerable reduction from their peak around mid-1948.

The contraction of deposit liabilities continued into the year 1949. In the first half of 1949, the demand for bank credit touched an all-time high, while deposits of banks declined further. Overall, the deposit liabilities of scheduled banks had fallen by ₹109 crore in 1949.[5] Thus, the fast-moving developments in pre-Independence 1947, the post-WWII economic adjustments during 1947–1949 resulting in simultaneous contraction of bank deposits and expansion of the lending portfolios of banks, and rapid changes in post-Partition 1947 had caused the banking system to remain in a fluid state. This unregulated system began to slowly shift to a regulated system with the nationalization of RBI in 1948 and the passage of the BCA in

1949. At the same time, the story of bank failures had continued; the number of bank failures rose to 55 in 1949, adding up to the total number of bank failures in 1947–1949 to 138.[6]

2.3. Changing Composition of Bank Categories

The division of the country and consequent shifting of some banks from Pakistan to India and a few from India to Pakistan, churning of non-scheduled banks among different categories and elimination of some of them, and the classification of foreign banks into scheduled and non-scheduled banks led to the ever changing numbers among the categories of banks.

The Inspection Ordinance and the Restriction of Branches Act in 1946 had begun to expose the unsound practices followed by several banks. Prior to 1948, non-scheduled banks comprised those banks which had been classified as banking companies under Section 277F of the Indian Companies Act. It also included those banks which were registered in the Indian States (which had not acceded to the Indian Union) and had no branches in the Indian Union. Prior to March 1949, any company that used the words 'bank', 'banker' or 'banking' as part of its name was deemed to be a banking company, irrespective of whether or not banking was, in actual fact, its principal business. Under the BCA, 1949, banking was precisely defined. As a result of various restrictions imposed by the Act, several banking companies declared themselves as non-banking companies to get excluded from the category of banks. The doubtful quality of the statistics received from the banks, hitherto, seemed to improve over these three years. The enactment of the BCA led to a new series of statistics, as banks were now legally required to submit returns about their businesses. This further led to a revision of banks in different categories.

Table 2.1 brings out the changing and declining numbers of scheduled and non-scheduled banks for the years 1946–1949, as reported in STs 1947, 1948 and 1949.

Table 2.2 summarizes the status of commercial bank categories in India over the four-year period.

Table 2.1 *Changing Numbers of Scheduled and Non-scheduled Banks: 1946–1949*

Sr. No.	Source	1946			1947			1948			1949		
		S	NS	T	S	NS	T	S	NS	T	S	NS	T
1	ST 1947	80	610	690	81	557	638	–	–	–	–	–	–
2	ST 1948	79	552	631	82	550	632	79	542	621	–	–	–
3	ST 1949	78	562	640	81	544	625	79	540	619	78	507	585

Sources: ST 1949, Introduction, p. v., for 1946–1949; ST 1950, for 1949*.
Notes: S = Scheduled; NS = Non-scheduled; T = Total.

Table 2.2 *Status of Commercial Bank Categories: 1946–1949*

Serial No.	Categories of Banks	1946	1947	1948	1949	1949*
1	**Indian Banks**	640	625	619	585	599
	1. Scheduled	78	81	79	78	78
	2. Non-scheduled	562	544	540	507	521
2	**Foreign Banks**	28	23	20	20	21
	1. Scheduled	16	16	16	16	16
	2. Non-scheduled	12	07	04	04	05
3	**Total Banks**	668	648	639	605	620
	1. Scheduled	94	97	95	94	94
	2. Non-scheduled	574	551	544	511	526

Sources: ST 1949, Introduction, p. v., for 1946–1949; ST 1950, for 1949*.

Just as we had concluded that the data on the number of banks and their classification for the years 1946–1949 could be reasonably assumed to have reached a state of finality, ST 1950 proved that conclusion incorrect by changing the 1949 figures surprisingly upward.

III. FILLING THE INSTITUTIONAL GAPS

2.4. Reserve Bank of India in Public Ownership

As noted in the last chapter, RBI had asked its Research Department towards the end of 1946 to examine the issue of nationalization of the Bank. The Research Department in its Note in early 1947 summed up its argument by stating, 'the case for nationalisation at the moment seems to be weak and inconclusive'. Meanwhile, in January 1947, the government had received notice of a resolution, from Mohan Lal Saksena, a member of the legislature, recommending to the Governor-General in Council 'to take necessary steps to nationalize the RBI and the Imperial Bank of India as a prelude to nationalization of banking and insurance in India'.

The Finance Department, GOI, wrote to RBI once again on 25 January 1947 asking for the promised Note by their research department and the views of RBI on nationalization of Imperial. In his reply on 31 January, the Governor, C. D. Deshmukh, expressed his fears that the Central Board of the RBI would not be prepared to make any recommendations at its forthcoming meeting on 11 February 'in view of the short time and also in the absence of any indication regarding Government's policy with regard to the whole question of nationalisation'.[7] The governor also wrote that similar considerations applied in the case of Imperial Bank. The governor concluded that, 'I am not in a position to let Government have the Bank's views on the question of nationalisation of the Reserve and Imperial Banks. I am still less able to make recommendations regarding the general question of the nationalisation of all banks in India'.

It is not known what happened to the resolution on nationalization that had been moved by a member, but the demand for nationalization of RBI did not recede. Soon thereafter, that is, on 18 February 1947, another member of the Legislative Assembly moved a resolution to the effect that 'the RBI be taken over by government, converted into a State bank and run as such'. This resolution was moved 'not because the member concerned was dissatisfied with the bank's working but because he considered that the monetary organization of the country should be of national concern and should not be confined to a limited number of shareholders "who are none but capitalists".' The resolution seemed to have the strong support of both the major parties in the legislature. Winding up the debate, the Finance Member, Liaquat Ali Khan, observed that it was evident that there was a general desire for the nationalization of the Bank. He went on to say:

> I also notice that this desire is not so much on account of any deficiencies that have been discovered in the present set-up of the Bank, but it is due on the general grounds that an institution playing such a vital part in the economic life of the country should be nationalised to secure proper coordination and integration of currency, credit and monetary policy with the Government's financial and economic policy.

He went on to observe that he hoped no member desired that 'the Central Bank of the country should become a handmaid of the Government of the time.'

While presenting the national budget on 28 February 1947, Liaquat Ali Khan announced the government's decision to nationalize RBI. Thereafter, 'The question of nationalization did not appear to have been referred to the Bank by the Government for some months, presumably owing to the sweeping political changes that took place, culminating in the partition of the country'. In January 1948, after Independence, R. K. Shanmukham Chetty, the first finance minister of independent India, requested RBI Governor, C. D. Deshmukh, to set down his personal views on the subject of nationalization of Reserve Bank and Imperial Bank. The governor in his reply, apart from narrating administrative and procedural issues, being minor issues, stated that 'it was not possible to be dogmatic about the nationalisation issue one way or the other, and on a final analysis, it did not much matter whether the Bank was run as it was then constituted, or was nationalised'. But in the end, consistent with his previously stated position, the governor expressed his opposition to nationalization.

On 4 February 1948, a member of the Legislative Assembly raised this subject again, and the finance minister responded that 'Government proposed to take steps to see that the nationalisation of the Reserve Bank was effected as soon as possible after September 30, 1948, when the Bank was to cease to be the common banker to India and Pakistan.' Two days later, on 6 February 1948, the finance minister wrote to the governor stating that, as the latter was aware, the decision to nationalize RBI was taken last year and it was left to the present government to just implement it. He also wrote that he would still like to receive the suggestions of the Central Board of the Bank. Accordingly, the matter was considered by the Central Board on 23 February 1948 which expressed itself in a resolution stating that 'it will not be in the interests of the country to nationalise the Reserve Bank of India and such a step may be fraught with very great danger which cannot be fully foreseen at present,...' The Finance Ministry wrote back to the governor stating 'the Government of India, having given careful consideration to the views of the Central Board, do not see sufficient justification for re-visiting their decision to nationalise the Bank'.

On 2 September 1948, a Bill called The Reserve Bank (Transfer to public ownership) Bill, 1948 was moved for consideration in the Legislative Assembly. The debate which followed was rather brief. 'The Bank was accused of having been throughout the slave of—the maid of the old Lady of Threadneedle Street—the Bank of England.' Winding up the debate, the finance minister assured the House that 'we would see to it that the Reserve Bank of India continues to function as a fully autonomous body.' The Act came into force on 1 January 1949.[8]

2.5. Reserve Bank of India and Bank Credit to Agricultural Sector

The discussions on this theme in Chapter 6 had recorded the fact that the activities of RBI in this sphere did not blossom till about the 1950s. Resuming therefrom, it may be stated that the 1947–1949 years had hardly any significant developments to report on RBI's role in promoting grant of bank credit to agricultural sector.

For the record, reference may, however, be made to the remarks made by a member, Mr Manu Subedar, in the Legislative Assembly on 18 February 1947, in reinforcement of his demand for nationalization of RBI, about the RBI's failure to improve the mechanism for dealing with agricultural finance and bringing about closer connections between agricultural operations and the Bank. Post its nationalization, the Bank was expected to play a more active role in promoting provision of agricultural credit and transferring its expertise to state cooperative departments.

2.6. Moves for Nationalization of Imperial Bank

The initial story of demand for nationalization of banks in India, which reportedly began to be made in the 1920s, has been narrated in Chapter 1. The demand met with its first success when the ownership of RBI was transferred to public ownership in 1949; but the nationalization of the central bank of a country falls in a different class. The demand for nationalization of Imperial Bank and other commercial banks continued to be asserted. Mention was made in Section III.2.4. supra of the government having received notice of a resolution in January 1947 to the effect that necessary steps should be taken to nationalize RBI and Imperial Bank as a prelude to nationalization of banking and insurance in India.

2.6.1. GOI versus Reserve Bank and Imperial Bank

It would have been observed in Section III.2.4 supra that, until the nationalization of RBI, correspondence between the Ministry of Finance, GOI and Governor, RBI (January 1947–January 1948) had linked the issues of nationalization of RBI and Imperial Bank together.

In response to the finance minister's letter to Governor, C. D. Deshmukh, in January 1948, the latter had responded by stating that it (that is, nationalization) was not a necessity on purely logical grounds. The governor had rebutted both the charges levelled against Imperial Bank: (a) it was over-conservative and almost wooden in its banking service and (b) it had not treated its Indian staff fairly and was generally backward in Indianization.

The governor's view was that government should hasten slowly and 'not bite more than we can chew'. The governor considered that instead of nationalization, it should be ascertained 'more painstakingly and accurately where exactly the present institution is going wrong and calling it to account.'

Further on, the governor dealt with the view of nationalizing the banking system too. He observed that

> If there is to be nationalisation ... it ought to apply to the system as a whole and not only to one unit (that is, Imperial Bank),[9] however important that unit may be.... The conditions in India did not call for such a kind of nationalisation at the present stage. There is no reason why we should at the beginning of our democratic existence, undertake an experiment which has not been undertaken

elsewhere, except in the U.S.S.R., where the entire economy is run on a communist basis.

In his concluding words, the governor observed, 'My advice, in brief, is, therefore, that we should wait for a year or two before rushing into nationalisation of the banking institutions...'

On 4 February 1948, Finance Minister, Chetty, largely on account of insistence from within the Congress Party, announced that, in respect of the Imperial Bank, the government accepted the policy of nationalization, but as that bank had branches outside India, government first proposed to examine carefully the various technical questions involved before implementing nationalization. The finance minister further announced that government did not have any intention to nationalize other commercial banks.

At the same time, the finance minister wrote to the Managing Director, Imperial Bank, A. R. Chisholm, informing him of the decision of the government. He also requested Chisholm to meet (Governor) Deshmukh and discuss with him 'the various questions that arise out of this decision'. The meeting between Deshmukh and Chisholm took place on 20 February 1948. At the very outset, the managing director pointed out that

[T]here was a considerable body of public feeling both for and against nationalisation and as far as I was concerned I could see nothing in favour of state control and everything against it and that it would result in the ultimate ruin of the bank if persisted with'.

He had added further that 'the net result could only be a drastic crippling of the profit-earning capacity of the institution and an undoubted drift of the cream of its business to its competitors'. According to the Reserve Bank governor, the decision to takeover had already been adopted at a meeting of a Congress sub-committee and some of the members had gone so far as to state that 'even if the Reserve Bank was not nationalized, they would still insist on the Imperial Bank being nationalized'.

In a letter dated 3 March 1948, Prime Minister, Jawaharlal Nehru, wrote, 'decision had already been taken to nationalise the Reserve Bank and the Imperial Bank after some months'.[10]

The Central Board of Imperial met in April 1948 to discuss the issue. After full consideration, the Board resolved, inter alia, that the government be informed that 'their proposal to nationalize the Bank, while leaving other Commercial Banks untouched, was regarded as totally unjustified and unnecessary'. The Board also resolved that 'it failed to understand why the Imperial Bank of India which is essentially a Commercial Bank should be singled out for nationalisation.' The resolution was forwarded to RBI for transmission to the government. While forwarding Imperial Bank's papers to the government, the governor added his own strong words stating that the nationalization would be a serious mistake. He added that 'nothing is to be gained, and much is likely to be lost, by nationalisation of Imperial Bank, at any rate, at this stage.'

The government considered the whole matter once again, and in early February 1949, Dr John Mathai, the new finance minister, announced that the government did not consider it feasible to proceed with the nationalization of Imperial Bank in view of possible repercussions on the investment market and the unsettled conditions in the country.

In a note for the committee of the Bank's Central Board in early March 1949, Chisholm also reported a 'realistic' statement of Vallabhbhai Patel, deputy prime minister, 'Government [had] neither the capacity nor the means to undertake nationalisation of any industry at present'. Chisholm felt that this statement would 'do much to restore confidence'. He added, '[I]t is a matter of deep satisfaction that the Bank may now be considered free to function as a Commercial Institution and that the danger of its being sacrificed on the altar of socialistic ideologies has meanwhile receded'.

It was said with reference to the above statement that '[a]lthough confidence may have been "restored" at least for a while, the demand for nationalisation continued and eventually led to the appointment of the Rural Banking Enquiry Committee (RBEC) by the Government of India in November 1949'.[11]

The RBEC was appointed mainly to suggest measures for the following:

- Extension of banking facilities in the rural areas
- Streamlining rural credit
- Mobilizing rural savings

The Committee submitted its report in May 1950.[12]

2.7. The Banking Companies Act, 1949: Finally!

The journey of the proposals for enacting a BCA till the year 1946 has been discussed in Chapter 1. Resuming therefrom, the report of the Select Committee on the Banking Companies Bill appointed in 1946 was presented to the Legislative Assembly in February 1947. The finance minister announced in the Dominion Parliament in January 1948 the withdrawal of this Bill as the government had decided to introduce a new one shortly. A fresh Bill incorporating several amendments was introduced in March 1948 and referred to a Select Committee. To provide for the regulation of the banking system meanwhile, the Banking Companies (Control) Ordinance, 1948, was promulgated in September 1948, bringing into immediate effect some of the important provisions of the Banking Companies Bill.

The Banking Companies Bill was finally passed by the Constituent Assembly of India on 17 February 1949. The Act came into force on 16 March 1949, marking the culmination of the efforts which had begun with the RBI's 'proposals for an Indian Bank Act' made in 1939. This Act consolidated the provisions concerning banking companies in the Companies Act, 1913, and various Ordinances and Acts which had been brought into force between 1946 and 1948; it also introduced some new provisions. Many of the underlying causes of weak banks and bank failures were taken care of by the passage of this law, especially by substantially strengthening RBI's powers of supervision and regulation of banks.

2.7.1. Select Provisions of the Act

- Banking was defined as 'the accepting, for the purpose of lending or investment, of deposits of money from the public, repayable on demand or otherwise, and withdrawable by cheque, draft, order or otherwise.'
- The Act applied to all banking companies, but not to cooperative banks, and was extended to all the provinces of India and to the acceding states.
- The Act delimited activities of banks by, in particular, prohibiting them from engaging, directly or indirectly, in trading, and prescribed certain conditions and a code of conduct for the business of banking.
- The Act prohibited non-banking companies from accepting deposits repayable on demand.
- It required that all banks working in the Indian Union are to be licensed. RBI was to be the authority for the issue of licences.
- It laid down minimum requirements relating to paid-up capital and reserves of a banking company.
- It empowered the RBI to exercise control over all joint stock banks in India, scheduled as well as non-scheduled. RBI might issue directions to banks in regard to their lending policies.

- RBI was given powers to inspect any bank on its own initiative.
- Requirements for cash reserve ratio (CRR) and statutory liquidity ratio (SLR) were clearly laid out.
- The Act prohibited interlocking of directorates among banking companies and the employment of managing agents. It prohibited unsecured loans to any of the directors or to firms and private companies in which the directors might be interested. The banks were required to submit to the RBI returns of the unsecured loans to public companies in which the directors might be interested.
- The Act widened the powers of RBI to enable it to come to the aid of banks in times of emergency.
- It made provisions for expeditious and effective proceedings for liquidation of banks. It also included provisions for facilitating amalgamation of banking companies.
- RBI was required to submit an annual report to the GOI on the trend and progress of banking in India (TP) with suggestions, if any, for strengthening the business of banking.[13]
- Every bank incorporated in India was required to prepare a BS and a PLA in prescribed formats in respect of all business transacted by it.[14]

IV. THE FINANCIALS: 1947–1949

The description of major developments in the economic and banking spheres provide the context in which the financials of Indian SCBs during the current period may be understood.

2.8. More but Still Inadequate Data for 1947–1948

Up to the year 1946, the available bank financial data comprised sparse but significant BS figures for equity and deposits on the liabilities side, money at call and short notice, investments and loans on the assets side, for Imperial Bank, exchange banks as a group and IJSBs as a group. There was no information about the PLA. ST 1948 changed that. While the BS content remained the same, the data presented was for Imperial Bank, SCBs other than Imperial and various categories of non-scheduled banks for three years 1946–1948. Data for exchange banks was omitted. But the welcome inclusion was the complete PLAs of Imperial Bank and the rest of the SCBs. After the enactment of the banking law in 1949, the financial picture became complete with the presentation of complete BS and PLA of Imperial Bank, major Indian SCBs, other Indian SCBs and foreign banks.

Another inadequacy of this period was that the figures for the years 1947 and 1948 for even the most relevant financial parameters including number of banks and number of branches, kept on changing. These figures changed from one ST to the following. It had been so noticed in the period up to the year 1946; it continued in the current period of 1947–1949. Referring to data availability for a study of trends, 'TP 1949' had the following to state as the reasons for, inter alia, non-comparability:

- Partition of India (change of geography),
- Changing extent of states/areas covered by the RBI and its laws with accession of princely states, etc.,
- Preparation of diverse statements from different sources within RBI,
- Inability and/or unwillingness on the part of some banks to provide accurate figures or to ensure their correct classification,
- Changing number of banks submitting returns from time to time and failure of banks to submit returns regularly and
- Changing number of banks in the 'SCB' category due to frequent entry and exit of banks from time to time.[15]

Compared to the paucity of bank data mentioned in Chapter 1 and the first couple of years of this period, that is, 1947–1948, a relatively less inadequate assessment became possible for the first time in the history of Indian banking because of the passage of one very essential requirement in the BCA in 1949, as aforementioned: Requiring every bank to prepare a BS and a PLA for every year and submit it to the central banking authority.

Full details for the year 1949 as per the prescribed format for BS were published for the first time in ST 1950. ST 1950 also published (PLA) data for SCBs for the years 1947–1949 and for foreign banks from 1949. In terms of providing full BS and PLA data, the year 1949 marked a welcome break from the past. However, figures for one important parameter for analysis, viz., bank employees, were still not available; this piece of data was published for the first time for public sector banks (PSBs) in 1969 and for all the banks in 1976.

2.9. The Financials of Indian SCBs

Three statements in the Annexure to this chapter contain relevant data for this section. Statement 2.1 provides BS main heads of Indian SCBs for three years. Foreign banks' data was not available for 1947–1948; hence, it got excluded. Statement 2.2 provides the PLA data of Indian SCBs and Statement 2.3 provides data for a few significant bank parameters of Imperial Bank.

As noted above, financials of foreign banks became available from 1949. The financial statements of foreign banks (limited to their Indian business) hardly showed any equity, as their equity resided in their corporate offices abroad. The BCA, 1949, required foreign banks to deposit with RBI an amount not less than ₹50,000, the minimum capital requirement for them. In compliance, these banks brought in that amount or more as equity. In 1949, the average Indian equity of 21 foreign banks was ₹100,000 and average net profit was in excess of ₹900,000. Hence, profitability analysis of foreign banks' Indian operations based on their miniscule Indian equity was a meaningless exercise; a better measure was return on assets (ROA). A usually better performance of foreign banks on several parameters compared to other bank sub-groups weighed strongly on the average performance of total SCBs (of course, not in this period).

Table 2.3 presents significant financials of Indian SCBs (Statements 2.1 and 2.2) for the years 1947–1949.

2.9.1. Transient Data Bank

One may notice the significant change in the data landscape in Table 2.3 from that in Tables 1.5 and 1.6 (in Chapter 1). Availability of full BS and PLA transformed the data set for analysis. Table 2.3 provides a reasonably complete picture of financial performance of Indian SCBs, taking in stock-and-flow parameters, mostly, from their financial statements. However, systematic closing down of non-scheduled banks and weak banks, and a few amalgamations, still-remaining inaccuracies of the data, and, to top it all, a tumultuous three years of political and economic change, made for a picture of transient financials in this very short period. The state of the economy which showed a decline in the first half of 1947–1949 had begun to improve for the better in the second half, as already described in Section II.2.2 supra.

2.9.2. Glaring Adverse Performance of Banks

The data in Table 2.3 shows decline in the size of the banking system (number of banks, TA and number of branches). These declines are supported by declines in the portfolios of deposits, advances and investment (Statement 2.1). Decline in deposits was reflected in changes in the ratios in which deposits appear as the denominator. Increase in C–I ratio was another adverse feature. Leverage 'improved' because TA had declined. It seems that leverage was measured in and around 1949 by relating equity to total deposits. The conventional norm of equity to deposits was 10 per cent.[16] Deposits of Indian SCBs in 1949 were ₹761

Table 2.3 Indian SCBs' Significant Financials: 1947–1949

Serial No.	Parameters	1947	1948	1949
1	Banks (number)	81	79	78
2	TA (₹ in crore)	1,044	1,136	869
3	Branches (number)	2,881	2,851	2,728
4	*Equity (₹ in crore)	59	63	63
5	Leverage	5.65	5.55	7.25
6	CASA: deposits (CASA–DEP) ratio	66	70	75
7	C–D ratio	41	42	44
8	I–D ratio	50	50	46
9	Investment: credit (I–C) ratio	120	119	103
10	Total income (₹ in crore)	29.82	29.73	26.72
11	Net interest income (NII) (₹ in crore)	16.56	17.47	14.32
12	Cost: income (C–I) ratio	62	68	76
13	Net interest margin (NIM) (%)	1.59	1.69	1.65
14	Operating profit (OP) after P&C (₹ in crore)	8.18	7.19	4.52
15	Net profit (profit after tax [PAT]) (₹ in crore)	5.23	4.79	3.27
16	ROA (OP on average assets (%)	0.78	0.66	0.45
17	Return on equity (ROE) (%)	14.35	11.79	7.17

Sources: Item 1: STs, various years; Item 3: Indian Banks' Association (IBA): performance highlights, various years, Bombay; items 2, 4, 10, 14 and 15: Annexure 2.1 and Annexure 2.2; items 5–9, 11–13 and 16–17: our workings from Annexure 2.1 and Annexure 2.2.

Note: For definitions of ratios in this and following chapters, see Ratios under Abbreviations.

crore, while equity was ₹63 crore; thus, leverage was 8.3 per cent, less than the convention. It seems also that the prevailing economic scenario in the country had made the bank depositors more risk-conscious to cause them to maintain high liquidity in their bank money by keeping their funds in current and savings bank accounts (CASA, hereinafter), resulting in an increasing level of CASA. It could also be explained by the need of bank customers to maintain high CASA balances to meet personal and business requirements in fast-changing economic conditions. All these changes were reflected in declines in ROA and ROE.

Thus, the Indian SCBs had recorded declines in their number, size of BS, number of branches, ROA and ROE. 'It was an all-round decline'. Another dire example of decline in performance of the banking system in 1947–1949 was the fact that 17 out of 41 largest banks of the country had recorded 'negative CAGR' during the three-year period. These 17 banks included SBI and PNB both affected, obviously, by Partition (see Tables 6.11 and 6.12.).

2.9.3. Market Share of Imperial Bank

It was shown in Chapter 1 that Imperial's market share in deposits and loans had been declining for several years up to 1946. Similar comparison is attempted for the year 1949.

Table 2.3 is based on the data of Indian SCBs which includes Imperial Bank. Comparing Statement 2.1 (Indian SCBs) with Statement 2.4 (Imperial Bank) on several parameters, it comes out that the Imperial's data has pulled down the Indian Total Scheduled Commercial Banks' (TSCBs) size and performance. Imperial's market share in several parameters is presented for the year 1949 in Part I of Table 2.4. In addition, comparisons of three other parameters are also made in Part II.

Of the five parameters in Part I, market shares in two parameters, deposits and advances, only are available for 1946 [Chapter 1, Section III.1.(2)(c)]. Imperial's share in deposits as well as advances had been declining since 1913 (on the basis of data for select years). In 1946, Imperial's share was 27 per cent in deposits and 20 per cent in advances. In 1949, as seen above, the shares were 33 per cent and

Table 2.4 *Market Share of Imperial Bank*

I. Market Share, 1949		
Parameters	*Market Share (%)*	
1. Branches	14	
2. TA	31	
3. Deposits	33	
4. Advances	27	
5. Total income	23	
II. Non-market Share Comparisons		
Parameters	*Imperial Bank*	*Total Indian SCBs*
6. C–I Ratio	81	76
7. ROA	0.31	0.45
8. C–D Ratio	36	44

27 per cent, respectively. But 1949 data does not include data of non-scheduled banks, whereas, the market shares in 1946 had been calculated after adding those banks' deposits and advances. On a rough basis, taking the share of non-scheduled banks in 1946 into 1949 data, Imperial Bank's share fell to 29 per cent and 23 per cent of deposits and advances, respectively. Still, it was higher in 1949 in comparison to 1946.

As regards the comparisons in Part II, Imperial Bank's performance was inferior to the performance of the aggregate (Indian TSCBs) on all the three counts.

V. THE 21ST-CENTURY BANKS: 1949

Continuing with our series of listing the 21st-century banks, the statement for 1949 is compiled in Table 2.5.

Table 2.5 *The 21st-Century Banks: 1949*

(Third in the Series)

Serial No.	Banks (Ranked by TA)	TA		No. of Branches	
		₹ in crore	Rank	Number	Rank
1	Imperial Bank of India	268.64	1	377	1
2	Central Bank of India	139.32	2	277	2
3	UCO Bank	91.95	3	81	6
4	Bank of India	65.26	4	33	18
5	PNB	52.07	5	246	3
6	United Bank of India	36.93	6	116 (1950)	4
7	Bank of Baroda	34.35	7	43	12
8	Allahabad Bank	31.59	8	76	7
9	Indian Bank	22.70	9	71	8
10	State Bank of Hyderabad	19.95	10	36	17
11	State Bank of Mysore	10.77	11	32	19
12	State Bank of Saurashtra	10.14	12	9	32
13	Indian Overseas Bank	10.14	12	40	14
14	State Bank of Bikaner & Jaipur (Bank of Bikaner)	9.15	14	43	12
15	Dena Bank	8.30	15	51	9
16	Canara Bank	8.21	16	40	14
17	State Bank of Bikaner & Jaipur (Bank of Jaipur)	7.80	17	49	10
18	State Bank of Patiala	7.17	18	40	14
19	Union Bank of India	6.11	19	6	37
20	Andhra Bank	5.71	20	45	11
21	State Bank of Indore	5.01	21	11	30
22	Syndicate Bank	4.86	22	85	5
23	State Bank of Travancore	4.70	23	15	25

(Third in the Series)

Serial No.	Banks (Ranked by TA)	TA		No. of Branches	
		₹ in crore	Rank	Number	Rank
24	New Bank of India	3.88	24	13	28
25	Corporation Bank	3.039	25	32	19
25	Corporation Bank	3.039	25	32	19
26	Bank of Maharashtra	2.44	26	20	21
27	Punjab & Sind Bank	2.11	27	8	35
28	Bank of Rajasthan	1.63	28	20	21
29	South Indian Bank	1.35	29	15	25
30	Jammu & Kashmir Bank	1.18	30	6	37
31	Karur Vysya Bank	0.95	31	15	25
32	Catholic Syrian bank	0.91	32	16	24
33	Vysya Bank	0.78	33	17	23
34	Oriental Bank of Commerce	0.72	34	6	37
35	Karnataka Bank	0.64	35	9	32
36	Nainital Bank	0.59	36	8	35
37	Ratnakar Bank	0.48	37	5	40
38	Tamilnad Mercantile Bank	0.46	38	5	40
39	City Union Bank	0.45	39	9	32
40	Vijaya Bank	0.44	40	13	28
41	Lakshmi Vilas Bank	0.39	41	10	31
42	Dhanlaxmi Bank	0.36	42	3	43
43	Federal Bank	0.05	43	4	42
Total		884		2,056	

Source: ST 1950, Table 29, 54–63.

Note: *Figure for 1948, as that for 1949 was not available.

This list added one more bank into it, that is, State Bank of Saurashtra, making it 43 banks in all. A bank named Bhavnagar Darbar Savings Bank established on 01 April 1902 was converted into a statutory corporation called State Bank of Saurashtra in 1950. On 01 July, the same year, four other Darbar banks were merged into it to form a bigger entity. As a result, State Bank of Saurashtra appears in Table 2.5 at serial number 12.

VI. AT THE CLOSE OF 1949

It is no coincidence that soon after India took charge of itself, first the Reserve Bank was nationalized and then the BCA was passed. This short period remains marked for attaining these two cherished goals of the Indian polity. Both these changes hugely strengthened the regulatory and supervisory structures of the banking system. The BCA also provided for publication of banks' annual financial statements and a lot of additional bank-related information. This enactment also required RBI to write an annual report on TP, both of which were a major boon to the building up of the data bank of the banking system.

During this period, 'bank failures' continued and even increased, due to the after-effects of the Partition, continued decline in the state of the economy and the enforcement of the BCA. The RBI had decided that, to protect public savings, it would be better to wind up weak, non-viable banks or merge them into stronger ones. The axe began to fall immediately on the weak and the wicked; and the number of non-scheduled banks began to fall, after their meteoric growth during the war period and after. The RBI continued to act with its firm hand into the 1950s.

In the first review of the TP in this period, TP 1949 referred to the adverse consequences of the Partition for the banking system, mostly in Punjab and Bengal. It also referred to a severe fall in deposits in 1949 coupled with high seasonal demand for bank loans creating a stringency of funds in the banking system. Despite the failure of a large number of banks (138, Section II.2 supra) and very poor financials of Indian SCBs (Section IV supra), TP 1949 concluded that 'the Indian banks have, on the whole, withstood the strain caused by the war and post-war economic conditions.' While offering suggestions to strengthen the banking system, TP 1949 had drawn attention to poor top managements of banks, their incorrect investment and lending policies, and loose supervision of branches. It concluded: 'To play their rightful part in the development of the country's economy, it is necessary that Indian banks should devote greater attention to a consolidation of their resources and to the building up of sound banking traditions'.[17]

The Imperial Bank continued to enjoy the position of the premier bank of the country (as most other SCBs were small in size). The demand for its nationalization was carried into the 1950s. Broadly, it may be said that, by the end of 1949, India had got its moorings and some sense of socio-political stability. RBI, through exercise of its new powers, could now begin to oversee the working of the banking system more closely.

Despite the transient changes in the economy and in the banking system, and its unsatisfactory performance, the banking system was beginning to look more organized at the end of this period. We could say that India, as a new nation, was now engaged in building up a new economy and a new banking system.

2.A. Annexure

Statement 2.1 *Main Heads of Indian SCBs' BS: 1947–1949*

				(₹ in crore)
S. No.	*Balance Sheet/Years*	*1947*	*1948*	*1949*
	Liabilities			
1	Own funds (Capital+reserves)	59	63	63
2	Deposits	906	874	761
3	Borrowings	0	0	21
4	Bills payable	0	0	12
5	Other liabilities	0	0	13
	Total liabilities/TA	**1,044**	**1,136**	**869**
S. No.	*Balance Sheet/Years*	*1947*	*1948*	*1949*
	Assets			
6	Cash and bank balances	169	163	160
7	Money at call and short notice	0	0	5
8	Investments	449	441	347
9	Advances	373	371	337
10	Fixed assets	0	0	8
11	Other assets (Non-banking assets+Other assets)	0	0	11

Sources: STs 1948, 1949.

Statement 2.2 *Main Heads of Indian SCBs' PLA: 1947–1949*

				(₹ in crore)
	PLA/Years	*1947*	*1948*	*1949*
	Income			
1	Interest earned	24.85	25.07	21.08
2	Non-interest income	4.97	4.66	5.64
3	Total income	29.82	29.73	26.72

			(₹ in crore)	
	PLA/Years	*1947*	*1948*	*1949*
	Expenditure			
4	Interest expended	8.29	7.60	6.76
5	Operating expenses	13.35	14.94	15.13
6	Total expenditure	21.64	22.54	21.89
	Profit			
7	OP (Before provisions and contingencies)	8.18	7.19	4.59
8	Provisions and contingencies	0.00	0.00	0.07
9	OP	8.18	7.19	4.52
10	Provision for tax	2.95	2.40	1.25
11	PAT	5.23	4.79	3.27

Sources: STs 1948, 1949.

Statement 2.3 *Principal Bank Parameters of Imperial Bank of India:* 1947–1949

Parameters	*1947*	*1948*	*1949*
1. TA (₹ in crore)	299	306	268
2. Total Income (₹ in crore)	–	–	6.07
3. Deposits (₹ in crore)	–	–	251
4. Advances (₹ in crore)	–	–	90
5. Branches (Number)	–	367	–
6. C–D ratio	31	35	36
7. C–I ratio	–	–	81.24
8. ROA	–	–	0.31

Sources: Items 1–4: STs, various years; item 5: IBA: highlights, 1948.

Note: Missing information had not been published, hence not available.

Notes

1. Description of the state of the economy during the years 1946–1949 below is based majorly on RBI, *Annual Reports 1946–1950.*
2. RBI, *Annual Report, 30 June, 1947,* 31.
3. C&F-1, 84.
4. ST, *1948,* 10; ST, 1949, 12.
5. The above narration of banking developments is mainly based on *ST, 1947,* Prefatory Note, vii, ix, xii; ST, *1948,* v, vi, ix; ST, *1949,* Introduction, x, xi.
6. C&F-1, Annex III.1, 139.
7. RBI History-1, 509.
8. Factual statements in this Section are based on the detailed story on the subject in Ibid., 505–524.
9. Words in parenthesis added by us.
10. SBI History-3, 586; Note 9, 631.
11. Ibid., 592.
12. For a more detailed chronological narration of developments in respect of nationalization of Imperial Bank between 1947 and 1949, read Ibid., Chapter 9, 583–592.
13. The first number of TP mandated as an annual report by RBI, under Section 36 (2) of the BCA, 1949, was published for the year 1949.
14. ST 1948, xviii-xx; Tannan, *Tannan's Banker's Manual,* vol. 2, 5.
15. TP, *1949,* 31.
16. Ibid., 34.
17. Ibid., 46, 51.

3

The First Transformation (1950–1968)

Three Strands of Change

I. ANOTHER STRESSFUL PERIOD

The 19-year period from 1950 to 1968 was extremely stressful for the country. The 1960s, particularly, was a decade of several successive shocks in the economic, political and social spheres. This period lost two prime ministers, fought wars with its neighbours and grappled with a major drought that lasted over 1965–1966.

A transformational nation-building change was the reorganization of the states of the country. GOI felt that the existing borders of the states were not suitable for administration. It, therefore, constituted a three-member high-level States Reorganisation Commission in 1953 to examine the issue of reorganization of the state borders. GOI implemented some of the recommendations of the Commission in 1956. It looked like the face and the spirit of the country were ever changing.

This period was extremely stressful for the economy. Economic planning at the national level had begun in 1951 with the launch of the first five-year plan. The emphasis of the plans on the establishment of heavy industries required large financial resources. The finances of the GOI were strained heavily by all these developments, causing its budgets to be supported by deficit financing. Such factors contributed to the creation of inflationary conditions which prevailed during a major part of this period. Rupee was devalued in 1966. RBI's existing methods of monetary control, given the undeveloped state of the money market, could not have been very successful in the circumstances. This necessitated the use of more blunt, direct credit controls to manage money supply and exercise needed controls over banks' policies like fixation of interest rates, etc. The weak banking system was to undergo major changes by shedding its several structural infirmities and by consolidating into a stronger system.

II. THREE STRANDS OF BANK TRANSFORMATION

Three significant strands of transformation ran along simultaneously in the banking system in this period.

1. The first strand of transformation was the strong intervention by the GOI in the banking system to push it into the rural sector.
2. The second strand of transformation comprised a package of direct instruments of monetary policy by RBI for exercising better control over policies of banks.
3. The third strand was interventions by RBI to weed out weak banks to consolidate the rest of the banks into a strong banking system.

Discussion on these matters follows:

3.1. Alignment of Banking Policies with National Goals

The political clamour for nationalization of banks and injection of bank credit into the rural economy since before Independence took concrete shape in this period. As the era of five-year plans to achieve a socialistic pattern of society began in 1951, steps to make bank policies align with national socio-economic goals began in right earnest. The main elements of transformation have been discussed further.

3.1.1. A Push into Rural Banking (RB)

The advent of a national government in the country put pressure on the RBI to accelerate its promotional role in spreading banking into undeveloped unbanked rural India. Facilitating availability of bank credit to agriculture and other activities in villages and semi-urban areas was by far the most important element of this role. Fresh ideas were needed to go forward. This led to the appointment first of the RBEC in 1949 and then the Committee of Direction of All-India Rural Credit Survey (called AIRCSC) in 1954. AIRCSC called for radical changes in the commercial banking structures and organizations which specifically included the nationalization of Imperial Bank. As a result, the number of rural branches went up from 540 (13 per cent of the total bank branches) at the end of December 1952 to 1,247 (18 per cent of the total bank branches) at the end of December 1967. The amount of agricultural credit by commercial banks rose from ₹12 crore (2.1 per cent of the total bank credit) at end-March 1951, to ₹57 crore (2.2 per cent of the total bank credit) at end-March 1967, an increase merely of 0.1 per cent. This was 'in sharp contrast to almost doubling of the share of industry from 34 per cent in 1951 to 64.3 per cent in 1967'.[1]

3.1.2. Nationalization of Imperial Bank

As noted above, the AIRCSC proposed that the Imperial Bank of India should be brought into public ownership and entrusted with the responsibility for spreading banking facilities to the remote regions of the country. The Committee also proposed that this State-sponsored, State-partnered commercial banking institution, to be called SBI, would be formed by amalgamating Imperial with 10 state-associated banks in the former princely states. SBI was to be the principal bank for extending modern commercial banking to rural parts of India.

The government accepted this recommendation of AIRCSC. The finance minister announced on 20 December 1954 that this was the first step towards the establishment of an integrated commercial bank catering to the entire country. He also confirmed the decision of the government that other parts of the banking system would remain in the private sector. It was decided that the shareholding of SBI would vest in the RBI alone, and not in the GOI. Accordingly, a bill to constitute SBI was passed and SBI was inaugurated on 1 July 1955. At its inauguration, RBI ended up with a holding of 92 per cent of the shares of SBI, the rest continuing to be held by some of the old shareholders of Imperial Bank.[2] In 2008, the GOI took over the stake held by RBI (to eliminate the existing conflict of interest and the impropriety of RBI, the regulator and supervisor of banking system, holding the ownership of a commercial bank).

On 30 June 1955, just before its take over, Imperial Bank's TA (BS size) stood at ₹248 crore and deposits at ₹211 crore.[3] The number of its branches was 453 on 31 December 1954.

3.1.3. Nationalization of State-associated Banks as SBI-subsidiaries

Four years after the formation of SBI, it was decided to constitute the major state-associated banks as subsidiaries of SBI. In 1959, the State Bank of India (Subsidiary Banks) Act was passed which received the assent of the president on 10 September 1959.[4] The following eight banks operating earlier in princely states were taken over as the subsidiaries of SBI—State Bank of Hyderabad, State Bank of Travancore, State Bank of Mysore, State Bank of Indore, State Bank of Saurashtra, State Bank of Bikaner, State Bank of Jaipur and State Bank of Patiala. On 1 January 1963, the State Bank of Bikaner and State Bank of Jaipur were amalgamated as State Bank of Bikaner and Jaipur. Thus, the number of SBI subsidiaries was reduced to seven.[5]

That brought one-third of the commercial banking system of the country into the nationalized sector.[6] On completion of the integration of its subsidiaries into SBI, the sizes of the subsidiaries of SBI and the SBI Group were as under:

	SUBs-SBI	SBI Group
31 December 1960		
1. TA (₹ in crore)	125	742
2. Total deposits (₹ in crore)	104	682
3. Total branches (Number)	490	1,391

SBI was required to open 400 branches within five years of its nationalization; it opened 416. For the next five years, SBI Group was required to open another 300 branches; it opened 309. Of the 1,608 branches opened by the SBI Group between end-December 1955 and end-December 1968, over 80 per cent were opened in rural and semi-urban centres.

3.1.4. Market Shares of SBI/SBI Group

Market shares of SBI/SBI group (PSBs) in the Indian banking sector in 1955, 1960 and 1968 are shown in Table 3.1. It may be noted that

Table 3.1 *Market Share of PSBs in the Indian Banking Sector: 1955, 1960 and 1968*

		1955		1960		1968	
Serial No.	Para-meters	Indian Banking Sector* (72)** (₹ in crore)	Public Sector (SBI) (1) (% Share)	Indian Banking Sector (77) (₹ in crore)	Public Sector (SBI Group) (8) (% Share)	Indian Banking Sector (58) (₹ in crore)	Public Sector (SBI Group) (8) (% Share)
1	TA	1,030	25	1,937	38	4,839	32
2	Deposits	894	25	1,732	39	4,393	31
3	Advances	497	21	1,005	29	2,870	33
4	Branches (no.)	2,772	17	4,081	34	7,321	32

Notes: * Indian banking sector here means all Indian SCBs only.
** Figures in parenthesis are number of banks.

the market shares of the SBI group in three parameters out of four in 1968 were less than those market shares in 1960.

'The formation of the State Bank group remains perhaps the most enduring outcome of the Report of the AIRCSC'.[7]

3.1.5. Social Control of Banks

Two major disquieting features of the banking system had been identified in the 1960s:

1. Neglect of agriculture and
2. Nexus between banks and industry

The issue of resolving neglect of agriculture by banks was being actively addressed by the government and RBI since 1947. It picked up speed as noted supra particularly with nationalization of Imperial Bank. But the second issue did not seem to have received attention. 'There was apprehension that a few business houses might acquire control over a significant proportion of country's banking assets' by having controlling interest in banks and misallocating bank credit in favour of their conglomerates. Hence, the 'concept of social control' over banking was born in 1967. Its main object was to achieve a balanced spread of the precious resource of bank credit, especially to the priority sectors of rural economy, small scale industry, exports, etc. The National Credit Council was set up in early 1968 to assist the State and RBI to allocate bank credit according to plan priorities. Banking laws were amended to exercise control over the appointment and composition of top managements of banks. But even before this concept had taken roots, it was given up on the presumption of its non-operability and 14 major banks were nationalized.

3.2. Shift to Direct Instruments of Credit and Monetary Policy

RBI took several steps to shift to direct instruments of credit and monetary policy.

1. Inflationary conditions and shortages of agricultural products had prevailed almost constantly throughout this period. The Wholesale Price Index (1939=100) rose from 397 in June 1950 to 450 by the end of March 1951. The new Wholesale Price Index (1952–1953=100) rose from 111.8 in 1950–1951 to 191.2 in 1966–1967. This phenomenon had impelled RBI to tighten its monetary policy by making use of various instruments of direct and indirect credit controls on the banking system. The bank rate, which had stayed at 3 per cent, seemingly unshakeably, since November 1935, was raised to 3.5 per cent in November 1951. It stayed there until 1957, to be raised a number of times, thereafter, to reach 6 per cent in 1965 and to be lowered to 5 per cent in March 1968.

2. An administered interest rate structure was imposed on banks. The objectives of RBI policy—to prevent application of low rates of interest on speculative activities and high rates on productive activities, and prevent diversion of large credit to big business—resulted in a complex interest rate structure. The new structure fixed interest rates according to depositor and according to borrower as per a set of criteria.
3. This system was coupled with a 'voluntary' inter-bank agreement in 1958, with RBI acquiescence, on a structure of rates on bank deposits to eliminate 'harmful' competition among banks. This led to a 'considerable inflexibility' in the interest rate structure.
4. As a result, 'the interest rates ceased to function as a signal of monetary policy'. Complexities were accentuated by the introduction of (a) a scheme of selective credit controls in 1956 to curb speculative activity in commodities and its constant tinkering, and (b) a Credit Authorisation Scheme in 1965 to prevent larger borrowers from pre-empting scarce credit.[8]
5. A scheme of deposit insurance to protect bank depositors was introduced from 1 January 1962.

3.3. Bank Consolidation: Pruning Weak Banks

The substantive change in India's geography due to Partition, the integration of 538 princely states into the Indian Union and reorganization of states' boundaries and consequent changes in its banking landscape had accentuated the running story of bank failures. Reinforced by the enactment of the BCA, one of the foci of RBI in the current period came to be to strengthen and consolidate the commercial banking structure, primarily through liquidation and amalgamation of weak banks. This process picked up speed in the mid-1950s and continued through this period.

Weak banks could be classified into two categories:

1. Non-scheduled banks (primarily) and
2. State-associated banks operating in former princely states. After these states were merged into the Indian Union, these banks had come under the regulatory regime of RBI.

The processes of their restructuring and consolidation are narrated briefly hereunder.

3.3.1. Weak Banks in the Indian Union

RBI began to wield its powers accorded by BCA to wind up weak and non-viable banks or merge them into stronger banks. Several legal hurdles came in the way. The BCA had to be amended several times to clear the hurdles.[9] As a result, hundreds of banks, particularly non-scheduled banks, went through the exit door.

3.3.2. Weak State-associated Banks

As per RBI's admittedly incomplete count, 54 state-associated banks (state-owned or commercial banks) existed in the former princely states in March 1952. These banks differed hugely in terms of ownership form, size, nature of organization, functional arrangements between them and relationships with their respective governments. Majority of them were 'weak, moribund or on the verge of liquidation'. As a result of RBI actions, some of them were converted into cooperative banks, some others were brought under the Companies Act and many of the rest were either liquidated or amalgamated. Of the 10 'non-weak' banks originally proposed to be converted into subsidiaries of SBI, Bank of Baroda and Bank of Rajasthan were left out to operate as independent PSBs; the other eight, eventually, seven, were taken over by SBI as its subsidiaries. Thus, the huge exercise of 'integration of the banking systems' of the princely states into the Indian banking system had been completed by RBI in a short span of a couple of years.

3.3.3. The Structural Transformation

At the beginning of 1950, the number of Indian scheduled banks and non-scheduled banks were 78 and 521, respectively, totalling 599. At the end of 1968, the corresponding figures had got reduced to 58 and 17, a total of 75 banks.[10] Thus, the structural transformation of commercial banking into a slim and healthy system was more or less complete.

3.4. Related Banking Matters

3.4.1. The Banking Regulation Act (BRA), 1949

The BCA had to be amended 10 times in this period to remove its inadequacies identified in implementation, to tighten regulatory requirements in order to facilitate the application of credit control measures, and to ease the processes of liquidation, merger and consolidation of banks. The Act was also renamed as 'BRA, 1949', in 1965 to reflect its main purposes.

3.4.2. Raising Capital Adequacy Norms

Capital adequacy (CA) requirements for banks in India were practically non-existent till the early 1950s. The BCA (1949) required banks to maintain a prescribed minimum amount of capital; banks were also required since 1962 to transfer one-fifth of their annual profits to a reserve fund until the latter equalled their paid-up capital. RBI, in its annual inspections of banks, used to use a comprehensive method of assessing the BS of banks to measure their adequacy of capital. In 1954, this issue of CA was raised with RBI, interestingly, by the Chairman of the Indian Banks' Association. The Association suggested that the minimum capital and reserves requirement should be quadrupled. RBI examined this proposal and after assessing other present-day methods of raising CA standards, rejected it. Its argument was that that the safety of depositors' money depended largely on the quality of management of banks, the composition of a bank's assets, and efficient control and supervision over banks. It said that the BCA had gone a long way in meeting these needs and the implementation of the contemplated scheme of deposit insurance would be an additional safeguard. Thus, we saw a proposal by the recognized banks' association to raise capital requirements being rejected by the central bank of the country.

The collapse of Palai Central Bank in 1960 affected several aspects of RBI's policy towards commercial banks (including CA norms). The then RBI governor took personal interest in evolving CA standards. He wanted to raise the prevailing standards. But his proposals did not outlast his tenure at RBI, and this subject receded into the background. The issue again raised its head in RBI in November 1967, but conflicting views from within the organization meant that further progress would remain stalled.[11]

III. THE FINANCIALS: 1950–1968

A fuller analysis of financials became possible for the years 1950–1968 as financial statements became available in STs from 1950. This section seeks to analyse the financials (financial management and financial performance) of SCBs for the 19 years of this period. The parameters used for assessment are five absolutes in Table 3.2 and seven ratios in Table 3.3. The 12 parameters taken together should provide a reasonably full picture of the changes in the banking system in terms of financial management and performance.

Table 3.2 SCBs' Significant Financials: 1950–1968 (Continued)

Serial No.	Parameters	1949	1950	1951	1952	1953	1954	1955	1956	1957	1958	1959
1	Banks (no.)	94	91	92	91	89	88	89	89	91	93	94
2	TA (₹ in crore)	1,073	1,067	1,134	1,051	1,046	1,151	1,279	1,418	1,658	1,880	2,159
	Percent increase year over year (YOY)		(0.6)	6.3	(7.3)	(0.5)	10.0	11.1	10.9	16.9	13.4	14.8
	CAGR		(0.6)	2.8	(0.7)	(0.6)	1.4	3.0	4.1	5.6	6.4	7.2
3	Total Branches (no.)	2,788	2,779	2,646	2,671	2,670	2,746	2,838	2,953	3,263	3,623	3,922
	Percent increase YOY		(0.3)	(4.8)	0.9	(0.0)	2.8	3.4	4.1	10.5	11.0	8.3
	CAGR		(0.3)	(2.6)	(1.4)	(1.1)	(0.3)	0.3	0.8	2.0	3.0	3.5
4	Total income (₹ in crore)	37	37	43	44	44	47	53	62	76	86	94
	Percent increase YOY		–	16.2	2.3	–	6.8	12.8	17.0	22.6	13.2	9.3
	CAGR		–	7.8	5.9	4.4	4.9	6.2	7.7	9.4	9.8	9.8
5	PBT (₹ in millions)	68	62	77	59	57	60	70	85	97	90	75
	Percent increase YOY		(8.8)	24.2	(23.4)	(3.4)	5.3	16.7	21.4	14.1	(7.2)	(16.7)
	CAGR		(8.8)	6.4	(4.6)	(4.3)	(2.5)	0.5	3.2	4.5	3.2	1.0

#, – = Less than 1 per cent.

Table 3.2 SCBs' Significant Financials: 1950–1968 (Concluded)

Serial No.	Parameters	1960	1961	1962	1963	1964	1965	1966	1967	1968	1968/1949 (Times)	CAGR
1	Banks (no.)	93	82	80	79	76	76	75	73	73	–	–
2	TA (₹ in crore)	2,232	2,318	2,581	2,870	3,296	3,673	4,287	4,731	5,396	5.03	8.9
	Percent increase YOY	3.4	3.9	11.3	11.2	14.8	11.4	16.7	10.4	14.1		
	CAGR	6.9	6.6	7.0	7.3	7.8	8.0	8.5	8.6	8.9		
3	Branches (no.)	4,150	4,390	4,608	5,004	5,499	5,902	6,382	6,781	7,446	2.67	5.3
	Percent increase YOY	5.8	5.8	5.0	8.6	9.9	7.3	8.1	6.3	9.8		
	CAGR	3.7	3.9	3.9	4.3	4.6	4.8	5.0	5.1	5.3		
4	Total income (₹ in crore)	104	114	130	149	176	229	298	343	382	10.32	13.1
	Percent increase YOY	10.6	9.6	14.0	14.6	18.1	30.1	30.1	15.1	11.4		
	CAGR	9.9	9.8	10.1	10.5	11.0	12.1	13.1	13.2	13.1		
5	PBT (₹ in millions)	115	126	100	101	119	117	321	329	344	5.06	8.9
	Percent increase YOY	53.3	9.6	(20.6)	1.0	17.8	(1.7)	174.4	2.5	4.6		
	CAGR	4.9	5.3	3.0	2.9	3.8	3.4	9.6	9.2	8.9		

Sources: Banks: STs, various years; branches: IBA, performance highlights, Bombay, various years; other parameters: Annexure, Statements 3.1 and 3.2.

Table 3.3 SCBs' Significant Financial Ratios: 1950–1968 (Continued)

Serial No.	Ratios	1949	1950	1951	1952	1953	1954	1955	1956	1957	1958
1	Leverage	5.87	5.79	5.61	5.92	5.90	5.37	4.88	4.48	4.10	3.75
2	Credit: Deposit	49	52	65	57	57	56	61	70	62	54
3	Investments: Deposit	43	44	38	41	41	39	40	36	34	42
4	Net Interest Margin	1.77	1.85	1.82	1.93	1.97	1.83	1.78	1.73	1.66	1.59
5	Cost: Income	75.77	78	76	80	82	82	81	80	79	81
6	Return on Assets	0.61	0.58	0.70	0.54	0.54	0.55	0.58	0.63	0.63	0.51
7	Return on Equity	10.79	9.97	12.29	9.41	9.18	9.73	11.26	13.44	14.68	13.05

Table 3.3 SCBs' Significant Financial Ratios: 1950–1968 (Concluded)

Serial No.	Ratios	1959	1960	1961	1962	1963	1964	1965	1966	1967	1968
1	Leverage	3.30	3.22	3.26	3.23	3.05	2.81	2.76	2.43	2.23	2.09
2	Credit: Deposit	52	62	63	64	65	67	67	65	66	67
3	Investment: Deposit	43	36	32	33	32	31	30	29	29	29
4	Net Interest Margin	1.55	1.74	1.86	1.90	1.98	2.07	2.23	2.69	2.79	2.82
5	Cost: Income	85	81	82	87	87	88	90	80	82	84
6	Return on Assets	0.37	0.52	0.55	0.41	0.40	0.38	0.34	0.81	0.73	0.68
7	Return on Equity	10.66	16.02	17.04	12.62	12.77	13.16	12.11	31.27	31.39	31.54

Source: Annexure: Statements 3.1 and 3.2.

3.5. The Financials

3.5.1. Five Parameters (Table 3.2)

3.5.1.1. Number of Banks

The number of banks in 1950, the first year of this period, was 91; 75 of them were Indian SCBs and 16 were foreign SCBs. The two groups need to be separately looked at. Between 1950 and 1960, the number of Indian banks fluctuated between 72 and 78. The number in 1961 declined to 67 and continued to decline, thereafter, to reach 58 at the end of 1968. It seems that the process of weeding out weak banks had begun in right earnest from the year 1961. The number of foreign banks varied between 14 and 17 between 1951 and 1968, and stood at 15 in 1968.

3.5.1.2. TA (BS Size)

BS size of SCBs in absolute terms grew 5.03 times over this period. Its compound annual growth rate (CAGR) was 8.9.

In the three years out of the first four, 1950–1953, BS size was less than that of 1949, last year of the previous period. It picked up from 1954 and continued upwards at unsteady rates. It was a period of 'unsteady growth' of banks' BS.

3.5.1.3. Total Branches

The number of branches grew 2.67 times over this period. Its CAGR was 5.3.

In the first five years, 1950–1954, the number of branches was less than that of 1949. It picked up from 1955 and continued to grow till 1968. Thus, the pattern was the same as TA.

3.5.1.4. Total Income

Total income grew 10.32 times in this period. Its CAGR was 13.1. Its annual rate of growth, like the preceding parameters, was unsteady, fluctuating all through.

3.5.1.5. Profit before Tax (PBT)

PBT grew 5.02 times and CAGR growth was at 8.9 in this period. It recorded negative rate of growth in 7 out of 19 years of this period. Among the positive years, the annual rate of growth varied between 1.0 per cent and 174.4 per cent. No statistical measures are needed to gauge the high rate of annual volatility of this parameter over this period.

3.5.2. Seven Ratios

Leverage: Leverage of SCBs, which was 5.87 in 1949, that is, end of the preceding period, declined to 5.79 in 1950. It continued to decline, thereafter, to 4s, then to 3s and finally to 2s to close in 1968 at 2.09. While CAGR of TA was nine during this period, that of equity was three. Thus, one of the major parameters of financial strength had fallen to low levels.

Credit–Deposit Ratio and Investment–Deposit Ratio: The investment portfolio of a bank is partly a statutory portfolio (required to meet the requirements of SLR) and partly an autonomous investment portfolio. The yield on this portfolio is usually not as high as that on the credit portfolio; but sometimes it can be more. An object of the investment portfolio is to be a reservoir of surplus funds to be drawn to meet credit demand and other liquidity needs. Hence, the C–D portfolio is very commonly the larger portfolio (with a larger contribution to the bank's income). The opposite can also happen in times credit demand becomes slack, so that the funds released by the advances portfolio may be ploughed to the investment portfolio. In a sense, then, as stated above, these two portfolios are contrarian twins. A common norm for credit plus investment portfolios is that it should not exceed 100. Actually, given the fact that banks are subject to the monetary instrument of CRR, a general rule of thumb shall be that the available funds for these two portfolios shall be 100 less CRR. A ratio of more than 100 shall mean that banks get to raising additional funds from more risky external sources and their market risk increases.

In the period under review, the C–D ratio was more volatile in the 1950–1959 period; it moved into the 60s only during 1960–1968. The two ratios added to more than 100 in 1951, 1955 and 1956. Years of relatively high C–D ratio should mean years in which credit was in high demand. CAGR of deposits, advances and investments was 9, 11 and 7, respectively during this period, hence this period saw a rising C–D ratio and a declining I–D ratio.

Net Interest Margin: NIM is an important element in measurement of 'operating efficiency' of banks. High NIM of banks in a banking system could mean that banks are not necessarily operating in a competitive market; they may be operating in an administered rate of interest regime. Whether it is one or the other depends on the prevailing banking environment. But if some banks earn high NIM, while some others show low NIM, it should be obvious which banks are being run more efficiently.

The 1950–1968 period was a period of administered rates, and we are looking at the NIM of a group of banks, not individual banks. Hence, NIMs would have been regulated NIMs. NIM was 1.85 in 1950 and remained below two up to 1963. During 1964 and 1968, it was above 2 and ended at 2.82, the highest NIM of this period. One might like to compare these movements with movements in the next ratio, the C–I ratio.

Cost–Income Ratio: C–I ratio measures the relationship between operating costs and income (net interest income + non-interest income) of a bank. Operating costs as a percentage of income yields the C–I ratio. While NIM measures the operating efficiency of the upper part of income statement, C–I ratio measures the operating efficiency of the lower part of the income statement.

C–I ratio was 78 in 1950 and showed a steady rise over the years to hit 90 in 1965, before declining to the 80s.

Broadly, as C–I ratio rose in the 1960s, NIM also rose. This being the period of an administered regime, relative rates were difficult to compare.

Return on Assets and Return on Equity: ROA is the single composite measure of the operating efficiency of the performance of any business unit. It is based on the bottom lines of the PLA (PAT) and the BS (TA). It combines the partial measures of NIM and C–I ratio into PBT. ROE is the other composite measure which measures the profitability of an enterprise for its equity shareholders. It is based on PBT from the PLA and equity (net worth) from the BS. It incorporates the benefit of leverage (risk-taking), hence should be larger and more volatile than ROA. But in times of low profits or losses from operations, ROE would fall to low or negative levels.

ROA of SCBs remained less than 1.0 per cent, a commonly accepted norm for ROA, throughout this period. It was 0.58 per cent in 1950 and 0.70 per cent in 1951. It remained in the 0.50–0.60 range until 1957. It began to decline until it dipped to 0.34 per cent in 1965. It had increased to 0.81, 0.73 and 0.68 in the last three years.

ROE was 9.97 per cent in 1950. Between 1951 and 1965, it ranged between 9.18 per cent (1953) and 17.01 per cent (1961). It rose sharply to 31.27 per cent in 1966, 31.39 per cent in 1967 and 31.54 per cent in 1968.

It may be possible to conclude that while ROA was not high, ROE had risen sharply in the later part of this period. Our conclusion: ROE rose to higher levels not only because of increasing profits but also because of declining equity.

It is reasonable to conclude from a review of Tables 3.3 and 3.4 that there was inadequate profit retention and/or inadequate induction of fresh capital. Possibly, one outcome of that state was that the BRA was amended to require banks to transfer 20 per cent of their post-tax profits every year to their reserves. Despite that, CA had continued to be inadequate.

3.6. Depth and Range of Branch Network

One measure of the real growth of banking can be gauged by assessing the depth and range of the branch network. The number of branches of SCBs had declined in the 1947–1949 period. This decline had continued from 2,788 in 1949 to 2,779 in 1950 and 2,746 in 1954. The network began to grow in 1955 and closed at 2,838. Expansion began after 1955, rising by more than 350 branches every year on average to close at 7,446 branches in 1968. Thus, branches in this period had grown by slightly less than three times the number in 1949.

Branch expansion policy of RBI had by then begun to target at correction of regional maldistribution in the branch network, so as to ensure larger network in unbanked centres and less developed states of the country. Still, in April 1969, out of 2,700 towns in the country, 600 were not covered by commercial banks. Further, out of nearly 600,000 villages, 5,000 only were estimated to be served by commercial banks.[12]

3.7. Broad Conclusions

Apart from the conclusions arrived at and stated for each of the twelve parameters above, it may be concluded, in sum, that the financials of the banking system had grown in the 19-year period but at unsteady rates. In the first 4–5 years of the period, several 'absolute' parameters had declined in continuation of the 1947–1949 trends. Administered interest rate structure in this period was possibly an important explanatory variable.

IV. THE 21ST-CENTURY BANKS: 1968

Table 3.4 produces the status of 42 banks at the end of 1968.

Table 2.4 consisted of 43 banks. Two of those banks, State Bank of Bikaner and State Bank of Jaipur got merged in 1963; hence the 1968 listing comprised 42 banks.

Table 3.4 *The 21st-Century Banks: 1968*

(Fourth in the Series)

Serial no.	Banks (Ranked by TA)	TA		Branches	
		₹ in crore	Rank	Number	Rank
1	SBI	1,279	1	1,544	1
2	Central Bank of India	526	2	504	3
3	Bank of India	468	3	234	8
4	PNB	458	4	531	2
5	Bank of Baroda	384	5	314	4
6	UCO Bank	307	6	314	4
7	Canara Bank	188	7	302	6
8	United Bank of India	170	8	164	14
9	Dena Bank	149	9	214	10
10	Union Bank of India	142	10	213	11
11	Syndicate Bank	139	11	254	7
12	Allahabad Bank	133	12	132	17
13	Indian Overseas Bank	124	13	179	13
14	Indian Bank	108	14	216	9
15	Bank of Maharashtra	91	15	137	16

(Continued)

Table 3.4 (Continued)

(Fourth in the Series)

Serial no.	Banks (Ranked by TA)	TA ₹ in crore	Rank	Branches Number	Rank
16	State Bank of Bikaner & Jaipur	71	16	208	12
17	State Bank of Hyderabad	68	17	157	15
18	State Bank of Travancore	54	18	130	18
19	Andhra Bank	54	19	121	19
20	State Bank of Mysore	50	20	113	20
21	State Bank of Patiala	49	21	83	23
22	State Bank of Saurashtra	42	22	88	22
23	State Bank of Indore	27	23	53	28
24	Corporation Bank	24	24	75	25
25	New Bank of India	21	25	37	32
26	Oriental Bank of India	20	26	27	35
27	Bank of Rajasthan	17	27	58	27
28	Vijaya Bank	15	28	89	21
29	South Indian Bank	15	29	78	24
30	Karnataka Bank	11	30	61	26
31	Jammu & Kashmir Bank	9	31	14	39
32	Karur Vysya Bank	8	32	45	30
33	Vysya Bank	8	33	30	34
34	Catholic Syrian Bank	7	34	44	31
35	Punjab & Sind Bank	6	35	16	38
36	Lakshmi Vilas Bank	6	36	48	29
37	Federal Bank	5	37	35	33
38	Dhanlaxmi Bank	3	38	20	37
39	City Union Bank	2	39	25	36
40	Tamilnad Mercantile Bank	2	40	9	40
41	Ratnakar Bank	2	41	7	41
42	Nainital Bank	1	42	7	41
Total		5,263		6,930	

Source: ST 1968, pp. 54–63.

V. SUMMARY: 1950–1968

Both for the economy and the banking system, it was a period of 'volatile volatility' due to several upheavals in the country. It is indeed creditable that, in the midst of the turmoil, the banking system could attain an enormous set of transformations. Those three transformations, as already described, need just to be noted below:

3.8. Rise of Public Sector Banking and its Push into Rural and Priority Sectors

By far, the important transformational changes were (a) the nationalization of Imperial Bank of India as SBI in 1955, (b) conversion of eight state-associated banks into SBI's subsidiaries to form the SBI Group in 1960, (thus making this Group equivalent to about one-third of the banking industry) and (c) the push of this Group into rural sector and priority sector lending (PSL).

This was a welcome action for banks to enter for bringing about social and economic changes in the life of the underprivileged and underprovided strata of the society. Nothing significant, however, had been achieved by the SBI Group by 1968.

3.9. Direct and Complex Instruments of Monetary Policy

RBI set the interest rates that banks could pay and charge; it also allocated bank credit according to borrower and his needs. An inter-bank agreement on deposit rates was enforced. There was no competition, except perhaps in respect of customer service.

3.10. Pruning Weak Banks

A major achievement of RBI was the weeding out of weak banks through their liquidation or amalgamation with strong banks. This was a surgical action that made the banking system stronger.

3.10.1. Financial Development of the Economy

At the end of 1968, it is possible to offer a few comments on the financial development of the economy.

1. The ratio of deposits to national income is considered to be a good index of the degree of development of banking and growth of institutional savings in a country. This ratio had increased from 9 per cent in 1951 to 16 per cent in 1968.[13]
2. Bank deposits had risen from 37 per cent to 53 per cent of aggregate monetary resources (currency plus deposits) and from 12 per cent to 38 per cent of gross savings of the household sector between 1951 and 1967.[14]
3. Share of bank deposits owned by the household sector in gross financial savings rose from 1.94 per cent in 1950–1951 to 12.94 in 1955–1956 to 27.14 in 1965–1966.[15]

Number of deposit accounts had climbed by 1.29 crore to 1.62 crore between 1 January 1951 and 31 March 1968, most of these being personal accounts. Per capita deposits of banks had risen from ₹24 to ₹81.[16]

Notes

1. C&F-1, Table 3.39, 94; RBI, *TP, 1968–1969*, Table 19, 48.
2. Much of the narration above is based on RBI History-2, 334–344.
3. SBI History-3, vol. 3, 644.
4. TP, 1959, 15.
5. The facts in this paragraph are based on RBI History-2, 379–389.
6. C&F-1, 93.
7. RBI History-2, 317.
8. C&F-1, 398.
9. RBI History-2, 398.
10. STs, 'Statistics at a Glance', 1967–2010-11.
11. RBI History-2, 406–408.
12. TP, *1968–1969*, 53.
13. STs, 'Statistics at a Glance', 1967–2010-11.
14. RBI History-2, 507.
15. TP, *1968–1969*, 43–44.
16. Ibid.

3.A. Annexure

Statement 3.1. Main Heads of SCBs' BS: 1950–1968

Statement 3.2. Main Heads of SCBs' PLA: 1950–1968

Statement 3.1. Main Heads of SCBs' BS: 1950–1968

(₹ in crore)

Main Heads/Years	1950	1951	1952	1953	1954	1955	1956	1957	1958	1959	1960	1961	1962	1963	1964	1965	1966	1967	1968
Liabilities																			
1 Own funds (Capital+reserves)	62	64	62	62	62	62	64	68	70	71	72	76	83	88	93	101	104	106	113
2 Deposits	925	925	898	912	1,005	1,091	1,172	1,448	1,674	1,952	1,974	2,085	2,306	2,554	2,906	3,266	3,907	4,298	4,845
3 Borrowings	32	48	39	22	23	48	107	85	74	61	97	67	84	92	145	114	108	116	195
4 Bills payable	18	19	16	15	18	26	27	26	28	33	32	36	38	42	37	45	45	43	60
5 Other liabilities	31	78	35	35	45	52	50	31	35	41	57	55	69	94	116	148	122	169	184
Total Liabilities/TA	1,067	1,134	1,051	1,046	1,151	1,279	1,418	1,658	1,880	2,159	2,232	2,318	2,581	2,870	3,296	3,673	4,287	4,731	5,396
Assets																			
6 Cash and bank balances	139	141	128	115	142	139	139	182	187	216	225	232	233	254	313	338	389	424	489
7 Money at call and short notice	13	13	16	13	20	12	14	52	43	35	45	49	60	64	73	73	88	101	106
8 Investments	406	348	366	375	396	433	417	493	709	846	710	663	754	820	903	982	1,141	1,229	1,390
9 Advances	483	606	515	516	566	665	821	894	902	1,015	1,216	1,321	1,484	1,667	1,938	2,182	2,552	2,832	3,254
10 Fixed assets	10	10	10	10	11	11	11	13	16	17	20	22	25	30	36	36	43	59	67
11 Other assets (Non-banking assets+other assets)	16	17	17	16	17	19	17	24	23	30	33	36	38	44	49	62	73	86	89

Source: STs of all years.

Statement 3.2. Main Heads of SCBs' PLA: 1950–1968

(₹ in crore)

Particulars	1950	1951	1952	1953	1954	1955	1956	1957	1958	1959	1960	1961	1962	1963	1964	1965	1966	1967	1968
Income																			
1 Interest earned	27.15	29.88	32.09	32.98	34.85	38.85	45.21	56.79	67.27	74.24	81.88	89.19	103.05	118.70	142.13	189.43	252.31	287.35	322.80
2 Non-interest income	9.41	12.95	12.08	11.48	12.44	14.49	17.18	18.91	18.81	20.07	22.48	25.30	27.43	30.27	33.72	39.33	45.29	55.37	59.70
3 Total income	36.56	42.83	44.17	44.46	47.29	53.34	62.39	75.70	86.08	94.31	104.36	114.49	130.48	148.97	175.85	228.76	297.59	342.72	382.50
Expenditure																			
4 Interest Expended	7.41	9.27	11.83	12.34	13.83	16.09	20.73	29.24	37.37	40.78	43.06	46.11	54.11	61.82	73.85	107.51	137.19	155.55	170.70
5 Operating expenses	22.60	25.42	25.96	26.17	27.29	30.15	33.09	36.63	39.27	45.37	49.53	55.62	66.20	76.08	90.03	109.22	128.27	154.24	177.38
6 Total expenditure	30.01	34.69	37.79	38.51	41.12	46.24	53.82	65.87	76.64	86.15	92.59	101.73	120.31	137.90	163.88	216.73	265.46	309.79	348.07
Profit																			
7 OP (Before provisions and contingencies)	6.25	7.75	5.92	5.74	6.04	7.00	8.50	9.70	9.03	7.69	11.56	12.73	10.15	11.00	11.88	11.83	32.13	32.93	34.42
8 Provisions and contingencies	0.04	0.05	0.00	0.05	0.03	0.01	0.03	0.04	0.09	0.14	0.10	0.16	0.12	0.09	0.02	0.08	0.00	0.00	0.00
9 OP	6.21	7.70	5.92	5.69	6.01	6.99	8.47	9.66	9.03	7.55	11.46	12.57	10.03	10.91	11.86	11.75	32.13	32.93	34.42
10 Provision for tax	1.27	1.36	1.51	1.25	1.46	1.45	2.20	2.73	0.00	1.73	3.65	1.60	0.55	0.42	0.73	0.48	19.59	22.10	22.43
11 PAT	4.94	6.34	4.41	4.44	4.55	5.54	6.27	6.93	9.03	5.82	7.81	10.97	9.48	10.49	11.13	11.27	12.55	10.83	11.99

Source: STs of all the years.

4

The Second Transformation (1969–1990-91)

Bank Nationalization, Focus on Rural Banking

I. THE DEFINING EVENT OF INDIAN BANKING

The nationalization of the 14 largest PSBs of the country on 19 July 1969 has been termed as the defining event of Indian banking, as also 'The single most important economic decision taken by any government since 1947.... Not even the reforms of 1991 are comparable in their consequences–political, social and, of course, economic'—to this event.[1] The raison d'être of this decision was extremely significant for an equitable national socio-economic-political development. The next nationalization of six banks was announced on 15 April 1980. But the first nationalization—of Imperial Bank of India—had taken place on 1 July 1955, to be followed by the nationalization of eight smaller banks as SBI's subsidiaries on 10 September 1959.

4.1. The Journey of Bank Nationalization (Three Nationalizations, Three Rationales)

It is instructive to traverse the journey of the three nationalizations by piecing together the rationale behind each of them.

4.1.1. The First Nationalization—State Bank of India: 1955, 8 Subsidiaries: 1959

As narrated in Chapter 1 as well as later, nationalization of Imperial Bank had been demanded by the Congress Party and others repeatedly since much before Independence, based on the socialistic ideology of state ownership. But it was vociferously opposed by its British bosses. C. D. Deshmukh, the then governor of RBI, supported the Imperial; he was strongly opposed to the ideological argument behind it. But when it was proposed on the argument of using the size and resources of this bank for extending banking to rural India, especially agriculture, the same Deshmukh, then the finance minister of the central government, openly embraced the proposal and Imperial was nationalized. Four years later, eight weak banks from princely states were taken over by SBI as its subsidiaries. Thus, the proximate but a strong, real argument of expanding banking into rural India was deployed to nationalize Imperial and eight weak banks. This brought one-third of the commercial banking system under the nationalized sector.[2]

4.1.2. The Second Nationalization—14 Banks: 1969

Go back to the last page of the last chapter of *RBI History-3*; it reads, inter alia, 'an uneven spread of two major banking resources, that is, branches and credit, still prevailed' (at the end of 1968). This was despite the fact that the State Bank Group had been nationalized 13 years ago and social control had been introduced in 1967. 'In

September 1967, the supporters of nationalisation received a shot in the arm from an unexpected quarter. The report of the Industrial Planning and Licensing Policy Committee that had been set up by the Planning Commission categorically advocated state control of banks.'

'...I should express my doubts about the viability of carrying through the above suggestions so long as many of the major credit institutions are under the direct control and/or influence of those who might suffer under the suggested arrangements. It would be difficult to undertake credit planning unless the link to control of industry and banks in the same hands is snapped by nationalisation of banks', said its author, R K Hazari, then a professor of economics at the University of Bombay.[3]

This report and Hazari's earlier in-depth empirical studies on the subject for the Planning Commission seemed to serve as a trigger to the political advocates of nationalization. Around the same time, there was a growing discomfort among some of the top political brass of the Congress Party that the instrument of social control was simply a diversionary tactic to prevent the nationalization of banks. Meanwhile, the loss of power by the Congress Party in one-third of the Indian states intensified the power struggle within the Party. It came to head in 1969 when Indira Gandhi, the then prime minister of a weakened government, used the issue of social control versus nationalization to project her image as a radical reformer and a leader of the poor.

I. G. Patel, secretary in the Ministry of Finance, wrote in his memoirs,

[S]ometime in July 1969, I was sent for by the Prime Minister. No one else was present. Without any fanfare, she asked me whether banking was under my charge. On my telling her it was, she simply said, For political reasons, it has been decided to nationalise the banks. You have to prepare within 24 hours the bill, a note for the Cabinet and a speech for me to make to the nation on the radio tomorrow evening. Can you do it and make sure there is no leak? ... the message was clear that no argument from me was required. I summoned courage, however, to make two suggestions: to leave the foreign banks alone, and nationalise only the major ones.... She immediately agreed and added that she could trust the details to me.[4]

The following 14 banks, each with deposits of over ₹50 crore, were nationalized on 19 July 1969: the Central Bank of India Ltd, the PNB Ltd, the Bank of India Ltd, the Bank of Baroda Ltd, the UCO Ltd, the Allahabad Bank Ltd, the Dena Bank Ltd, the Indian Bank Ltd, the United Bank of India Ltd, the Canara Bank Ltd, the Union Bank of India Ltd, the Syndicate Bank Ltd, the Bank of Maharashtra Ltd and the Indian Overseas Bank Ltd.[5] The advocacy for nationalization of banking on socio-economic rationale which had persisted consistently since before Independence had found its fulfilment in uneasy political circumstances. But this action went against the affirmation by the finance minister of India (at the time of the nationalization of Imperial Bank in 1955) of 'the government's intention not to disturb other parts of the banking system which would remain in the private sector'. (See Chapter 3, p. 90)

This act of nationalization raised the total number of PSBs to 22. Together, this brought 83 per cent of the total deposits, 84 per cent of the total credit and 82 per cent of the total branches of the banking system under the nationalized sector.[6]

4.1.3. The Third Nationalization—6 Banks: 1980

To quote I. G. Patel, the then governor, RBI, again at some length:

Such is the irony of life that one of the first steps I had to recommend to Mrs Gandhi was that she should nationalise another swathe of private banks. The Reserve Bank had the responsibility to supervise private banks and to ensure their compliance with social control norms as well as with law. ... Some of them, like the Punjab and Sindh Bank and the Vijaya Bank had become the personal fiefdoms of individuals who disregarded all rules and advice with impunity. ... I decided that the 'only practical way to tackle the problem was to nationalise the banks' which had now reached the cut-off point of the 1969 Act. Mrs Gandhi readily accepted the advice.... But it must be said.... That this particular initiative for the second phase of nationalisation came entirely from me.[7]

The six banks which were nationalized on 15 April 1980 were: The Andhra Bank Ltd, Corporation Bank Ltd, The New Bank of India Ltd, The Oriental Bank of Commerce Ltd, The Punjab & Sind Bank Ltd and Vijaya Bank Ltd. The criterion applied was that these banks had demand and time liabilities as on 14 March 1980 of not less than ₹200 crore.[8]

It brought the total number of PSBs to 28 by which the share of this sector rose from 83 per cent of the total deposits and 84 per cent of the total credit to 91 per cent of the total deposits and 91 per cent of the total credit of the banking system.[9]

II. OTHER ECONOMIC-BANKING DEVELOPMENTS

4.2. Statist Controls on the Economy: 1969–1981

Statist controls on the economy took off rapidly after the 1969 nationalization. The period 1969–1980/1981 was marked by widespread state ownership and regulation (perhaps, overregulation) of the economy. Following bank nationalization, general insurance and coal mining were also nationalized. A monopolies law was passed and shackles put on 'big business'; their industrial capacities were sealed at existing production levels. Salaries of top corporate executives were capped. The Foreign Exchange Regulations Act was amended to control foreign companies. Price controls were imposed on a large number of goods. Imports of many commodities were 'canalized' through government agencies. Labour laws were tightened, adversely affecting trade and commerce. Private wholesale trade in food grains was banned. Finance Minister, Indira Gandhi, said in her 1970 budget that 'the budget framework was consistent with the political, economic and social realities of our country. The fiscal system had to serve the ends of greater equality of incomes, consumption and wealth'.[10] But from the year 1974, some of the above steps were reversed. 'Price controls were lifted, monopolies law was rendered irrelevant, many foreign exchange controls were eased, (and) companies were allowed "automatic" expansion of capacity…'. T. N. Ninan termed 1974 as the 'invisible turning point'.[11]

But there was no turning point in the banking system. The implementation of the objectives of bank nationalization continued relentlessly. In pursuance of promoting RB and PSL, several structural and schematic changes were introduced. (See Section III). Targets for expansion of branch network in rural areas and for lending to weaker sections of the society had been set and were being pursued.

One of the outcomes of huge plan expenditure during the 1970s and 1980s was that the GOI's budget was expanded by using the banking sector as a source of funds. The RBI had to raise CRR from 5 per cent to 15 per cent over the years 1973–1989 in order to counter the impact of deficit financing.[12] An Additional CRR of 10 per cent was also introduced in 1983. The banks also became a captive source of funds when GOI asked RBI to raise SLR. Between 1970 and 1990, SLR was raised from 26 per cent to 38.5 per cent.[13] Thus, the two ratios combined amounted to 63.5 per cent of the bank funds, the highest ever, for several years. Fiscal policy, then, completely dominated monetary policy; in fact, there was total dominance of the central government over RBI. RBI's autonomy had been severely dented.

The 13-year period, 1969–1981, was also witness to some other big events; these included the Bangladesh War, two severe oil shocks and severe droughts. It had also seen nine finance ministers at GOI and eight governors at RBI. Not surprisingly, this period had passed through high rates of volatility of annual economic growth and inflation. The average rates of economic growth and inflation in the 1970–1971 to 1979–1980 decade were 2.9 per cent and 9.0 per cent respectively.[14]

4.3. Excessive Lending to Large Borrowers: Two Study Groups

The objective of breaking the nexus between banking and industry by bank nationalization seemed to have been achieved by removing 'big business' from ownership and governance of banks. But bank funds had continued to flow to large trade and industry.

On 11 October 1968, National Credit Council had constituted a study group under the chairmanship of V. T. Dehejia, the then chairman of SBI, to examine 'the extent to which credit needs of industry and trade are likely to be inflated and how such trends could be checked'. The study group submitted its report in September 1969. 'A major finding of the Group was that there was a tendency on the part of a number of industrial units to utilise short-term bank credit and other current liabilities for acquisition of non-current assets'.[15] According to the Group, the prevalent lending system of banks appeared to have greatly assisted this tendency on the part of many borrowers. The system, it observed, was found convenient as banks placed emphasis on the security aspect. Despite the recommendations of the Group and RBI's steps to amend the prevailing situation, the practice of using short-term bank funds under the cash credit system for long-term uses had continued to persist.

In 1973–1974, when demand for bank credit rose sharply while production was not rising and inflation touched the unprecedented level of 31 per cent, RBI concluded that time was ripe to bring about reforms in the bank credit system. In July 1974, RBI constituted a study group under the chairmanship of Prakash Tandon, the then chairman of PNB, to frame guidelines for the follow-up of bank credit. The group was also asked, inter alia, to suggest criteria applicable to companies (borrowers) regarding their satisfactory capital structure and sound financial basis in relation to borrowings, and to make recommendations regarding the sources for financing the minimum working capital requirements. Dehejia study group had already brought out the finding of large borrowers using short-term funds for long-term purposes, thus causing current ratio to fall below 1. The major recommendation of Tandon study group was to take measures to raise current ratio of borrowers steadily to above 1. This would fulfil the basic tenet of a strong BS. Several recommendations were made to convert the borrower BS to that level. This recommendation would also ensure releasing banks' resources for lending to other classes of borrowers including PSL.

4.4. Decontrol and Deregulation: 1981–1991

The period 1981–1990-91 was the era of decontrol and deregulation without a planned framework. Slow and steady deregulation began in three areas—industry, trade and taxation, besides exchange rate management. Twenty-five broad categories of industries were de-licensed. Industrial and stock exchange reforms were carried out.

The proliferation of different lending institutions and schemes under directed credit programmes plus the operation of commercial banks including Regional Rural Banks (RRBs) and cooperative banks had led to a complex set of interest rate structures. It was found that about 200 rates of interest were in effect by the middle of 1980s. It was then that the structure of interest rates at the short end began to be rationalized.[16]

The vast 'banking system shift' from urban areas to rural and semi-urban areas resulted in huge expansion of banking transactions over a much larger geography. Banks' lines of command and control got stretched to breaking point, and smaller bank branches were now manned by untrained, junior personnel. The potential consequences of this serious organizational problem came to be realized in the early 1980s. RBI took up the task to consolidate the banking system and to build on the gains of the 1970s. Key elements: slowdown in branch expansion, drawing up of comprehensive action plans by banks to rewrite their systems and procedures, actions to relieve policy-related constraints on bank profitability by raising coupon rates of government bonds and interest on cash balances held with RBI, allowing greater flexibility in bank service charges, and strengthening the capital base of banks.

In the beginning of the 1980s, most of the financial markets were still characterized by controls, mispricing of financial products, restrictions on the flow of transactions, barriers to entry, low liquidity and high transaction costs, many of them are the characteristics of less-developed financial markets. These features severely inhibited the growth of the financial markets and reduced the allocative efficiency of the resources channelled through them. The proliferation of directed credit programmes, the administered interest rate structure, fast (non-viable) branch expansion and substantial increases in statutory pre-emptions had an adverse impact on profitability. Monetary policy was not yet attuned to the use of market-based indirect instruments.

Relaxation of controls on the financial markets including the banking system began in 1981. Several actions were initiated throughout the 1980s, particularly from the mid-1980s, which essentially started the process of liberalization of the banking system. Major policy changes were introduction of treasury bills, recreating the money market, and rationalization and partial deregulation of interest rates. BRA was amended in 1984 to address the decline in the role of banks due to disintermediation; banks were allowed to undertake merchant banking activities through the setting up of subsidiaries. Widespread diversification into new instruments of deposits and credit was permitted. Banks were permitted to open new subsidiaries to run new financial services such as mutual funds, equipment leasing, housing finance, and provision of services of venture capital, factoring and portfolio management. By the end of June 1991, banks had set up 25 subsidiaries for these diverse activities. Banks were allowed to open overseas branches. Selective credit controls were dismantled. Credit Authorisation Scheme was abolished in 1989.

As a result of the steady stream of reforms, the average rates of economic growth and inflation in the 1980-81–1989-90 decade had improved to 5.8 per cent and 8.0 per cent respectively.[17]

4.5. Other Regulatory Matters

4.5.1. Consolidation of Banks: Pruning Weak Banks

The pruning of the remaining weak banks, post actions taken during 1950–1968, was continued in this period. At the end of last period (1968), the number of Indian SCBs and non-scheduled banks was 58 and 17 respectively, a total of 75. At the end of 1980, their respective numbers were 62 and 3. At the end of 1990–91, their number was 53 and 3 respectively, a total of 56 and a total reduction of 19 banks. It would seem that the RBI had almost completed the task of pruning weak banks through amalgamations and liquidations.

4.5.2. Capital Adequacy

The relentless pursuit of targeted expansion of bank branch network in rural and semi-urban areas, and increase in PSL at subsidized rates of interest put heavy adverse pressure on PSBs' profits. Declining (actual) profits (unknown to the public as real position of PLAs was hidden from them) resulted in declining equity and, hence, declining leverage of bank BS. The resulting financial weaknesses of PSBs alarmed even the majority bank owners, that is, the GOI. Therefore, it evolved a scheme to contribute to the capital base of nationalized banks. Its implementation began in 1985 and GOI had contributed ₹2,600 crore till 1990–91. SBI's authorized capital had been raised from ₹200 crore to ₹1,000 crore, and its paid-up capital had been revised from ₹150 crore to ₹200 crore.

Till 1990–91, CA norms for banks were not uniform. The capital structure of PSBs was governed by their respective enactments. For private sector banks (PrSBs), the required capital was linked to their geographical locations. Foreign banks were required to have, as at the end of each accounting year, foreign funds equivalent to 3.5 per cent of the deposits deployed in Indian business. There were, of course, prescriptions regarding maintenance of statutory reserves. This was the status until 1991, when the GOI accepted the recommendations of the Committee on the Financial System (CFS) on adopting new CA standards.[18]

III. BANKING FOR RURAL DEVELOPMENT

4.6. Policies, Programmes and Schemes

Post nationalization, the banking system underwent a major structural change. The main objectives of bank nationalization were to (a) expand the banking system to the unbanked geography of the country so as to reach banking services all over the country and (b) serve the credit needs of its poorest everywhere, particularly to provide small loans in the 'priority sectors' of the economy. The rural and tribal parts of the country were the dominant focus of this coverage. The underlying propellant of the banking system in this period, therefore, was the twin expansion of: (a) its rural and semi-urban branch infrastructure and (b) PSL in rural India. This process continued until around the mid-1980s. From the mid-1980s, this transformation seemed to have been slowed with a view to consolidate what had been achieved, to rectify some of the actions which had not worked and to undo some of the restrictive impositions on banks.

4.6.1. Differentiating Priority Sector Lending from Rural Banking

It is appropriate here to bifurcate rural development banking into its two major programmes. We divide them into: (a) RB and (b) PSL, a conceptual division not made usually. Both may overlap here and there, but still it is felt necessary to do so in order to set goals and to measure achievements in this very broad area of rural development banking.

'RB' refers to banks doing the business of banking through their presence in rural India. Banks open branches in the 'geographic areas' called rural areas and tribal areas, and, at a minimum, conduct their basic banking functions of collecting deposits from and granting loans to the residents in these areas. Such loans will usually comprise lending for all the economic activities, big and small, including agriculture.

'PSL' comprises lending for activities defined as priority sector by the State. The concept of 'priority sector' was born in 1967 with the advent of the concept of social control over banks. The scheme of social control was announced in the Parliament in December 1967 in order to ensure more equitable distribution of the financial resources of the banking system. The idea was to grant relative priorities to occupations followed by small farmers and poorer classes of the populace in the country, which were hitherto neglected by the banking system. The scope of priority sector was expanded from time to time. Thus, in 1975, priority sector referred to sub-sectors of agriculture, small scale industries (SSI), road and water transport operators, retail trade and small business, professionals and self-employed and education.[19] In 1985, this concept was expanded to also include indirect finance to other priority sectors, pure consumption, and housing loan to weaker sections and SCs/STs.[20]

From the above description, it should be clear that while RB meant banking in the rural parts of the country (and included lending to the defined priority sectors in rural India), PSL meant lending to the weakest sections of the society for specified economic sectors all over the country, including tribal areas and, particularly, less developed areas. While RB was conducted from the rural branches of banks, PSL could be conducted from all branches of all the banks. Under the push by the GOI and RBI to reach the economically weakest sections of people of the country, minimum targets were prescribed for the expansion of rural branches and for minimum lending to the priority sectors. Both these classes of banking were targeted to grow at rates faster than in the past and at rates faster than the rates of growth of total bank branches and aggregate bank lending respectively.

In 1969, a 'new branch licensing policy' was written which shifted the focus of branch expansion to rural and semi-urban centres. A new scheme called 'Lead Bank Scheme' (LBS) was also launched. Under LBS, the nationalized banks and three PrSBs were designated as lead banks of several districts, each from all the districts of the country (except metropolitan and union territories). Each lead bank was to prepare a district credit plan (DCP) of each allotted district to incorporate programmes to (a) mobilize deposits, (b) deploy credit to the priority sector and (c) become the principal instrument of branch expansion. Each district had to achieve a minimum C–D ratio of 60 per cent.

Several other steps were taken to expand lending to the priority sector. In the early 1970s, while 81 per cent of the borrower accounts of banks were for an amount of ₹10,000 or less, they accounted for only 4 per cent of outstanding bank credit. RBI promoted a 'Credit Guarantee Corporation' in 1971 to provide guarantees against defaults in repayments by small borrowers. A 'Differential Rate of Interest Scheme' (DRI) was launched in 1972 under which 1 per cent of each bank's advances at the end of the previous year had to be lent to the poorest of the poor in rural areas at an interest rate of 4 per cent. In 1974, banks were advised that their PSL should reach the level of at least one-third of their outstanding credit by March 1979. Later, this target was raised to 40 per cent. Also, banks were advised to earmark at least 10 per cent within this target for lending to the weaker sections.

While all the above measures resulted in improvement in PSL, it was below expectations. The assessment was that commercial bank staff was not attitudinally attuned to the needs of small and poor farmers. A new genre of banks called RRBs was, therefore, set up in 1976 to meet the credit needs of the weakest sections of the society such as small and marginal farmers, and landless labourers. In July 1982, the National Bank for Agriculture and Rural Development was born at the apex level to be dedicated to rural credit, and the Agricultural Credit Department of RBI was wound up.

Under the 'service area approach', a new strategy for rural lending was introduced in 1989 as a part of the LBS for improving the quality of lending by the banks. This approach aimed at a planned and orderly development of an identified command area which would enable the branch to focus on proactive lending. To its end, branches were to prepare annual credit plans.

Thus, the experimentation with potentially more effective schemes and programmes continued throughout this period. It still continues.

4.7. Achievements

The analysis of achievements in pursuit of these objectives during 1969–1990-91 is divided into 3 parts:

1. Branch network expansion (Table 4.1),
2. Growth of RB (Table 4.2) and
3. Growth of PSL (Table 4.3).

4.7.1. Branch Expansion

Table 4.1 shows the branch network of the banking system, according to bank groups and population groups, as on 31 March 1991.

As read from Table 4.1, the share of rural branches in total branch network was '58 per cent'. As against this, there were 1,860 rural branches out of the total branches of 8,322 on 19 July 1969, that is, '22 per cent' of the total.[21] Going by Table 4.4, the number of branches of SCBs, alone (not considering RRBs), had grown by 40,530 by

Table 4.1 SCBs' Branch Network—31 March 1991

Bank Groups	Rural	Semi-urban	Branches Urban	Metropolitan	Total
1. 28PSBs	20,463	9,116	6,713	5,438	41,730
2. RRBs	13,447	921	145	5	14,518
3. All PSBs	33,910	10,037	6,858	5,443	56,248
4. PrSBs	1,262	1,250	745	543	3,800
5. All Indian SCBs	35,172	11,287	7,603	5,986	60,048
6. Foreign Banks	–	2	9	130	141
7. Non-SCBs	20	16	11	–	47
8. All Banks	35,192	11,305	7,623	6,116	60,236

Source: ST 1990–91, Table 31, p. 73 (derived).

Table 4.2 Growth of RB (1969–1991): Select Years

As at the End of	No. of Bank Offices		Credit Outstanding		Deposits		C–D Ratio (%)	
	Rural	% of Total	Rural (₹ crore)	% of Total	Rural (₹ crore)	% of Total	Rural	All-India
June 1969	1,443	18	115	3.3	306	6.3	37.6	71.9
Dec.*1972	5,109	36	257	4.6	540	6.5	47.6	79.9
June 1975	6,807	36	534	6.0	1,026	9.0	52.0	71.4
June 1980	15,105	47	2,643	10.7	4,644	12.5	56.9	66.1
June 1985	30,185	59	7,278	13.8	10,411	13.4	69.9	66.1
Mar. 1991	35,206	58	18,599	14.9	31,010	15.4	59.9	60.0

Sources: 1969: C & F-1, Table 3.27, p. 102; the rest: RBI, BSR, various years.

Note: *Data for 1970 and 1971 not available, hence 1972 taken.

Table 4.3 Growth of PSL (1969–1991): Select Years

As at the End of	Priority Sector Advances (₹ in crore)	(Growth %)**	Share of Priority Sector Advances in Total Advances (%)
June 1969	504	—	14.9
June 1970	838	66	21.2
June 1975	2,292	173	27.5*
June 1980	7,278	218	37*
June 1985	19,829	172	44.9*
Mar. 1991	44,572	125 ,	39.2*

Sources: RBI, BSR, 1975, 1980, 1985 and 1991.

Note: * Percentage is of non-food credit; ** Each growth percentage is over the preceding figures.

March 1991, more than 6 times the 7,446 branches at the end of 1968. It may be noted that, on a much smaller base, branches had grown at less than 3 times during the period 1950–1968.[22]

Thus, branch infrastructure in rural India had grown about 19 times, while the total network in the country had grown a little over 7 times in this period. This scale of development had not occurred before and may not occur again.

4.7.2. Growth of Rural Banking

Nationalization had generated strong confidence of the public in the banking system which had contributed to the system's fast growth. Table 4.2 shows the growth of RB.

Bank offices had multiplied by 24 times, credit outstanding by 51 times and deposits by 93 times. C–D ratio had increased from 37.6 per cent to 59.9 per cent while All-India C–D ratio had declined from 71.9 per cent to 60 per cent since June 1969 to March 1991. It may be concluded that 'RB had recorded a stellar growth on the three parameters. It had laid a strong foundation for its future growth and for the economic well-being of the rural populace'.

4.7.3. Growth of Priority Sector Lending

Table 4.3 shows the growth of PSL.

The rate of growth of PSL was higher than that of the total advances over the period. The share of PSL in total advances had gone on increasing up to June 1985 when it had crossed the target of 40 per cent. In the last period of about six years, there had been a slight slowdown to 39.2 per cent of non-food advances.

IV. NON-DISCLOSURE IN FINANCIAL STATEMENTS

4.8. Evolution of Non-disclosure Practices: 1969–1991

Nationalization had cast onerous responsibilities on banks, particularly PSBs, of targeted accelerated PSL and branch expansion. Low lending rates, high manpower and other operating expenses, increases in bad and doubtful debts, and low coupon rates on gilts adversely affected the financial statements. There were telltale signs of the impact on the face of these financial statements, despite the fact that actual figures were being hidden. Bad times breed bad practices to hide the adverse impact on profitability and financial condition, mostly with the 'acquiescence/approval' of the owners and regulators, and even auditors. Several methods were used to hide poor performance:

1. Summarized PLA format
2. Inadequacy of provisions
3. 'Adjustments' of revenue and expenditure
4. Appendment of 'negative notes' to BS
5. Drawing upon of secret reserves.

4.8.1. Summary of Profit and Loss Account Format

First and foremost, the PLA format was changed in 1970 (to remain in force until 1988–89) to make it very brief, so as to exclude most details of income and expenditure including all provisions. Until 1965, the BS showed an omnibus item titled 'others (including provisions)' under the head 'other liabilities'. This item of 'others' did not appear from 1966–1978. It re-appeared from 1979 until 1988–89.

Hence, there was a complete shutout of amounts of provisions, if any. The summary of PLA allowed the authorities concerned to hide and manipulate income and expenditure items in any way they wanted to. That was possibly a method to hide actual data and to show some 'manufactured' data to the readers. This became evident from the following descriptions.

4.8.2. 'Adjustments' of Revenue and Expenditure

Hiding provisions and/or declining performance require 'adjustments' in some revenue and expenditure items. An analysis of select data of 28 PSBs for the year 1984 from ST 1984 was made to unearth the methods used for the purpose. Revenue and expenditure items were 'adjusted' (not disclosed in the PLAs) to make undisclosed provisions for bonus, gratuity, staff welfare, income tax, etc. and to transfer to/from secret reserves.

- Revenue items were adjusted to the extent of ₹885 crore;
- Expenditure items were adjusted to the extent of ₹179 crore;
- This left a balance of ₹706 crore;
- It can be surmized that this amount was used to make provisions, etc. of ₹678 crore;
- The balance of ₹28 crore got accounted for by (a) withdrawal of ₹6 crore from their secret reserves (by some banks) and (b) transfer of ₹34 crore to their secret reserves by some other banks.

4.8.3. Non-disclosure of Provisions

Till 1965, the PLAs of banks showed provisions including reserves (provisions) for bad and doubtful debts on their PLAs. But there was an exception. Even in those years, SBI Group was following the practice of non-disclosure of provisions on their PLAs. In the period

1966–1969, PLAs showed provision for taxation only and no other provisions. In the period 1970–1990-91, the new prescribed format of PLA did not provide space for stating provisions. There was no way to ascertain whether provisions were actually made or not, whether those were adequate or not, and where those were located (hidden). Hence, the authenticity of profit figures in this period could not be vouched. An attempt was made to get an idea of the likely estimate of non-disclosure in those years by comparing PLA figures of 1989–90 and 1990–91 (the last two years of non-disclosure) with corresponding figures of 1991–92 (the first year of disclosure):

Year	Total Income (₹ in crore)	Profit before Provisions (₹ in crore)	Provisions (₹ in crore)	Profit after provisions (₹ in crore)
1989–90	22,571	489	–	489
1989–91	26,563	606	–	606
1989–92	39,753	7,091	5,811	1,280

The comparative figures are self-explanatory. Note that the amount of published provisions, ₹5,811 crore, was more than 11 and 9 times the profits shown for 1989–90 and 1990–91 respectively. To us, it seems that the extent of adjustments in PLAs in years up to 1990–91 was huge and hiding of provisions was larger still.

It can also be stated that the authenticity of any ratios/relationships of which one of the variables was a profit figure in the years of non-disclosure was questionable. The declining ROAs and ROEs of banks in this period would actually have been lower than shown.

4.8.4. Appendment of Notes to the Balance Sheet

It was noticed that the number of 'notes' appended to the BS had begun to increase in this period. A study was undertaken to identify the nature and magnitude of this practice among the 28 PSBs. It was found that the total number of these notes had increased from 46 in 1969 to 308 by 1988–89, from an average of 2 per bank to 11 per bank. Most of the notes were instrumental in introducing ambiguity in the required amount of provisions and postponing recognition of losses (which was obviously the intent of top managements of banks); some notes included changes in accounting practices which would cause recognition of income, early and postpone recognition of losses to a later day. These notes were 'negative'.

4.8.5. Use of Secret Reserves

Commercial banks are run on public money and public trust. Being a highly leveraged enterprise, a decline in the profit of a bank results in a sharper decline in its profitability and, consequently, in its market value. That is why banks are highly regulated institutions, formed under special banking laws, and regulated and controlled by central banks of the country.

One of the devices banks deploy to prevent declines in their performance from being exposed in the public domain is to create 'secret reserves'. In good times, it is an accepted practice for banks to transfer a part of their profits to secret reserves, to be used to write off losses in bad times. It ensures a certain level of stability in banks' published financial results.

The STs of six years, 1979–1984, happened to publish a statement from which actual unadulterated financial data of the banks could be derived. Our study found that some banks had drawn upon their secret reserves to bolster their financial results in these years. It was another indicator of the declining fortunes of banks during the current period. But, interestingly, some banks had transferred profits to their secret reserves also; and those amounts were much larger than the amounts transferred back from these reserves by, possibly, some other banks.

In view of the above reality, the elaborate financial analysis attempted in section V, below, has to be taken with a large pinch of salt.[23]

4.9. From Non-disclosure to Disclosure

Committee to Consider the Issues

Having turned a blind eye to the growing deterioration in the levels of presentation and disclosures in the financial statements of banks and its negative impact for more than a decade, RBI decided that its stance on this matter may need to be changed. In 1982, it appointed a committee chaired by A. Ghosh, the then deputy governor, RBI, to examine the 'desirability of greater or full disclosure in the published accounts of banks and related issues'. The committee called 'the Committee to Consider Final Accounts of Banks' (C-FAB, hereinafter) submitted its report in 1985.[24] GOI acted on the report in January 1991. Following up on the recommendations of C-FAB, it issued a notification to make amendments in the Third Schedule of the BRA, incorporating changes in the formats of bank financial statements with the objective of providing some transparency of bank performance. Additionally, banks were advised to disclose their 'principal accounting policies' regarding key areas of their operations, including making of provisions and adjustments made before disclosing net profit, at one place, along with the notes appended to their financial statements for the year ended 31 March 1991 onwards on a regular basis.[25] Thus, the implementation aspect of the recommendations was taken care of. Rationale of the recommendations and related aspects are discussed at some length, more appropriately, in Chapter 5.

V. THE FINANCIALS: 1969–1990-91

The financials (financial management and performance) of SCBs for 22 years are analysed in this section. The parameters and the methodology used are the same as in Chapters 3 and 4, and the sequence of analysis also follows them. Five financial absolutes of size and performance are analysed in Table 4.4, and seven ratios which supplement and deepen that analysis are presented in Table 4.5. The 12 financial variables taken together provide an adequately full picture of the banks' financials to yield meaningful conclusions. This financial analysis adds to the banking analysis in the preceding sections.

4.10. The Financials

4.10.1. Five Parameters (Table 4.4)

Number of banks: The number of banks at the beginning of this period was 73. It comprised 58 Indian banks and 15 foreign banks. It rose steadily to 81 in 1981, and then began to decline to end up at 76 in 1990–91, the last year of the period. In this period, the number of Indian banks had declined to 53, while the number of foreign banks had increased to 23. It seems that the process of consolidation of Indian PrSBs was complete by 1990–91.

Total assets: The consolidated BS of the banking system grew every year of this period at rates varying between 13 to 28 per cent per annum. It grew from ₹54 billion in 1968 to ₹2,866 billion in 1991, 53 times over the whole period. Its CAGR from 1969 to 1975 grew between 13 and 18, and from 1976 to 1990–91 at 20 every year. CAGR for the full period was 20.

Total branches: Total branches grew from 7,446 at the beginning of this period to 47,976 at its end. Post nationalization of 14 banks, banks were required to add to their branches at high-targeted numbers, particularly in rural and semi-urban centres. Bank branches increased

Table 4.4 SCBs' Significant Bank Parameters: 1969–1990-91 (Continued)

Serial No.	Parameters	1968	1969	1970	1971	1972	1973	1974	1975	1976	1977	1978	1979
1	Banks (number)	73	73	73	74	74	74	74	73	73	74	75	75
2	TA(₹ in billions)	54	61	74	85	100	124	145	177	226	272	342	412
	Percent increase YOY		13	21	15	18	24	17	22	28	20	26	20
	CAGR		13	17	16	17	18	18	18	20	20	20	20
3	Branches (number)	7,446	8,867	11,040	12,888	14,630	16,387	18,050	20,293	23,037	25,759	27,725	29,099
	Percent increase YOY		19	25	17	14	12	10	12	14	12	8	5
	CAGR		19	22	20	18	17	16	15	15	15	14	13
4	Total income (₹ in crore)	382	427	494	616	727	904	1,252	1,571	1,926	2,311	2,678	3,338
	Percent increase YOY		12	16	25	18	24	38	25	23	20	16	25
	CAGR		12	14	17	17	19	22	22	22	22	21	22
5	PAT(₹ in millions)	120	120	140	170	170	180	250	310	400	310	360	440
	Percent increase YOY		0	17	21	0	6	39	24	29	-23	16	22
	CAGR		0	8	12	9	8	13	15	16	11	12	13

Table 4.4 SCBs' Significant Bank Parameters (1969–1990-91) (Concluded)

Serial No.	Parameters	1980	1981	1982	1983	1984	1985	1986	1987	1988–89*	1989–90	1990–91	1990–91/1968 (Times)	CAGR
1	Banks (number)	77	81	79	80	79	79	79	78	78	74	76	–	–
2	TA (₹ in billions)	492	598	705	836	996	1,185	1,383	1,638	2,075	2,479	2,866	53.07	20
	Percent change YOY	19	22	18	19	19	19	17	18	27	19	16		
	CAGR	20	20	20	20	20	20	20	20	20	20	20		
3	Branches (number)	31,365	33,547	34,906	36,559	38,240	40,355	40,559	41,356	44,146	47,545	47,976	6.44	9
	Percent change YOY	8	7	4	5	5	6	1	2	7	8	1		
	CAGR	13	12	12	11	11	10	10	9	9	9	9		
4	Total income (₹ in crore)	4,233	5,315	6,274	7,181	9,124	10,552	12,450	14,810	22,729	22,571	26,563	69.54	21
	Percent change YOY	27	26	18	14	27	16	18	19	53	(1)	18		
	CAGR	22	22	22	22	22	22	21	21	23	21	21		
	PAT (₹ in millions)	520	640	790	850	1,000	1,210	2,230	2,820	4,360	4,890	6,060	50.50	20
	Percent change YOY	18	23	23	8	18	21	84	26	55	12	24		
	CAGR	13	14	14	14	14	15	18	18	20	19	20		

Sources: Banks: STs, various years; branches: IBA, performance highlights, various years, Bombay; other parameters: Annexure, Statements 4.1 and 4.2.

Note: *By a notification dated 30 December 1988 (1 day before the end of the calendar year, that is, the 12-month accounting/ financial year of banks), GOI notified to change the financial year of banks to the government's financial year, that is, April 1 of a year to March 31 of the following year. Consequently, the financial year of banks for 1988 changed to 1988–1989, consisting of 15 months (1 January 1988 to 31 March 1989).

Table 4.5 SCBs' Significant Bank Ratios: 1969–1990-91 (Continued)

Serial No.	Ratios	1968	1969	1970	1971	1972	1973	1974	1975	1976	1977	1978	1979
1	Leverage	2.09	1.87	1.62	1.51	1.34	1.14	1.24	1.25	1.22	1.16	1.08	1.06
2	C–D	67	69	72	67	62	65	65	68	70	65	64	62
3	I–D	29	28	28	29	32	30	30	29	29	29	29	29
4	NIM	2.82	2.79	2.54	2.78	2.75	2.64	2.84	2.82	2.20	2.10	1.97	2.04
5	C–I	84	85	95	95	96	96	96	96	95	96	96	96
6	Return on average assets	0.68	0.63	0.21	0.22	0.18	0.16	0.19	0.20	0.20	0.12	0.12	0.12
7	Return on average equity	31.54	32.06	11.89	13.92	13.03	13.06	15.56	15.67	16.18	10.48	10.43	10.97

Table 4.5 SCBs' Significant Bank Ratios: 1969–1990-91 (Concluded)

Serial No.	Ratios	1980	1981	1982	1983	1984	1985	1986	1987	1988–89	1989–90	1990–91
1	Leverage	1.07	1.04	1.17	1.16	1.07	1.56	1.77	1.94	1.82	1.94	2.24
2	C–D	62	64	64	62	63	60	58	57	61	62	62
3	I–D	29	28	28	30	28	30	32	34	34	34	34
4	NIM	2.11	2.11	2.11	1.12	2.40	2.29	2.21	2.14	2.50	2.03	1.96
5	C–I	97	96	96	96	97	97	95	94	94	93	93
6	Return on average assets	0.12	0.12	0.12	0.11	0.11	0.11	0.17	0.19	0.24	0.21	0.23
7	Return on average equity	10.82	11.15	10.90	9.53	9.83	8.31	10.39	10.01	12.52	11.38	10.78

Source: Annexure, Statements 4.1 and 4.2.

by 19 per cent in 1969 (= Pre-nationalization nearly six-and-half months, post-nationalization five-and-a-half-months) as against 6.3 per cent in 1967 and 9.8 per cent in 1968. This number increased at 22 per cent and 17 per cent in 1970 and 1971 respectively. Thereafter, rates of growth kept on declining at fluctuating rates. The growth rate in 1990–91 was just 1 per cent. 'Obviously, the targets of branch expansion were lowered to reduce overheads to improve the bottom line. Overall, the branches in this period had multiplied 6.44 times, at a CAGR of 9.'

Total income: Total income of SCBs had grown from ₹382 crore at the beginning of this period to ₹26,563 crore at the end of 1990–91—a rise of more than 69 times. Annual growth rates varied from 12 per cent to 27 per cent. 'Three special mentions' need to be made: (a) the growth rate in 1974 was above the range of growth aforementioned. It was 38 per cent. The reason was the increase in the interest rates of deposits and lending. Also, the employee costs increased due to upward revision in the dearness allowance of employees. Hence, both the total income and the total expenditure went up by about 38 per cent. (b) Over the years 1984–1986, interest rates on banks' CRR balances, interest rates on food procurement funds used by banks and coupon rates on gilts were raised. This raised the total income of banks steadily over these years. (c) As a result of change in accounting year from the calendar year to the government's financial year, the accounting year of January 1988 to December 1988 (12 months) was changed to 01 January 1988 to 31 March 1989 (15 months). Hence, the results of 1988–89 covered a period of 15 months and, therefore, its income would arithmetically be higher by a proportion of one-quarter. One, therefore, finds the growth rate of 1988–89 to be 53 per cent, as against the rates of the previous year 1987 (19%) and the following year 1989–90 (−1%). Its CAGR was 21.

Profit after tax: This parameter, being the bottom line of a PLA, recorded a higher level of volatility than other parameters. PAT recorded an annual percentage change varying from 23 per cent to 00 per cent to 29 per cent. Exceptional variations beyond the above variations were 39 per cent in 1974, 84 per cent in 1986 and 55 per cent in 1988–89. Overall, PAT increased 50 times over this period. CAGR was 20.

4.10.2. Seven Ratios (Table 4.5)

Leverage: Leverage of SCBs was 2.09 at the beginning of this period. Stiff targets to fast track PSL and to open more branches in rural areas caused profits and profitability to decline over the years. Leverage in 1969 declined to 1.87 and went on declining till around 1984. Extent of actual declines over the period could not be ascertained as the formats/contents of published financial statements were changed, which camouflaged actual figures in BS and PLA.

Leverage improved from 1985 as a few deregulatory steps were taken by RBI, as noted earlier, to improve bank profitability. As a result, leverage improved for the better to close at 2.24 in 1990–91.

Credit–Deposit Ratio and Investment–Deposit Ratio: As is in their nature, the two ratios continued to move in tandem. The combined ratios of these two added up to 96 per cent at the beginning of 1969. It increased to 97 by the end of that year and rose to 100 per cent in 1970, the highest of this period. From 1970, SLR began to be raised to force banks to invest more in gilts, as GOI required funds to meet its budgetary requirements. Additionally, the yield on gilts was kept low, below the market rates, to keep the costs of financing government's budgets low. From 1973, CRR also began to be raised to keep inflation under control. Taken together, CRR and SLR were raised to their highest levels warranted by law. As CRR reached its highest possible limit of 15 per cent + 10 per cent incremental, the combined two ratios never touched 100 again in this period. When yields on gilts began to be raised in mid-1980s,

I–D ratio began to go up at the cost of the C–D ratio. Table 4.5 tells this story clearly.

Net Interest Margin: NIM, one of the two major determinants of the bottom line, was a pretty volatile figure in this period. It was 2.82 per cent at the beginning of 1969, fluctuated around this figure until it was 2.82 per cent again in 1975, and began to fall to reach 1.12 in 1983. It began to rise again till it stood at 2.5 per cent in 1988–1989. It closed at 1.96 per cent at the end of this period. Overall, it fell to below 2.0 per cent in three years. Culprits for low NIMs in this period were the same as mentioned above.

Cost–Income Ratio: This period saw a very high C–I ratio throughout. At the beginning of the period, this ratio was 84. It was 85 per cent in 1969. In 1970, it shot up to 95. Between 1970–1986, C–I ratio remained at 95–97. Some changes in 1986, as noted earlier, raised NIM somewhat. It raised the income component of C–I, so that C–I dropped to 94 and then to 93. As repeated again and again, the obvious reasons for the high levels of this parameter were the rapid growth of RB and PSL, sharply raising operating costs; interest yields, owing to subsidized interest rates on PSL, declined. This had adversely affected bank profitability.

Return on Assets and Return on Equity: ROA was 0.68 per cent in 1968 and 0.63 per cent in 1969. It fell sharply to 0.21–0.22 in 1970–1971 and continued to slide, so that it was 0.11 in 1983–1985. From 1986, the year in which reversal of fortunes was brought about it began to rise, so that ROA ended this period at 0.23, although still low.

ROE was 32 per cent in 1968 and in 1969, the first year of this period. It fell sharply to 12–13 per cent from 1970 onwards, rose to 16 per cent in 1974–1976, before resuming the slide to 10–11 per cent, and to fall to its lowest level of 8 per cent in 1985. From 1986, it rose to 10–13 per cent and ended this period at about 11 per cent. It is to be noted that even this (low) level of ROE had been reached on low levels of equity (which forms the denominator of the ROE equation).

4.11. Concluding Remarks

The positive achievements narrated in the preceding section were attained at the cost of deterioration of banks' financials. This progress was exacted at a heavy cost in terms of decline in productivity and efficiency of the system. It led to severe decline in profitability leading to negative equity of several banks. As a result, it affected the ability of the banking system to expand further.[26]

It would have been noted from the income and the BS parameters of the total income, PAT, NIM, C–I ratio, ROA and ROE in Tables 4.4 and 4.5, and the analysis following, that the years 1974, 1986 and 1988–89 were the three inflexion points for them, where the income curve moved upwards. Two major actions which the banks were tasked to undertake after nationalization, that is, fast branch expansion into rural and semi-urban India and rapid increase in PSL (at low, below-cost interest rates), affected the profitability of banks adversely. As and when the authorities found that the banks were close to going into the red, some actions would follow to shore up their bottom lines. Those actions took place in a few years, particularly in 1986, and their impacts on the PLAs would occur in those and the following years. As described in Section II.3 supra, banks were allowed around the mid-1980s to diversify into merchant banking activities, etc., which contributed to an increase in bank income.

VI. THE 21ST-CENTURY BANKS: 1991

Table 4.6 produces the status of 42 banks as on 31 March 1991. This table is a little different in its content in that while it lists TA as on 31 March 1991, it lists branches as on 31 March 1989 (see the note and source of Table 4.6.).

Table 4.6 The 21st-Century Banks: 1991

(Fifth in the Series)

Serial No.	Banks (ranked by TA)	TA (1990–91) ₹ in crore	Rank	Branches (1988–89) Number	Rank
1	SBI	91,511	1	7,937	1
2	Bank of India	22,693	2	2,080	5
3	PNB	18,813	3	2,752	2
4	Bank of Baroda	18,514	4	2,106	4
5	Canara Bank	17,656	5	1,945	6
6	Central Bank of India	15,330	6	2,720	3
7	UCO Bank	11,626	7	1,751	7
8	Indian Bank	11,282	8	1,167	11
9	Indian Overseas Bank	9,331	9	1,152	13
10	Syndicate Bank	8,528	10	1,474	10
11	Union Bank of India	8,499	11	1,740	8
12	Allahabad Bank	7,854	12	1,509	9
13	United Bank of India	6,498	13	1,164	12
14	Andhra Bank	4,223	14	906	16
15	Bank of Maharashtra	4,390	15	1,071	14
16	Dena Bank	3,932	16	1,051	15
17	State Bank of Patiala	3,622	17	548	23
18	Vijaya Bank	4,066	18	702	18
19	State Bank of Hyderabad	3,649	19	652	20
20	Oriental Bank of Commerce	3,556	20	502	25
21	Punjab & Sind Bank	3,263	21	657	19
22	State Bank of Bikaner & Jaipur	3,151	22	718	17
23	State Bank of Travancore	2,975	23	634	21
24	New Bank of India	2,375*	24	567	22
25	Corporation Bank	2,322	25	431	26
26	State Bank of Mysore	2,012	26	527	24
27	State Bank of Indore	1,827	27	320	28

(Continued)

(Continued Table 4.6)

(Fifth in the Series)

Serial No.	Banks (ranked by TA)	TA (1990–91) ₹ in crore	Rank	Branches (1988–89) Number	Rank
28	State Bank of Saurashtra	1,782	28	308	29
29	Jammu and Kashmir Bank	1,578	29	NA	–
30	Vysya Bank	1,396	30	283	32
31	Federal Bank	1,053	31	333	27
32	Bank of Rajasthan	1,090	32	292	31
33	Karnataka Bank	776	33	270	33
34	South Indian Bank	647	34	300	30
35	Catholic Syrian Bank	533	35	229	34
36	Tamilnad Mercantile Bank	444	36	115	38
37	Karur Vysya Bank	436	37	155	36
38	LakshmiVilas Bank	385	38	168	35
39	City Union Bank	196	39	80	39
40	Dhanlaxmi Bank	142	40	124	37
41	Nainital Bank	134	41	48	41
42	Ratnakar Bank	99	42	57	40
Total		304,189		41,545	

Sources: 'TA' is sourced from ST 1990–91, Table 47, pp. 110–219; unlike previous years, ST 1990–91 did not provide branch data for each bank. Hence, the branch data has been sourced from the closest previous year, that is, 1988–89, from ST 1988–89, Table 55, pp. 160–227. ST 1989–90 was not published.

Note: * 'TA' of New Bank of India for 1990–91 was not published; hence, this figure has been taken from ST 1988–89.

VII. 1969–1991: REVOLUTIONARY CHANGES

This period had begun with PSBs gaining dominance in the banking system in 1969. This dominance expanded in 1980 with the nationalization of another six banks. By the end of 1990–91, this dominance was at its peak. (Table 4.7.) RB gained traction, and share of RB and PSL increased substantially. Both developments, in consonance with the government's national goals, have gone together.

A brief account of performance on the aforementioned developments follows.

4.12. Growth of the Banking System

Let us first review the growth in size of SCBs (includes foreign banks) over this period:

	31 Dec. 1968	31 March 1991	1991/1968
a. Total assets	5,396	286,556	CAGR 20
(₹ in crore)			
b. Branches (no.)	7,446	47,976	CAGR 09

Put in another way, TA had grown 53 times and branches 6 times (Table 4.4).

As an indicator of fast banking development in the economy, deposits/national income had risen from 16 per cent in 1968 (Chapter 3) to 48 per cent in 1990–91.[27] The aggregate deposits of SCBs at the end of June 1991 were equivalent to about 35 per cent of the country's GDP.[28]

Table 4.7 Market Share of Public Sector Banks in Indian Banking Sector: Complete Dominance: 1969, 1980 and 1990–91

Serial No. (A)	Parameters	1969		1980		1990–91	
		Indian Banking Sector (58)* (₹ in crore)	Public Sector (22) (% share)	Indian Banking Sector (62) (₹ in crore)	Public Sector (28) (% share)	Indian Banking Sector (53) (₹ in crore)	Public Sector (28) (% share)
1	TA	5,532	93	47,577	95	270,152	96
2	Deposits	5,008	93	42,477	95	220,244	96
3	Advances	3,398	94	26,105	95	136,572	96
4	Branches (no.)	8,736	83	31,233	87	47,825	92

Sources: Parameters: STs of various years: for financial data.

Note: * See Table 3.1 for explanations.

4.13. Dominance of Public Sector Banks

Nationalization of 14 banks in 1969, the first year of this period, completed two decades on 18 July 1989, close to the end of this period. It will be educative to review the outcomes of this transformative event in its first 20 years.

It is interesting that nationalization of banking had been advocated for several decades on ideological grounds. But, when it happened on three different dates, the proximate reason of each was different. It was the 1969 nationalization which turned out to be extremely popular, controversial and utilitarian. It was the boldest decision in the financial history of independent India. Dr C. Rangarajan had observed much later that 'the functional and geographical coverage of the system that followed that nationalisation was unparalleled.... Nationalisation brought about a change in the banking system that left its impact forever'.[29] Finally, the State controlled the commanding heights of the banking sector.

Table 4.7 provides data on market share of PSBs in 1969 (after nationalization of 14 banks), 1980 (after nationalization of 6 banks), and close of 1990–91 (end of this period).

Compare these figures with 1968 figures of PSBs (Table 3.1). The market shares of eight PSBs in the four parameters then was 31–33 per cent. With the nationalization of 14 banks in 1969, the market shares of 22 PSBs in the four parameters jumped sharply to between 83 and 94 per cent of the banking system. With the nationalization of another six banks in 1980, the 28 PSBs commanded 87–95 per cent of the banking market, rising to its pinnacle of 92–96 per cent by end-March 1991. The 25 private sector banks, left after the bigger ones had been nationalized, were very small in size. Their shares in 'TA', deposits and advances were 4 per cent in each. Their share in number of branches was 8 per cent.

4.14. Strong Shifts to Rural Banking and Priority Sector Lending

Focus on RB and PSL had spread Indian banking to a new geography. We have already analysed the accelerated rate of development of RB in terms of branches, credits and deposits, and PSL in Tables 4.1, 4.2 and 4.3. Comparing the data on two dates, June 1969 and March 1991, we get the following findings:

1. Rural branches had increased from 13 per cent to 58 per cent of the total branches in the country.
2. Advances had gone up from 3.3 per cent to 14.9 per cent.
3. Deposits were up from 6.3 per cent to 15.4 per cent.
4. C–D ratio was up from 37.6 per cent to 59.9 per cent.

Similarly, on the same dates, PSL had increased from 14.9 per cent to 39.2 per cent. The number of priority sector accounts in PSBs had grown from less than 0.3 million in June 1969 to 34.9 million by June 1991. By 1990–91, PSL had probably attained the correction which was sought to be achieved in the imbalance in the sectorial distribution of bank credit.

As a result of fast branch expansion, average population per branch had fallen from 65,000 in 1969, prior to nationalization, to 11,000 by the end of June 1991. The rapid rise in the rural C–D ratio had ensured that the funds generated in rural areas were used for the benefit of the rural populace only.

A closer look at the data on RB and PSL showed that targets set by the GOI/RBI had been achieved or were close to achievement. Having achieved the targets, some of the parameters had begun to slacken due to sharply declining profitability of banks, particularly, the PSBs. Hence, the need then was to transform the system of RB and PSL 'into a more selective and sharply focused arrangement taking into account the imperatives of societal concerns for assisting the truly weaker sections and tiny units'. Henceforth, the focus needed to be shifted to consolidation of achievements, hitherto, and qualitative development in the future. By the schemes as framed and targets as set, banks had been tasked to subsidize them. That meant banks had been booking losses in implementing these schemes. The non-performing advances (NPAs) in these areas were bound to increase. Hence, the task from now onwards was: Could RB be made a self-propelled and viable banking area for the future?

4.15. Negative Offshoots

This analysis cannot be complete without highlighting two negative offshoots of the accelerated growth of RB and PSL lending at subsidized interest rates. The very fast pace of all-round growth of banking and the political-cum-bureaucratic control of the PSBs had caused:

1. Significant deterioration of the PSBs' financial positions: declining profitability, growing NPAs and eroding capital bases; and
2. Rapid deterioration of corporate governance standards in these banks because of the control by the Ministry of Finance (and interventions by the political system through the Ministry) over banks' Boards of Directors and appointment of top bank management, and direct participation of political leadership in loan *melas* and related activities to gain political mileage.

While the repair of the first impact was already in the works by the end of this period, the second negative continued to live with government ownership and control. While government ownership had to remain, possibly at reduced levels, it called for a transparent and intense debate among the intelligentsia to find solutions for elimination of government control. The regulation and supervision of PSBs was best left to the central bank of the country.

Notes

1. RBI History-3, 13.
2. C&F-1, 93.
3. RBI History-3, 20.
4. Patel, *Glimpses of Indian Economic Policy*, 135.
5. TP *1968–69*, 1.
6. Ibid.
7. Patel, *Glimpses of Indian Economic Policy*, 165–166.
8. TP, *1979–80*, 51.
9. Ibid.
10. RBI History-3, 4.
11. The above two paragraphs are based on Ninan, '1974-The Invisible Turning Point'.
12. Based on the narration in C&F-1, Table 3.30.
13. Ibid., Table 3.31, 105.
14. RBI History-4, 38.
15. TP, *1969–70*, 73.
16. RBI History-3, 9.
17. RBI History-4, 412.
18. Section B.5 is based on TP, *1990–91*, 79.
19. RBI, BSR, 1975.
20. RBI, BSR, 1985.
21. TP, *1990–91*, Table II.22, 52.
22. Chapter 3, Table 3.1(D).3.
23. Section IV is based on a set of four research papers/articles written by the author. For a full version, see: (1) Chawla, 'Financial Statements of Public Sector Banks'; (2) Chawla, 'Bank Annual Reports' (3) Chawla, 'Turnaround in Nationalised Banks; (4) Chawla, 'Window-dressing'.
24. RBI, *Report of Committee to Consider Final Accounts*.
25. TP, *1990–91*, 81.
26. Paraphrased from *Committee on the Financial System 1991*, 22.
27. RBI, STs, 'Statistics at a Glance', various years.
28. TP, *1990–91*, 1.
29. RBI History-3, Preface.

4.A. Annexure

Statement 4.1. Main Heads of SCBs' BS: 1969–1990-91

Statement 4.2. Main Heads of SCBs' PLA: 1969–1990-91

Statement 4.1. Main Heads of SCBs' BS: 1969–1990-91

(₹ in crore)

Particulars/Years	1969	1970	1971	1972	1973	1974	1975	1976	1977	1978	1979	1980	1981	1982	1983	1984	1985	1986	1987	1988-89	1989-90	1990-91
Liabilities																						
1 Own funds (Capital+ reserves)	114	119	128	134	141	180	222	274	316	370	438	528	620	825	966	1,068	1,843	2,451	3,184	3,786	4,813	6,420
2 Deposits	5,516	6,455	7,698	9,291	11,199	13,079	15,650	19,740	24,063	30,381	36,658	43,764	52,913	61,397	72,946	85,962	101,871	120,716	138,871	170,313	202,582	232,010
3 Borrowings	200	453	300	230	539	599	1,004	1,580	1,542	1,477	2,166	2,475	3,165	4,654	5,493	7,136	7,886	8,222	12,003	17,863	24,025	27,326
4 Bills payable	68	92	93	124	157	226	225	273	512	863	888	1,098	1,258	1,583	1,677	2,125	2,446	2,934	2,881	5,479	7,060	7,873
5 Other liabilities	224	244	243	241	343	409	647	695	792	1,079	1,031	1,300	1,855	2,057	2,516	3,340	4,423	4,013	6,862	10,033	9,386	12,842
Total Liabilities/ Assets	**6,123**	**7,364**	**8,461**	**10,020**	**12,380**	**14,493**	**17,748**	**22,563**	**27,225**	**34,170**	**41,181**	**49,164**	**59,812**	**70,516**	**83,598**	**99,630**	**118,470**	**138,335**	**163,802**	**207,475**	**247,903**	**286,556**
Assets																						
6 Cash and Bank Bal.	513	609	715	818	1,269	1,452	1,694	2,011	2,931	3,974	5,421	6,418	7,788	8,911	9,990	14,145	17,483	18,736	22,499	31,166	36,164	40,398
7 Money at call and short notice	66	50	89	176	46	156	248	267	468	384	524	655	775	1,263	1,769	1,761	3,171	2,773	3,602	2,966	3,374	2,771
8 Investments	1,553	1,809	2,226	2,980	3,383	3,917	4,596	5,698	7,021	8,742	10,580	12,663	14,891	17,173	21,769	24,479	30,332	38,829	47,386	57,521	67,877	78,837
9 Advances	3,800	4,672	5,154	5,723	7,295	8,476	10,606	13,751	15,731	19,380	22,685	27,008	33,635	39,514	45,407	54,174	60,945	69,880	79,138	103,366	125,214	143,692
10 Fixed assets	76	87	102	110	124	139	157	180	205	228	258	296	358	440	532	644	732	868	975	1,225	1,392	1,599
11 Other assets (Non-banking assets+other assets)	114	138	176	213	262	353	447	655	869	1,463	1,712	2,124	2,364	3,216	4,131	4,427	5,807	7,249	10,202	11,231	13,881	19,260

Statement 4.2. Main Heads of SCBs' PLA: 1969–1990-91

(₹ in crore)

Particulars/Years	1969	1970	1971	1972	1973	1974	1975	1976	1977	1978	1979	1980	1981	1982	1983	1984	1985	1986	1987	1988–89	1989–90	1990–91
Income																						
1 Interest earned	361	413	521	620	770	1,072	1,355	1,658	2,008	2,337	2,931	3,754	4,759	5,659	6,519	8,342	9,647	11,272	13,391	20,602	20,464	23,940
2 Non-interest income	66	82	94	107	134	180	216	268	303	341	407	478	556	615	662	782	905	1,178	1,419	2,127	2,106	2,623
3 Total income	427	494	616	727	904	1,252	1,571	1,926	2,311	2,678	3,338	4,233	5,315	6,274	7,181	9,124	10,552	12,450	14,810	22,729	22,571	26,563
Expenditure																						
4 Interest expended	190	226	286	344	444	661	854	1,163	1,435	1,663	2,093	2,717	3,496	4,174	4,743	5,954	6,935	8,209	9,885	15,410	15,434	18,330
5 Operating expenses	201	254	312	365	442	566	686	723	845	978	1,201	1,463	1,756	2,021	2,352	3,071	3,496	4,018	4,643	6,883	6,647	7,627
6 Total expenditure	391	480	598	710	886	1,227	1,539	1,886	2,280	2,642	3,294	4,180	5,251	6,195	7,095	9,024	10,431	12,227	14,528	22,293	22,081	25,957
Profit																						
7 OP (Before provisions and contingencies)	36	14	17	17	18	25	31	40	31	36	44	52	64	79	85	100	121	223	282	436	489	606
8 Provisions and contingencies	0	0	0	0	0	0	0	0	0	0	0	0	0	0	0	0	0	0	0	0	0	0
9 OP	36	14	17	17	18	25	31	40	31	36	44	52	64	79	85	100	121	223	282	436	489	606
10 Provision for tax	25	0	0	0	0	0	0	0	0	0	0	0	0	0	0	0	0	0	0	0	0	0
11 PAT	12	14	17	17	18	25	31	40	31	36	44	52	64	79	85	100	121	223	282	436	489	606

Sources: Various STs.

5

The Third Transformation (1991-92–2010-11)
From Regulation to Liberalization

I. FIRST DECADE OF REFORMS: 1991-92–2000-01

This period marked the end of the 20th century and entry into the 21st-century, and, with that, the move from regulation to deregulation and liberalization. The third transformation was distinctly marked by turning a regimented banking system into a liberalized banking system based increasingly on a play of market-determined forces. This translated into deregulating the banking system and opening it up for the entry of new PrSBs and foreign banks and, thus, the induction of bank competition. The windows began to open.

Bank reforms began with a big bang in the first year of this period with the reports of two committees. Mention was made in Chapter 4 of the appointment and report of C-FAB, and commencement of implementation of its recommendations. CFS was appointed in 1991 and it reported in the same year. Its recommendations on reforms were significant and were taken up almost immediately for implementation. Most of this task was completed in the next few years and the burst of reforms was over. The third committee called the Committee on Banking Sector Reforms (C-BSR, hereinafter) was appointed in 1997 which reported in 1998. Its recommendations were in continuation of the CFS report.

5.1. Committee to Consider Final Accounts of Banks (Some Transparency, Some Opacity)

The main recommendations of C-FAB were focused on the matters of fuller disclosure and transparency in banks' financial statements, their consequential aspects dealing with secret reserves, loan loss provisioning and valuation of investment portfolios, grouping and off-setting practices in preparing those financial statements, and window-dressing. The principal recommendations and their implications are briefly described below:

5.1.1. Disclosure

C-FAB observed that '[I]n Indian conditions, the time is not yet opportune for practicing full disclosure in respect of secret reserves and loan loss provisioning'. At the same time, 'correct income should be reported in the profit and loss account and the amount transferred to contingencies may, therefore, be shown along with various other provisions … as a "conglomerate" item on the expenditure side'.

5.1.2. Financial Statements and Accounting Policies

C-FAB recommended versions of summary formats of the BS and PLA, by transporting the details of asset and liability items to schedules, enhancing, in the process, a uniform coverage by banks. The Committee also recommended that 'notes' are to be given in clarification of several important items, of which the Committee gave illustrations. The GOI notified on 26 March 1992 the substitution of new formats of the BS and PLA in the Third Schedule of BRA.

C-FAB also recommended that banks may disclose their accounting policies at one place under the head 'principal accounting policies'. The policies will cover, inter alia, subjects such as the basis of presentation of accounts, practices relating to loan loss provisioning and contingency funds, and adjustments made before disclosing net profit. As stated in Chapter 4, this recommendation was required to be implemented from the accounting year 1990–1991.

5.1.3. Implications of Changes

The amendments to formats translated into following changes in the financial statements:

The following contents of old format of the BS had to be changed in the new format:

- Portfolios of advances and investments were to be shown net of necessary provisions (without disclosing amounts provided as provisions). Besides this, other provisions, if any, were to be clubbed into the omnibus item of 'provisions and contingencies' under the head 'other liabilities' in the BS.
- Secret reserves were previously shown as 'contingencies' clubbed with 'current deposits' under the head of 'deposits'. Under the new format, the amount under 'contingencies' was to be transferred to 'provisions and contingencies', so that the item 'deposits' will be shown at its correct amount.
- The old format showed 2 contra items *viz.*, bills for collection being bills receivable, and acceptances, endorsements and other

obligations. As these items may or may not convert into actual liabilities/assets in the future, these items were taken out of the BS and were to be shown as contingent liabilities. These adjustments would reduce the size of the BS.

The effect of these rationalizations was that

- the PLA would show the 'correct' income of a bank.
- presentation of some asset/liability items in the BS would change for better.
- the subjective methods in estimating provisions which were practiced in the past would continue to be practiced, so that underestimation or overestimation of provisions could still prevail.
- the provisions and secret reserves of a bank would still remain hidden in the financial statements.[1]

5.2. Committee on the Financial System

Deregulate to Promote Efficiency and Competition

One of the earliest steps taken by the GOI after the policy of liberalization and deregulation of the economy was the appointment of CFS, chaired by M. Narasimham in August 1991. The high-powered CFS was tasked to examine all aspects of the working of the financial system. The GOI memorandum appointing the Committee stated, 'In recent years ... certain rigidities and weaknesses have developed in the system and these have to be addressed to enable the financial system to play its role in ushering in a more efficient and competitive economy'. The Committee submitted its report in November 1991. It presented a concise set of significant macro recommendations.

In a Note submitted and made part of the report, two members, M. Datta Chaudhuri and M. R. Shroff succinctly summed up the Committee's approach to the issue of financial sector reforms.

That approach was 'to ensure that the financial services industry operates on the basis of operational flexibility and functional autonomy with a view to enhancing efficiency, productivity and profitability'.[2]

The Committee proceeded to suggest multiple surgeries of the banking system to repair or even remove its diseased parts caused by ailments wrought by the past, particularly during the 1969–1990-91 period. The Committee's prescriptions became the basis of the banking sector transformation in the next several years.

5.2.1. Major Recommendations and their Implementation

The RBI and GOI got down to implement CFS recommendations from around 1 April 1992. Those may be classified under four heads:

1. Restore bank BS to health,
2. Remove monetary authority-imposed constraints to bank performance,
3. Reform bank policies, programmes and systems,
4. Undertake strategic reorganization and reconstruction.

5.2.1.1. Restore Bank Balance Sheet to Health

Income recognition and asset classification: The recommendations of CFS differed significantly from those of C-FAB in the sense that it advocated a set of objective criteria for income recognition and asset classification. These criteria reflected the prudential norms proposed by a Basel Committee of the Bank for International Settlements (BIS).

The prevailing eight-category health code system was replaced by a four-category system of classification of advances. The criteria for classification of advances were laid down. As a result, aggregate domestic NPAs of all PSBs which constituted 14.5 per cent of total outstanding at March-end 1992 based on the old health code system worked out to 23.2 per cent at March-end 1993.

Provisioning for non-performing advances: Banks were required to make provisions for NPAs at prescribed rates.

Capital adequacy: In order to lift the existing low capital bases of the banks to a higher minimum level, a system of capital to risk-adjusted assets ratio (CRAR) was introduced based on Basel proposals. Indian banks were required to achieve a minimum CRAR of 4 per cent by March 1993 and 8 per cent by 31 March 1996. Strict norms and datelines were prescribed for Indian banks with branches abroad and for foreign banks in India.

Disclosure and transparency: RBI did not accept the recommendation of CFS for full disclosure in the financial statements. It retained C-FAB's recommendations on non-disclosure of provisions and secret reserves which remained unchanged at March-end 2011.

5.2.1.2. Remove Monetary Authority-Imposed Constraints on Bank Performance

Reduction of statutory liquidity ratio and cash reserve ratio: CFS had recommended reduction of SLR to 25 per cent, the minimum limit, from the current 38.5 per cent, and progressive reduction of CRR from its current 15+10 per cent, but consistent with the requirements of monetary policy. Combined together, these two ratios had reached the historically high level of 63.5 per cent of net demand and time liabilities of the banking system by September 1990, leaving about one-third of its resources only for lending. CRR funds with the Central Bank yielded zero or a low rate of interest. SLR's investment in gilts yielded a return at less than the market rate. The impact was obviously on the system's profitability.

A phased reduction in both the ratios was undertaken between January and April 1993. SLR was brought down to the statutory minimum of 25 per cent by October 1997. CRR was also reduced to 4.5 per cent by 2004. The incremental CRR of 10 per cent was also withdrawn.[3] However, CRR was subsequently raised due to prevailing monetary conditions.

Deregulation of interest rates, lending limits and lending methods: In regard to the complex interest rate structure, which had been built over the previous decades, the process of reforms began in 1992 to rationalize and deregulate it. The basic thrust, as advocated by CFS, was to eliminate unnecessary complexity of the structure, provide transparency in interest rates, and, finally, to change negative real rates to positive real rates of interest.

RBI proceeded to make quick changes in deposit and lending rates from April 1992 over the next 6–7 years. Barring savings bank accounts, the structure of interest rates on domestic term deposits was made more and more flexible. Banks were given freedom to fix rates for term deposits above one-year maturity. Lending rates for credit limits of over ₹2 lakhs were deregulated. The net outcome was that banks had been given back their freedom to decide interest rates. Yields on gilts were steadily increased to 'close to market-related' rates. RBI granted full operational freedom to banks to assess the working capital requirements of borrowers. Also in April 1997, all instructions relating to maximum permissible bank finance were withdrawn. The lending method and related provisions introduced post Tandon Committee (1975) were done away with. Deregulation of interest rates and withdrawal of various regulations related, thereto, were a major element in the process of infusing competition in the banking system.[4]

5.2.1.3. Reform Bank Policies, Programmes and Systems

Restructure PSL and phase out directed credit programmes: One of the recommendations of CFS was that the relevance of directed credit programme should be re-examined and this programme should be phased out. CFS also recommended that the scope of the priority sector should be redefined to narrow its coverage to the smallest of the farmers, village and cottage industries, rural artisans, and the tiny sector of industry. It also added that the credit target of this redefined sector should be fixed at 10 per cent of aggregate credit.

RBI made a detailed analysis of the recommendations and found almost all the recommendations as non-feasible. Instead, RBI enlarged the eligible activities under the priority sector, deregulated interest rates and permitted alternate avenues of investment (including contributions to various rural infrastructure funds and institutions), thereby making PSL by banks more flexible than before.[5]

Branch licensing policy: CFS had recommended that the system of branch licensing should be abolished; banks should be given freedom to open or close branches (other than rural branches) or swap their rural branches with those of other banks.

Accordingly, RBI issued detailed guidelines in May 1992 by which banks were given greater freedom to open new branches, rationalize their branch network by relocating branches (without closing any rural branches), open specialized branches, set up controlling/administrative offices and open extension counters. RBI also decided in December 1994 to allow banks to install automated teller machines (ATMs) at licensed branches. Banks were also given freedom to install ATMs at other places after obtaining licence from RBI.

Induction of modern work technology: CFS reviewed the prevailing methods of operations of the Indian banking system which had changed little 'in the last two decades' due to various constraints. It referred approvingly to the views of the Rangarajan Committee on Computerisation (1988) that computerization must be looked upon as a means to improve customer service and efficiency which would lead to the growth and thus help to expand employment.[6]

Computerization of bank operations began in a big way in the early 1990s. Two areas in which use of technology increased significantly thereafter were computerization of branches and installation of ATMs. This development was to transform digitization of banks significantly soon in the following years.[7]

Allowing entry of new banks into the private sector: One of the important recommendations of CFS was that '[F]reedom of entry into the financial system should be liberalised and the Reserve Bank should now permit establishment of new banks in the private sector.' The implementation of this recommendation began from January 1993.

Allowing foreign banks to open more branches: CFS recommended that the policy with regard to allowing foreign banks to open branches in India either as branches or as subsidiaries should be more liberal, subject to the statutory requirement of reciprocity, etc. It said that this would have a beneficial impact from the point of view of improving competitive efficiency of the Indian banking system as also upgrading with technology.[8]

Foreign banks grew at their fastest in the 1990s; from 23 in 1990–1991, they had increased to 41 in 1997–1998. The number of their branches had increased from 151 in 1990–1991 to 196 in 1997–1998. But the competition in the banking system was still muted in this period.

Restructuring RBI's system of financial supervision: CFS suggested that the RBI's supervisory focus should be on the more relevant segments needing closer checks such as prudential norms, statutory requirements, and qualitative and quantitative checks on credit portfolios. The Committee suggested the separation of the regulatory and supervisory functions, and the establishment of a quasi-autonomous Banking Supervisory Board under the aegis of RBI.

The RBI proceeded to implement those recommendations including the setting up of the Board for Financial Supervision. RBI also undertook a review of its inspection system of banks and a new approach to on-site inspection was adopted.[9]

5.2.1.4. Issues in Strategic Reorganization and Reconstruction

CFS made a few drastic recommendations:

- End duality of control over banks by RBI and the Ministry of Finance.
- Eliminate political interference in appointment of chief executives of PSBs and directors on the boards of these banks.
- Eliminate differential treatment of PrSBs and PSBs.
- Reconstruct/reorganize PSBs into a few large banks.
- Set up subsidiaries of PSBs to take over their rural branches.
- Introduce new institutional arrangements to remove bad loans from the BS of PSBs.
- Restructure RRBs and allow them to engage in all commercial banking businesses.
- Owing to their deep ramifications in terms of political purpose or institutional conflicts or economic rationale 'many recommendations were kept virtually in cold storage for several years. Several of these were still pending for action at March-end 2011'.

5.2.2. Committee on the Financial System: Closing Remarks

The narration given previously has attempted a summary of actions taken/not taken by GOI/RBI on CFS recommendations. Two significant recommendations made by CFS were not acted upon by the GOI. One was to 'end duality of control over banks by RBI and the

Ministry of Finance'. This was a 'positive' recommendation which the GOI did not act upon and had not acted upon until 2017–2018. The second recommendation was to dilute PSL. This was a 'negative' recommendation and the GOI rightly did not accept it. Action on several other recommendations was still a work in progress. The issues of providing for NPAs and 'inadequacy' of CA were to remain on the active agendas of GOI, RBI and the affected banks for many years. The 'big achievement' of CFS was that it put heavy pressure on, and provided a handle to the GOI and RBI to get going on deregulation and liberalization of the financial sector.

5.3. Committee on Banking Sector Reforms

Another phase of banking reforms began with the constitution of another committee in December 1997, again headed by M. Narasimham, called the C-BSR. It was tasked to review the progress of implementation of financial reforms recommended by CFS and to suggest further measures to strengthen the banking system, covering areas of banking policy, institutional structure, supervisory system, and legislative and technological changes.[10] C-BSR submitted its report in April 1998.

5.3.1. Main Recommendations and Their Implementation

RBI considered the recommendations of this Committee, in consultation with GOI. Most of the recommendations were focused on: (a) elimination of weaknesses in implementation of CFS recommendations, and (b) upgrading and extending those recommendations. The CFS Report was a comprehensive package, and it was inevitable that those recommendations were reinforced as a result of rapidly changing events in global banking. Many of the decisions made on the C-BSR were announced in RBI's monetary and credit policy review in October 1998. Below is a listing of main recommendations followed by actions taken, thereon, by RBI.

1. *Recommendation*: A minimum target of 9 per cent CRAR should be achieved in 2000 and of 10 per cent by 2002.

   RBI announced that banks should achieve a minimum CRAR of 9 per cent as on 31 March 2000.

2. *Recommendation:* A general provision of 1 per cent on standard assets should be introduced. This measure was envisaged to mitigate the procyclical behaviour of banks.

   RBI required banks to make a general provision on standard assets of a minimum of 0.25 per cent in the year ended on 31 March 2000. It was subsequently raised steadily to 1 per cent.

3. *Recommendation:* There is a need for disclosure in a phased manner of the maturity pattern of assets and liabilities, and of movements in the provisions of NPAs.

   Banks were advised by RBI to put in place a formal Asset-Liability Management (ALM) system effective 1 April 1999.

4. *Recommendation:* CA requirements should incorporate market risk in addition to credit risk. Risk weights were also recommended on central and state government securities and approved securities, whether part of SLR or outside SLR.

   RBI made these prescriptions in October 1998. Risk management was thus further strengthened.

5. *Recommendation:* The definition of NPAs should be tightened further and government guaranteed advances should be brought into the ambit of income recognition, asset classification and provisioning norms.

   RBI revised the norms with some modifications.

6. *Recommendation:* With cleaning up of the BS, steps should be taken to prevent/limit emergence of new NPAs.

   Banks were advised by RBI to put in place appropriate risk management systems and practices to prevent re-emergence of fresh NPAs.

7. *Recommendation:* The government will need to guarantee bonds for Tier II capital to enable banks to issue such bonds. Government guarantee would make these bonds eligible for SLR investment.

    RBI: PSBs are encouraged to raise Tier II capital. Government guarantee to these instruments does not seem appropriate.[11]

8. *Recommendation:* Weak banks, as defined by the Committee, should be examined case by case and considered for revival or merger or other options, including their closure.

    A working group on restructuring weak banks was appointed in 1999. The Group submitted its report and was acted upon in the Union Budget for 2000–2001.

    Implementation of above recommendations over the next few years is detailed in Part II below.

9. *Other recommendations:* C-BSR again raised some major issues such as consolidation and mergers of PSBs, and granting functional autonomy to banks. 'But most of those issues remained untouched to a large degree and continued to sit in cold storage at the end of the first decade of reforms'.

II. SECOND DECADE OF REFORMS (2001-02–2010-11): CONTINUITY AND CONSOLIDATION

The two Narasimham Committees, particularly the first, had laid out a full menu of changes in the banking system recommending a total breakout from the past. Change is a constant, and reforms remained on the active agenda of RBI in this period.[12]

Actions to implement recommendations on the following major issues were expected to continue in the second decade:

1. Implement measures to reduce NPAs and improve CA in accord with the prevailing Basel guidelines

2. Manage weak banks
3. Expand RB and PSL
4. Continue with the opening of new PrSBs
5. Take additional steps to promote competition
6. Resolve issues in ownership and governance of banks.

Discussion follows in seven parts, A to G, below:

5.4. Non-performing Advances and Capital Adequacy of Banks

5.4.1. Basel Guidelines and Steps to Their Implementation

Until 1990–91, capital standards for different classes of banks were laid down and assessed in specific details. This was described in Chapter 4. In 1988, a Basel Committee had laid down a framework for CA standards worldwide. It had adopted a weighted risk-assets approach. That Committee set the minimum capital standards at 8 per cent to be achieved by the end of 1992. Based on those recommendations, the RBI had, under consideration, a proposal to introduce the risk–asset ratio system for banks for measuring their CA.[13]

It was then that CFS was appointed. As noted above, it made recommendations, inter alia, on capital adequacy (CRAR) based on Basel proposals. These recommendations were further strengthened by C-BSR in 1998.

In June 1999, Basel announced a New Capital Adequacy Framework to replace the old capital adequacy Accord of 1988. The new accord was based on three pillars: (a) minimum capital requirements, (b) supervisory review of CA and (c) effective use of market discipline. The new accord also suggested that banks have to provide additional charge on various kinds of risk including credit risk, market risk, operations risk and interest rate risk.[14]

The implementation of the new framework required additional capital infusion by banks. This issue gained

> [I]n importance in view of Government ownership of banks and the ability of the PSBs to raise capital either internally or from the market. It appears that even after allowing for additional infusion of capital through internal generation and access to subordinated debt, the gap between additional requirement and the leeway available to raise capital from the market was likely to remain quite sizeable.[15]

This gap could neither by filled by the RBI (for reasons of monetization) nor by the GOI (for reasons of tight fiscal condition). Therefore,

> [A] strong case existed for raising the legislative ceiling for market participation in equity capital of PSBs. In this context, pronounce-ment in the Union Budget 2000–01 that the Government would reduce its holdings in PSBs to 33% while ensuring that banks retain their public character, assumed importance.[16]

(This proposed reduction of government holdings to 33 per cent had not been made until October 2018. Suggestions to this effect continue to be made in the media.)

In April 2007, final guidelines for implementation of the New Capital Adequacy Framework (Basel II) by banks were announced. Some of the major initiatives included issuing guidelines on stress testing by banks and enhancement of disclosure norms to strengthen Pillar 3 of the new framework. Risk weights and provisioning require-ments for lending to sensitive sectors were enhanced.

5.4.2. Status of Non-performing Advances and Capital Adequacy in 1998 and 2011

5.4.2.1. *Non-performing Advances*

As a result of various measures taken, gross NPAs (GNPAs) of PSBs had declined from 23.2 per cent at end-March 1993 to 14.4 per cent of gross advances by end-March 1998. Net NPAs (NNPAs) to net advances also declined and stood at 7.3 per cent at end-March 1998. GNPAs and NNPAs as per cent of TA were 6.4 per cent and 3.0 per cent, respectively. Nearly one-half of the NPAs of PSBs were on account of the priority sector. Share of priority sector in GNPAs had come down from 50 per cent at end-March 1995 to 46.6 per cent at end-March 1998.[17]

At March-end 2011, NPAs of SCBs stood at the following levels:

GNPAs/Gross advances were at 2.25 per cent and NNPAs/Net advances were at 0.97 per cent.[18] These ratios were an improvement over those of the previous three years. It meant that asset quality of banks had steadily improved.

In December 2009, banks were advised by RBI to achieve a provisioning coverage ratio of 70 per cent of their NPAs by end-September 2010. As on 31 March 2011, the required ratio was below 70 per cent in the case of PSB group.

It may be noted that legal and institutional arrangements (Debt Recovery Tribunals and Settlement Advisory Committees) for the recovery of NPAs, particularly of PSBs, continued to be strengthened, and systems and procedures for recovery continued to be simplified from year to year, but still NPAs continued to remain high.

5.4.2.2. Capital Adequacy

At March-end 1998, all banks except five (one PSB and four PrSBs) had achieved the stipulated CRAR of 8 per cent.[19] Overall, CA ratio of PSBs was 11.53 per cent at that date.

Under Basel I and II, CRAR of all bank groups remained well above the stipulated norm of 9 per cent as at March-end 2011:

	Basel I	*Basel II*
SCBs	13.0	14.2
PSBs	11.8	13.1
a. Nationalized banks	12.2	13.5
b. SBI Group	11.0	12.3
	Basel I	*Basel II*
PrSBs	15.1	16.5
a. Old	13.3	14.6
b. New	15.5	16.9

Source: TP 2010–11, Table IV.13, p. 74.

5.4.3. Capital Adequacy: Recapitalization of PSBs

Recapitalization of nationalized banks by GOI had begun from the year 1985 as capital bases of these banks had been declining for some years on the account of fast growing BS and declining profitability.[20] Implementation of reforms led to substantial increase in banks' capital requirements. GOI had to make contributions to the capital of nationalized banks from the years beginning from 1992–93. Total amount of capital injected into the 19 PSBs by GOI during 1992–93 and 1998–99 was 20,446.12 crore, of which ₹5,729.3 crore (28% of the total) was injected the three weak banks—Indian Bank, UCO Bank and United Bank of India—identified by Verma Committee.[21] No contributions were made in 1999–2000 and 2000–01. ₹1,300 crore was contributed to the capital of Indian Bank in 2001–02. (No data on recapitalization for years 2002-03–2010-11 was available in RBI's TPs.)

5.4.4. Capital Adequacy: Partial Privatization of Public Sector Banks

GOI allowed PSBs to go to the capital market to raise equity since capital infusion by the government was inadequate. This was the beginning of another big policy reversal by the State: partial privatization.[22]

Thus, the reason for privatization was not ideological but the fact that GOI had no other source left. Perhaps, this also provided the State the opportunity to slowly begin freeing the banks from State ownership. It was laid down that the government ownership would remain at least at 51 per cent of equity of every nationalized bank, thus retaining control over banks.

SBI was the first PSB to tap the capital market with an equity-cum-bond issue of ₹3,212.18 crore in December 1993. Preceding this, 'The State Bank of India Act, 1955', was amended by an ordinance in October 1993 to enhance the scope of the provision for partial private shareholding. BCAs (Acquisition and Transfer of Undertakings), 1970/1980, were amended with effect from 15 July 1994 permitting the nationalized banks to raise capital up to 49 per cent from the public. Oriental Bank of Commerce was the first nationalized bank to access the capital market with an equity issue of ₹387 crore in October 1994. Over the years 1993–2002, 12 PSBs had raised capital through public issues of ₹6,501 crore. Besides, some banks had raised subordinated debt for their Tier II capital.[23] Public equity issues by PSBs during 2004-05–2007-08 amounted to ₹27,283 crore. Equity rights issues by PSBs amounted to ₹4,332 crore in 2010–2011.[24] Amount raised by PSBs through private placements in 2007–08 and 2008–09 was ₹52,413 crore. Private placements by PSBs were ₹20,916 crore in 2009–10 and ₹23,762 crore in 2010–11.[25]

Legal and non-legal amendments had to be made by the GOI from time to time to enable banks go in for public equity/bond issues. The GOI promulgated another ordinance in January 1995 to amend the BCAs, 1970/1980, for enabling the banks to reduce their paid-up capital. GOI provided ₹1,506.21 crore during 1995–96 towards writing down of the capital base of two banks for the adjustment of their losses. Such actions had to be repeated in later years.[26] Write-off of accumulated losses against paid-up capital reduced capital and raised earnings per share (EPS) to enable banks to make public issues. Loss write-offs against capital amounted to 6,037 crore by March-end 1999[27] and ₹6,334 crore by March-end 2000.[28] Some banks were also able to return capital to the GOI. Such amounts totalled to ₹690 crore by 2000–01.[29] The shareholding of the GOI and RBI in SBI constituted 1.8 per cent and 59.7 per cent respectively of its total capital at March-end 1999. The ownership pattern of nationalized banks varied from bank to bank at March-end 1999. Out of 19 banks, 14 were still held 100 per cent by GOI. Only five banks had made public issues by 31 March 1999; GOI ownership in them varied between 66.5 and 76.6 per cent.[30] Government shareholding in PSBs ranged roughly between 57 per cent and 85 per cent, though the minimum statutory requirement is 51 per cent.[31]

5.4.5. A Leverage Ratio under Basel III

"In an attempt to increase the systemic resilience by strengthening capital standards at individual bank level, Basel III's regulatory capital framework had proposed a non-risk-based leverage ratio as a backstop to the risk-based capital requirement. It was proposed to test a minimum Tier I leverage ratio of 3% beginning 2013 capturing both on-and-off balance sheet exposures."[32]

5.5. Management of Weak Banks

The *Working Group on Restructuring Weak Public Sector Banks* had concluded that a comprehensive restructuring strategy dealing with operational, organizational, financial and systemic aspects would be the most appropriate for the three identified weak banks. Subsequently, the Union Budget for 2000–01 announced that each weak bank-specific Financial Restructuring Authority (FRA) would be constituted. Under the proposed framework, the statutes governing PSBs would be amended to provide for supersession of the Board of Directors on the basis of recommendations of the Reserve Bank and constitution of a FRA for such a bank. 'The Government would consider recapitalisation of the weak banks to achieve the prescribed capital adequacy norms, provided a viable restructuring programme acceptable to the Government as the owner and the Reserve Bank as a regulator is made available by the concerned banks'.[33]

5.6. Rural Banking, Priority Sector Lending and Financial Inclusion

Programmes of RB and PSL continued at a declining pace during 1991–2011 compared to the previous period of 1969–1991. Priority sector comprised agriculture, small scale industries (SSI), small road and transport operators, retail trade, professional and self-employed persons, State-sponsored organizations for SCs and STs, education, housing, consumption loans, micro-credit, loans to software, and food and agro-processing sector in this period. The stipulated target of 40 per cent of net bank credit for lending to the priority sector by domestic SCBs both in the public and private sectors stayed in this period. Within this, a target of 18 per cent of net bank credit stipulated for lending to agriculture continued. The stipulated target of 32 per cent of net bank credit for foreign banks stayed too.[34] During 2006–2007, the guidelines on the priority sector were revised in order to improve credit delivery.

The growth of RB and PSL during 1990-91–2010-11 is presented in Tables 5.1 and 5.2.

Table 5.1 Growth of RB (1990-91–2010-11): Select Years

As at the End of March	Rural Bank Offices		Credit Outstanding: Rural				Deposits: Rural				C–D Ratio (%)	
	Number	%	Amount ₹ in crore	%	Accounts Number ('000)	%	Amount ₹ in crore	%	Accounts Number ('000)	%	Rural	All-India
1991	35,206	58	18,599	14.9	NA		31,010	15.4	NA		60.0	59.9
1992	35,269	58	20,692	15.1	NA		35,750	15.0	NA		55.4	57.9
1996	32,981	51	29,012	11.4	NA		61,313	14.4	NA		58.6	47.3
2001	32,640	48	54,431	10.3	22,457	43	139,431	14.7	131,722	31	53.5	39.0
2006	30,610	43	126,078	8.3	28,576	33	226,061	10.8	139,570	29	55.8	71.5
2011	33,367	36	295,814	7.3	39,130	32	493,266	9.2	250,254	31	59.9	75.7
	(5%)		1490%		74%		1491%		90%			26%

Source: RBI, *Basic Statistical Returns* (BSR), Tables 1.1 and 1.3, various years.

Notes: % in the Table is the percentage of the total (all population groups) of the specific parameter; NA = Not Available. Data for number of accounts became available from 1999. In that year, number of accounts of credit and deposits in rural branches were (in thousands) 24,434 (46.7% of the total) and 122,660 (30.2% of the total) respectively.

Table 5.2 Growth of PSL (1990-91–2010-11): Select Years

As at the End of March	Priority Sector Advances (₹ in crore)	Share of Priority Sector Advances As % of Total Advances
1991	44,572	37.7
1992	47,318	37.1
1996	80,831	32.8
2001	182,255	35.5
2006	548,774	37.2
2011	1,337,333	33.9
	2011/1991 = 30 times	

Source: RBI, BSR, Table 1.1, various years.

Let us first read Table 5.1:

1. Instead of increasing, total number of rural branches steadily declined over the period to close at a total decline by 5 per cent; the number had declined from 58 per cent to 36 per cent of total (All-India) branches;
2. Credit outstanding had increased substantially, by 14.90 per cent over the period, but as percentage of total bank credit, it had declined from 15 per cent to 7 per cent;
3. Total amount of rural deposits also increased substantially, by 14.91%, but as a percentage of total bank deposits, it had declined from 15 per cent to 9 per cent;
4. Rural C–D ratio, which was 60 per cent in 1991, had steadily declined to 55.8 per cent by 2006 but had picked up to nearly 59.9 by 2011;
5. The data on number of bank deposit and credit accounts became available after 1999. It tells us of the number of persons with bank accounts. It is found that number of rural credit accounts increased over 2001–2011 by 74 per cent, but, as a percentage of total India credit accounts, the figure had declined from 43 per cent to 32 per cent. The number of rural deposit accounts had increased over the

same 10-year period by 90 per cent and, as a share of total India accounts, it had remained steady at about 31 per cent.

6. Broad conclusions which can be drawn are:
   a) Banks consolidated their branch network in this period;
   b) Deposits and advances in these branches increased substantially, though at a declining rate. It, therefore, also means that deposits and advances per branch increased over this period;
   c) While the C–D ratio of rural branches did not increase, that of all branches of banks did increase by about 26 per cent; and,
   d) It points to steps by banks to improve their operating efficiency and profitability. It also perhaps indicates that the growth potential of deposits and loans in rural areas may be shrinking; but it may be too early to reach conclusions.

Table 5.2 shows that PSL advances increased every year; they increased over 30 times in this period. At the same time, the share of these advances in total bank advances had fluctuated YOY and had overall declined from 37.7 per cent in 1991 to 33.9 per cent in 2011. This seems to confirm the broad conclusions drawn from Table 5.1 that the banking system was in a consolidation mode, was in the mode to improve operating efficiency and/or the growth potential of PSL may be shrinking.

5.6.1. Non-performing Advances in the Priority Sector

Priority sector loans grew by 21 per cent in 2010–11.

In the same period, its impaired assets increased by 28%. Thus, asset quality of exposures to the priority sector, especially agriculture, continued to compare unfavourably with the overall NPA ratio of the banking sector. Consequently, the gross NPA ratio for the sector deteriorated from 3.3% to 3.5%. Gross NPA Ratio in respect of credit to agriculture segment rose to 3.3% in year ending March 2011 from 2.4% in year ending March 2010. This deterioration was attributable to a rise of 60% in agriculture NPAs as against a growth of 18% in agriculture credit.[35]

5.6.2. New Concept of Financial Inclusion

'RBI used the term "financial inclusion" for the first time in India in its monetary policy statement of 2005–06.'[36] It advised banks 'to make available a basic banking "no-frills" account with low or nil balances as well as charges, to expand the outreach of such accounts to vast sections of the population'. Financial inclusion is a wider countrywide concept beyond RB and PSL. Action followed and, 'According to the information available with the Reserve Bank, about five lakhs "no-frills" accounts were opened till March 31, 2006.'[37] Since then, GOI and RBI, in particular, continued to pursue the spread of this concept through the addition of new instruments of inclusion and appointment of working groups to make regular assessments of financial inclusion and to further promote its coverage. Besides, RBI took additional initiatives for promotion of this concept by introduction of the business correspondent (BC)/business facilitator (BF) model, promotion of financial literacy-cum-counselling, and adoption of Information and Communication Technology (ICT) solutions for achieving greater outreach. RBI appointed a committee in 2009 to review the LBS for providing special focus on financial inclusion.[38] It was obvious that RBI had adopted the broadest approach aimed at 'connecting people' with the banking system and not just credit dispensation.

Table 5.1 provided a view of progress of financial inclusion in rural India by showing increase in number of deposit accounts between 2001 and 2011. Table 5.3 supplements that information by showing March-end 2011 progress of financial inclusion:

TP 2010–11, the source of information in Table 5.3, continues: 'Yet, the extent of "financial exclusion" is staggering. Out of every 1000 persons, only 99 had a credit account and 600 had a deposit account as at March-end 2010'.[39] Thus, the task ahead was also staggering; and it had staggering potential too.

Table 5.3 *Progress of Financial Inclusion: 2011*

Indicator	2010–11
1. Credit-GDP	54.6
2. Credit-Deposi	76.5
3. Population per bank branch	13,466
4. Population per ATM	16,243
5. Population having deposit accounts (%) (2009–2010)	61.2
6. Population having credit accounts (%) (2009–2010)	9.9
7. Population having debit cards (%)	18.8
8. Population having credit cards	1.49
9. Branches opened in Tier III–VI centres/Total new branches (%)	55.4
10. Branches opened in unbanked centres/Total new branches	(%) 9.7

Source: TP 2010–11, Table IV.37, p. 94.

5.7. New Private Sector Banks

5.7.1. A New Breed of Banks is Born

A fact worth noting is that while there was no legal ban on entry of new banks in the banking system,[40] no new banks had been licensed after the nationalization of 14 banks in 1969.[41]

One of the important recommendations of CFS was that 'freedom of entry into the financial system should be liberalised and the Reserve Bank should now permit establishment of new banks in the private sector.'[42] This major policy reversal began in January 1993, when RBI issued a set of guidelines for establishing new PrSBs 'in order to enhance competition in the financial system'.

5.7.2. Chronology of New Banks

Subsequent to the issue of guidelines, nine entities were granted 'in principle' approval to set up banks in 1993, and six banks were established in that year itself; those were: UTI Bank, IndusInd Bank, ICICI Bank, Global Trust Bank, Centurion Bank and HDFC Bank. By the end of 1994–95, their first year of operations, these six banks had opened 30 branches, collected ₹2,655 crore of deposits and made a net profit of ₹42 crore. In 1995–96, three more banks, Times Bank, Bank of Punjab and IDBI Bank, had started operations. The 10th bank, Development Credit Bank (formerly Development Cooperative Bank) was granted an 'in principle' approval in January 1995 after its conversion into a SCB. It was included in the list of 'old' PrSBs by RBI. Two more banks had been granted 'in principle' approval, making it 12. But, by the end of 1995–96, nine new banks had started their operations. The story of moving numbers of new banks, thereafter, till the end of 2010–11 was as follows:

1. 1999–2000. Times Bank was merged into HDFC Bank, reducing the number of banks from nine to eight.
2. 2002–03. Kotak Mahindra Bank was set up. Number of banks = nine.
3. 2003–04. Development Credit Bank was moved from 'old' to 'new' banks, making it 10 banks.
4. 2004–05.
   (a) Global Trust Bank, a failed bank, was taken over by Oriental Bank of Commerce, a PSB.
   (b) IDBI Bank was made a PSB.
   (c) A new bank named YES Bank was set up. Total number = nine.
5. 2005–06. Bank of Punjab and Centurion Bank were merged to become Centurion Bank of Punjab, reducing the number to eight.
6. 2006–07. UTI Bank was renamed as Axis Bank.
7. 2008–09. Centurion Bank of Punjab was taken over by HDFC Bank, reducing the total number of banks to 7. The number

remained at seven at the end of 2010–11. These seven running banks were:

ICICI Bank, HDFC Bank, Axis Bank, IndusInd Bank, Kotak Mahindra Bank, YES Bank and Development Credit Bank.

5.7.2.1. Licensing of New Banks

A discussion Paper on *Entry of New Banks in the Private Sector* was issued by RBI in August 2010. On finalization, it was to become the basis for licensing of new banks in the private sector.

5.7.3. Performance of New Banks

Table 5.4 provides a three-parameter financial profile of the new PrSBs over the 16-yearperiod, 1995–96 to 2010–11. Two parameters, TA and number of branches, provide a snapshot of the size and growth of this bank group, and the third parameter, that is, ROA summarizes the profitability of this group. These banks, nine at the beginning and seven at the end of this period grew from the size of ₹90 billions to ₹10,898 billion, 121 times over this period at a CAGR of 38. Obviously, this group grew its TA from a high growth rate of 79 per cent on a small base in the beginning to a more or less declining rate to close at 28 per cent annually and a CAGR of 38 on a much larger size at the end. In terms of the other measure of growth, that is, the number of branches, the speed of growth, though at a varying rate, was equally fast. From the addition of 66 branches in 1996–97, this bank group added 1,742 branches in 2010–11 to end up at 6,973 branches in 2010–11, a CAGR of 35. Similarly, it recorded ROA of 1.85 per cent in 1995–96, to progress broadly at a declining trend, to rise again to close at 1.34 per cent in the last year. This was a stellar performance compared with those of other bank groups (Compared under analysis of financials, infra). Starting

Table 5.4 Profile and Progress of New PrSBs: 1995-96–2010-11

Serial No.	Parameters	1995–96	1996–97	1997–98	1998–99	1999–00	2000–01	2001–02	2002–03	2003–04	2004–05	2005–06	2006–07	2007–08	2008–09	2009–10	2010–11	2010–11/1995–96 (times)	CAGR
1	Banks (no.)	9	9	9	9	8	8	8	9	10	9	8	8	8	7	7	7	–	–
2	TA (₹ in billions)	90	161	258	385	589	788	1,745	1,922	2,466	2,944	4,217	5,848	7,456	7,955	8,818	10,898	121	38
	Percentage growth, YOY		79	60	49	53	34	121	10	28	19	43	39	27	07	11	24		
	CAGR		79	69	62		54	64	55	51	47	47	46	44	41	39	38		
3	Branches (no.)	76	142	247	367	452	823	977	1,171	1,369	1,712	2,016	2,598	3,634	4,332	5,231	6,973	92	35
	Addition, YOY		66	105	120	85	371	154	194	198	343	304	582	1036	698	899	1,742		
	CAGR		87	80	69	56	61	53	48	44	41	39	38	38	36	35	35		
4	ROA (%)	1.85	1.77	1.55	1.03	0.97	0.81	0.44	0.90	0.83	1.05	0.97	0.91	1.01	1.10	1.22	1.34	–	–

Source: Banks: TPs and STs, various years; TA: TPs, various years; branches: TPs, IBA and banks performance highlights (annual publication), various years; ROA: TPs, various years. (ROA is based on PAT).

with clean slates, these banks employed officer-oriented high-skilled workforce, introduced modern methods of recruitment, compensation and promotions, and high levels of technology. In a short period of their operating lifespan, these banks were fostering higher levels of efficiency in the banking system and providing stiff competition to PSBs and old PrSBs. Soon, they were the change leaders of the banking industry.[43]

5.8. Promoting Bank Competition

One of the purposes of bank reforms was to promote competition among the banks. Reforms were introduced in 1992 and signs of competition began to appear soon thereafter:

1. New PrSBs opened their doors in 1994–95 and the 12th bank was opened in 2004–05. But competition forced three banks to merger or be acquired. One bank failed and RBI arranged it to be acquired by a PSB. It reduced these banks to seven by the end of 2010–11. The zigzag progress of these banks in the first 15 years of commencement of their operations in 1994–95 makes for an interesting story (already covered in Section D).
2. 24 foreign banks were operating in 1991–92; they increased to 44 in 1998–99 and then began to decrease to the end at 34 in 2010–11. Most foreign banks are small outfits. They move base for various reasons including low volumes and stiff competition.
3. There were 52 Indian SCBs in 1991–92; they rose by just one (excluding new nine ones) by 1995–96 and had declined to 40, mostly by mergers, by 2010–11.

Owing to increased competition, many banks resorted to sub-benchmark prime lending rates (BPLR) lending. Share of sub-BPLR lending to total lending had increased from 43 per cent in 2003–04 to 79 per cent by end-March 2007.[44]

5.8.1. Foreign Direct Investment in Private Sector Banking and by Foreign Banks

During the second phase of banking reforms, some additional steps were taken to strengthen competition in the banking sector. With the liberalization of the foreign direct investment (FDI) regime, FDI in private sector banking was brought under the automatic route. On 5 March 2004, it increased the FDI limit in PrSBs from 49 per cent to 74 per cent of the paid-up capital of the investee bank under the automatic route. Investment by foreign institutional investors (FIIs) was limited to 49 per cent within the FDI ceiling of 74 per cent. At all times, at least 26 per cent of the paid-up capital was required to be held by residents. At end-March 2007, non-residents held majority equity in seven old and new PrSBs.[45]

On 28 February 2005, RBI, in consultation with GOI, released the roadmap to operationalize the guidelines for FDI investment by foreign banks in India.

> The roadmap was divided into two phases. During the first phase between March 2005 and March 2009, a foreign bank was to be permitted to establish presence by way of setting up a wholly owned banking subsidiary or by conversion of the existing branches into a wholly owned subsidiary.[46]

Until 2016–17, no foreign bank had taken this route, probably because their subsidiary would fall under the full regulatory and supervisory regime of RBI, including CA requirements. The roadmap also laid out the conditions for permission to eligible foreign banks to acquire shareholding in Indian PrSBs.

5.9. Ownership and Governance of Banks

One of the defining reasons for nationalization of banks in 1969 was the realization that the link between industry and banks must be broken to prevent concentration of economic power in the hands of a few. Another reason was that the management of banks, including their Boards of Directors, should be in the hands of 'fit and proper' persons, persons who possessed required expertise and integrity. This is one reason why appropriate principles of ownership and control of new PrSBs needed to be framed too. RBI had issued appropriate guidelines on the subject in 2004 and earlier, but comprehensive guidelines were issued in February 2005 to cover all PrSBs and foreign banks foraying into acquiring ownership in Indian PrSBs.

But what about the PSBs? Continuing in their Note (p. 4 of Chapter 5) to the CFS Report, Datta-Chaudhuri and Shroff had added, 'We believe that ensuring the integrity and autonomy of operations of banks and DFIs is by far the more relevant issue at present than the question of their ownership'. The Note went on to opine that

[I]n line with the above and the concept of self-denial by the Government of its ownership rights, which the Committee has rightly advocated, we think that the Government should not appoint its officials on the boards of public sector banks and financial institutions. The Banking Division of the Ministry of Finance, as at present constituted, should consequently be abolished.[47]

Later, M. R. Shroff, in an interview, had observed, 'As Prof Chaudhuri pointed out, the government representative on a bank board is not a mere joint secretary; he has the majesty of the power of the state behind him'.[48]

Much later, GOI, at the initiative of RBI, amended the laws governing the nationalized banks and subsidiary banks of SBI to set the governance principles for them also. Those amendments included new sections providing for applicability of 'fit and proper' criteria for elected directors on the Boards of PSBs. Necessary guidelines were issued to the nationalized banks in November 2007.[49] The banking division still continued at the end of March 2011 with a change of its nomenclature. Its secretaries still continued to be nominated on bank boards.

5.10. Sundry Reforms

In continuation of the above, a few other reform measures need to be described here.

5.10.1. Categorization and Valuation of Investment Portfolios

RBI issued final guidelines on categorization and valuation of banks' investment portfolio, by which banks were required to classify the entire investment portfolio, including SLR securities, under three categories, viz., 'held to maturity', 'available for sale', and 'held for trading'. Out of these, 'held to maturity' portfolio was not to exceed 25 per cent of the total investment portfolio.[50]

5.10.2. Cash Reserve Ratio, Statutory Liquidity Ratio and Interest Rate Structure—Loans, Deposits and Gilts

These parameters, by their very nature, are tied to the dynamics of monetary policy and the economy in general and hence remained subject to change by RBI in either direction. More so in the context of the fact that those parameters had a complex past and still needed some rationalization. In April 2003, a scheme of BPLR was introduced by RBI for ensuring transparency in banks' lending rates as also for reducing the complexity involved in pricing loans.[51]

5.10.3. Technology

CFS had made recommendations for speedy digitisation of banking. In the early 1990s, use of technology was visible in computerisation of branches and installation of ATMs. However, most of those efforts were on a standalone basis. In 2002, banks had been urged to pay special attention to computerisation and networking of branches. By end-March 2007, about 86% of branches had been fully computerised, of which a little more than half of them were under core banking solutions. The number of ATMs (both on-site and off-site) at end-March 2007 was 27,088.

Electronic payments and settlement systems grew rapidly in this period. Implementation of real time gross settlement (RTGS) and national electronic fund transfer (NEFT) have enabled receipt of funds on a real time basis. The RTGS platform has contributed to improved cash management in banks. Technology has enabled banks to innovate new products and services such as phone banking and internet banking. In these and other ways, technology has contributed to making Indian banking more competitive, efficient and productive.[52]

5.10.4. Branch Authorisation Policy

The Branch Authorisation Policy was liberalized in September 2005. 'The system of granting authorisation for opening individual branches from time to time was replaced by a system of giving aggregated approvals on an annual basis.' It granted reasonable flexibility and freedom to banks in matters relating to shifting of branches and conversion of extension counters into branches.[53]

III. THE FINANCIALS: 1991-92–2010-11

The financials of SCBs for 20 years are analysed in this section. The parameters and the methodology used are the same as in Chapters 3 and 4 and the sequence of analysis also follows those chapters. Five financial absolutes of size and performance are analysed in Table 5.5, and seven ratios which supplement and deepen that analysis are presented in Table 5.6. Adding to the analysis of reforms attempted in the preceding pages, this analysis completes a full review of the reform period.

Table 5.5 SCBs' Significant Bank Parameters: 1991-92–2010-11 (Continued)

Serial No.	Parameters	1990–91	1991–92	1992–93	1993–94	1994–95	1995–96	1996–97	1997–98	1998–99	1999–00	2000–01	2001–02
1	Banks (number)	76	76	76	76	84	91	99	103	105	101	100	97
2	TA (₹ in billions)	2,866	3,372	3,761	4,352	5,068	5,989	6,701	7,955	9,505	11,104	12,950	15,355
	Percent change YOY		18	12	16	16	18	12	19	19	17	17	19
	CAGR		18	15	15	15	16	15	16	16	16	16	16
3	Branches (number)	47,976	48,347	48,976	48,970	49,430	50,245	50,870	51,734	52,769	53,094	53,122	53,379
	Percent change YOY		0.77	1.30	(0.01)	0.94	1.65	1.24	1.70	2.00	0.62	0.05	0.48
	CAGR		0.77	1.04	0.69	0.75	0.93	0.98	1.08	1.20	1.13	1.02	0.97
4	Total income (₹ in billions)	266	398	420	437	511	651	762	858	1,000	1,154	1,321	1,510
	Percent change YOY		50	6	4	17	27	17	13	17	15	14	14
	CAGR		50	26	18	18	20	19	18	18	18	17	17
5	PAT (₹ in millions)	6,060	12,800	(41,500)	(36,430)	22,230	9,210	44,700	64,510	46,600	73,730	64,990	11,5760
	Percent change YOY		111	(424)	(12)	161	(59)	385	44	(28)	58	(12)	78
	CAGR		111	NA	NA	38	9	40	40	29	32	27	31

Table 5.5 SCBs' Significant Bank Parameters: 1991-92–2010-11 (Concluded)

Serial No.	Parameters	2002-03	2003-04	2004-05	2005-06	2006-07	2007-08	2008-09	2009-10	2010-11	2010-11/1990-91 (Times)	CAGR
1	Banks (number)	92	90	88	85	82	79	80	81	81	—	—
2	TA (₹ in billions)	16,967	19,750	23,555	27,859	34,634	43,265	52,386	60,251	71,835	25.06	17
	Percent change YOY	10	16	19	18	24	25	21	15	19		
	CAGR	16	16	16	16	17	17	18	17	17		
3	Branches (number)	53,717	54,438	55,707	57,148	59,722	63,015	66,570	71,526	76,083	1.59	2.33
	Percent change YOY	0.63	1.34	2.33	2.59	4.50	5.51	5.64	7.44	6.37		
	CAGR	0.95	0.98	1.07	1.17	1.38	1.62	1.84	2.12	2.33		
4	Total income (₹ in billions)	1,721	1,838	1,902	2,208	2,762	3,689	4,638	4,943	5,712	21.47	17
	Percent change YOY	14	7	3	16	25	34	26	7	16		
	CAGR	17	16	15	15	16	17	17	17	17		
5	PAT (₹ in millions)	170,260	222,710	209,470	245,820	384,590	427,260	527,680	571,090	703,310	116.06	27
	Percent change YOY	47	31	(6)	17	56	11	24	8	23		
	CAGR	32	32	29	28	28	28	28	27	27		

Source: Banks: STs, various years; branches: IBA, performance highlights, various years, Mumbai; other parameters: Statements 5.1 and 5.2.

Notes: * 'PAT' figures have been used as figures for 'PBT' were not available.

Table 5.6 SCBs' Significant Financial Ratios: 1991-92–2010-11 (Continued)

Serial No.	Ratios	1990–91	1991–92	1992–93	1993–94	1994–95	1995–96	1996–97	1997–98	1998–99	1999–00	2000–01
1	Leverage	2.24	2.62	2.91	5.13	6.11	6.13	6.46	6.73	5.79	5.62	5.23
2	C–D	62	60	58	48	51	55	51	50	48	49	50
3	I–D	34	37	39	44	43	41	42	42	44	46	47
4	NIM	1.96	3.35	2.57	2.54	3.06	3.15	3.23	2.95	2.78	2.72	2.84
5	C–I	93	92	129	122	90	97	86	82	88	84	88
6	ROA	0.23	0.42	(1.16)	(0.90)	0.47	0.17	0.70	0.88	0.53	0.72	0.54
7	ROE	10.78	16.77	(41.99)	(21.92)	8.34	2.72	11.17	13.32	8.59	12.56	9.98

Table 5.6 SCBs' Significant Financial Ratios: 1991-92–2010-11 (Concluded)

Serial No.	Ratios	2001–02	2002–03	2003–04	2004–05	2005–06	2006–07	2007–08	2008–09	2009–10	2010–11
1	Leverage	5.48	5.74	5.9	6.35	6.58	6.33	7.29	7.02	7.14	7.10
2	C–D	54	55	55	63	70	73	75	74	74	77
3	I–D	49	51	51	47	40	35	35	36	36	34
4	NIM	2.57	2.77	2.86	2.83	2.81	2.94	2.32	2.40	2.38	2.68
5	C–I	82	78	77	79	78	69	73	74	74	74
6	ROA	0.82	1.05	1.21	0.97	0.96	1.23	1.10	1.10	1.01	1.06
7	ROE	15.24	18.76	20.82	15.74	14.77	19.12	15.98	15.44	14.31	14.96

5.11. Five Parameters

5.11.1. Number of Banks

The number of banks in this period of 20 years rose from 76 at the end of the last period to 81 at the end of the current period. The number had changed from 1994–95 from year to year and had risen to the highest of 105 in 1998–99, before beginning to decline. The main contributory factor was the new policy of liberalization adopted from 1992–93. New banks were allowed to be established, entry to foreign banks was freed and mergers were more freely permitted. The number of new banks rose from 6 to 9 to 10 before closing at 7, because of a few mergers. The number of foreign banks which stood at 24 at March-end 1991 rose to 44 before closing at 34 at March-end 2011. The numbers of banks in SBI Group declined from eight at the beginning to six at the close of the period, as two of the SBI's subsidiaries were merged into SBI. Among the nationalized banks, one bank was merged into another nationalized bank, and one bank—IDBI Bank, first classified as new PrSB was re-classified as PSB, the total remaining at 20. The number of old PrSBs declined from 25 to 14 in this period, mostly due to mergers. Thus, nine old PrSBs had been merged between January 1996 and June 2004.[54]

5.11.2. Total Assets

During the 20-year period, TA increased by 25 times over 1990–91 and by a CAGR of 17. The annual growth rate of the SCBs' BS size ranged from 10 per cent in 2002–03 to 25 per cent in 2007–08. The years 2006–07 to 2008–09 recorded the fastest annual growth rates of 24, 25 and 21 per cent respectively. These years were among the fastest growing years for the Indian economy.

5.11.3. Total Branches

'Overall, the number of branches increased from 47,976 in 1990–91 to 76,083 in 2010–11, that is, 1.59 times over the period, a CAGR of 2.33.' The process of change in number of branches was a mix of a period of consolidation (slowdown) for existing banks and fast expansion for new PrSBs.

5.11.4. Total Income

The year-on-year growth rate of total income, the third measure of size of banks, was a little volatile too, with the first year of 1991–92 recording the period's highest rate of 50 per cent. But this parameter recorded lows in the two 'big loss' years of 1992–93 and 1993–94. The years 2003–04 and 2004–05, and again the year 2009–10 also recorded low rates. Overall, 'total income registered a growth of 21 times and a CAGR of 17 in the period'.

5.11.5. Profit after Tax

Being the bottom line, subsuming the impact of all items of PLA, PAT was the most volatile of the preceding three variables, as it moved like a pendulum during this period. PAT recorded the heaviest losses of the whole period of our study in the two years of substantive reform, 1992–93 and 1993–94. It also recorded five years of negative growth year on year. At the same time, PAT picked up well in the second half of the period, a high growth period for the economy. The sum total: Its overall growth was by far the highest—116 times—and CAGR was also the highest at 27!

5.12. Seven Ratios (Table 5.6)

5.12.1. Leverage

Leverage of SCBs stood at 2.24 at the end of 1990–91, last year of the previous period. As reforms kicked in, losses on bad loans were written off and more provisions had to be made, equity got reduced further, particularly affecting the leverage ratios of PSBs. New CA requirements raised the need for additional capital further. As fresh capital contributions flowed in, leverage ratio went up slightly to 2.62 and 2.91 in 1991–92 and 1992–93 respectively. The compulsion to make additional contributions to equity continued and the leverage ratio began to rise. The leverage of SCBs rose to 5.13 at March-end 1994. It fluctuated thereafter to close at 7.10 at March-end 2011. It is to be noted that the leverage figures like other parameters are an amalgam of leverage of four sets of banks, that is, PSBs, old PrSBs, new PrSBs and foreign banks. Write-offs involved PSBs and old PrSBs. New PrSBs and foreign banks had higher leverage ratios and this fact raised the overall leverage figures. Thus, at March-end 2011, the 7.10 leverage ratio was the weighted average of: the leverage ratio of 16.49 of foreign banks, that of all (old and new) PrSBs at 9.91 and that of PSBs at 5.48.

It is interesting to note that as against the leverage of 7.10, CA of SCBs at March-end 2011 as per Basel-I was assessed at 13.0 and as per Basel-II at 14.20 (Section II.5.4.2.2 supra), which was exactly double of the leverage.

5.12.2–3. Credit-Deposit Ratio and I–D Ratio

Reading these two ratios together leads us to make the following observations:

1. The C–D and I–D ratios were 60 and 37 respectively in 1991–92, the year before the introduction of income recognition, provisioning and CA reforms. As the reforms began to clean up the bank BS and NPAs began to be brought into the open, provided for or written off, and banks cut down on new loans, C–D ratio fell to 58 in 1992–93 and further to 48 in 1993–94. Correspondingly, the I–D ratio increased to 39 in 1992–93 and further to 44 in 1993–94. It is interesting to note that during 1992–93 and 1993–94, SLR was reduced from 38.5 per cent to 34.75 per cent.

Normally, SLR reduction should result in disposal of equivalent gilts, release of funds going into increase in credit portfolio, thus a decline in I–D ratio and an increase in C–D ratio. Actually, I–D ratio had increased and C–D ratio had declined. The combined C + I/D ratio stood at 92 in 1993–94.

2. Between 1994–95 and 2003–04, the two ratios moved upwards in slow motion. I–D portfolio remained in the 41–44 range until 1998–99 and then moved slowly up until it stood at 51 in 2003–04. Correspondingly, the C–D portfolio moved slowly up to rise to 55 in 2003–04. The C + I/D ratio was 106 in 2003–04. In this period, SLR had been reduced from 34.75 per cent to 25 per cent.

3. The third phase recorded a sharp increase in C–D ratio from 2004–05 to close at 77, and a corresponding contrarian move of I–D ratio to hit 34 in 2010–11. SLR had been reduced from 25 per cent to 24 per cent. The combined ratio had reached 111.

Borrowings of SCBs in 1991–92/1992–93 were 9–10 per cent of deposits. As reforms came in, borrowings began to decline and reached 5 per cent by 2000–01. It began to rise from 2001–02 and had reached a high of 11–12 per cent of deposits in 2010–11, confirming that this period was a period of high economic growth and, therefore, high credit growth.

5.12.4. Net Interest Margin

NIM was unusually low at 1.96 per cent in the last year of the preceding period, and it was unusually high at 3.35 per cent in 1991–92, the first year of current period. The period from 1992–93 was to experience a deregulated regime. NIM fell to 2.57 in 1992–93 and to 2.54 in 1993–94. It rose again to 3.23 per cent in 1996–97, the highest in the deregulated era and then slid below 3 per cent which it never touched again in this period.

Thus, while NIM was less than 3 per cent in the complex and regulated interest rate environment of the previous period, it was less than 3 per cent (except for 3.23 per cent in 1996–97) throughout the deregulated current period environment. We might say that the new competitive environment of the banking system kept the NIM at less than 3 per cent. Of course, we are referring to the average NIM of SCBs. These are the averages for SCBs. But the major difference between the two periods would be that there was the prescribed uniformity of rates among banks in the regulated interest rate regime, and there were significant differences in the interest rate structures of banks in the deregulated regime. For example, look at the NIMs of new PrSBs in the following three years for which all the three figures for each year could be found:

Year	Average	Highest	Lowest
2006–07	2.10	4.21	1.41
2007–08	2.39	5.08	1.36
2008–09	2.79	5.33	1.80

Contrary to general expectations, differences in NIMs between banks could be huge, even in a deregulated environment in which tough competition among banks would prevail. May be, though, different banks were operating in differentiated credit and deposit markets.

5.12.5. Cost–Income Ratio

The C–I ratio is the other side of income ratio; it is an important indicator of a bank's profit margin.

C–I ratio was at a high of 93 in 1990–91 and 92 in 1991–92. In the two years of major reforms, 1992–93 and 1993–94, C–I ratio slid to negative at 129 and 122 respectively. The following years of 1994–95 to 2001–02 were volatile years for this ratio when it fluctuated between 97 and 82. C–I then went steady below 80 after 2001–02 and was 74 in 2010–11; these were the years of good profits for SCBs.

5.12.6–7. Return on Assets and Return on Equity

The SCBs had yielded ROA of 0.23 per cent in 1990–91 and 0.42 per cent in 1991–92, the last two years of the regulated era. As reforms inaugurated the deregulated environment, cleaning up some of the hidden losses of SCBs, the 'big' loss years of 1992–93 and 1993–94 showed negative ROAs of (1.16%) and (0.90%) respectively and the lowest positive ROA of 0.17 per cent in 1995–96. It fluctuated between 0.53 and 0.88 between 1994–95 and 2001–02 (except 1995–96). It crossed 1.0 per cent in 2002–03. ROA remained at around close to one in two years and above one for seven years.

For assessing ROE, the amount of net profit and the degree of leverage would matter. High profit and low leverage would maximize the ROE and vice versa. From 16.77 per cent in 1991–92, ROE slid to 41.99 per cent in 1992–93 and 21.92 per cent in 1993–94. From 1994–95 to 2000–01, ROE recorded positive returns from the lowest at 2.72 per cent in 1995–96 and the highest at 13.32 in 1997–98. From 2001–02 to 2010–11, ROE rose to a higher level to once cross 20 per cent to register 20.82 per cent in 2003–04; for the rest of the years, it stayed between 14.31 per cent and 19.12 per cent. For the closing years of this period, higher profits and high leverage produced above average profits with low risk.

Positive changes in the 12 financial parameters stated above were clear indicators that the banking system had shown improved performance.

Over and above this analysis, the following important information may be added:

Advances had grown 30 times and its CAGR was 19 over the 20-year period, despite the fact that this parameter had grown at rather low rates in the first decade of the period.

GNPAs to gross advances ratio at 2.25 per cent at the end of 2010–11 meant that asset quality of the banking sector had improved. NNPAs to net advances were at 0.97 per cent at the end of 2010–11, indicating higher level of provisioning for NPAs.

IV. THE 21ST-CENTURY BANKS: 2011

Table 5.7 lists 38 banks only, as the following 4 out of 42 banks were merged in this period:

1. New Bank of India was merged into PNB in 1993.
2. State Bank of Saurashtra was merged into SBI in 2008.
3. State Bank of Indore was taken over by SBI in 2010.
4. Bank of Rajasthan was merged into ICICI Bank in 2010.

V. SUMMARY REVIEW: 1991-92–2010-11

5.13. The Banking System Turns Around Again

The Indian economy provided a wholesome context during most of this period. Table 5.8 provides a short view of annual GDP growth and inflation rates in this period.

As can be viewed from Table 5.8, the five-yearly minima and maxima of GDP broadly increased over this period. Conversely, the

Table 5.7 *The 21st-Century Banks: 2011*

(Sixth in the Series)

Serial No.	Banks (Ranked by TA)	TA ₹ in crore	Rank	Branches Number	Rank
1	SBI	1,223,736	1	13,284	1
2	PNB	378,325	2	4,855	2
3	Bank of Baroda	358,397	3	3,352	4
4	Bank of India	351,173	4	3,303	5
5	Canara Bank	336,079	5	3,252	6
6	Union Bank of India	235,984	6	1,556	14
7	Central Bank of India	209,757	7	3,737	3
8	Indian Overseas Bank	178,784	8	2,167	10
9	UCO Bank	163,398	9	2,192	9
10	Oriental Bank of Commerce	161,343	10	1,640	12
11	Syndicate Bank	156,539	11	2,491	7
12	Allahabad Bank	151,286	12	2,373	8
13	Corporation Bank	143,509	13	1,268	17
14	Indian Bank	121,718	14	1,829	11
15	Andhra Bank	108,901	15	1,603	13
16	State Bank of Hyderabad	106,698	16	1,210	18
17	United Bank of India	90,041	17	1,556	14
18	Vijaya Bank	81,691	18	1,186	20
19	State Bank of Patiala	81,286	19	1,013	21
20	Bank of Maharashtra	76,442	20	1,505	16
21	State Bank of Travancore	70,977	21	797	24
22	Dena Bank	70,838	22	1,191	19
23	Punjab & Sind Bank	68,550	23	941	22
24	State Bank of Bikaner & Jaipur	62,954	24	909	23
25	State Bank of Mysore	52,032	25	700	26
26	Federal Bank	51,456	26	741	25
27	Jammu and Kashmir Bank	50,508	27	503	29
28	ING Vysya Bank (Vysya Bank)	39,014	28	504	28

(Continued)

Table 5.7 (Continued)

(Sixth in the Series)		TA		Branches	
Serial No.	Banks (Ranked by TA)	₹ in crore	Rank	Number	Rank
29	South Indian Bank	32,820	29	632	27
30	Karnataka Bank	31,693	30	483	30
31	Karur Vysya Bank	28,225	31	369	31
32	Tamilnad Mercantile Bank	16,117	32	232	36
33	City Union Bank	14,592	33	248	35
34	Dhanlaxmi Bank	14,268	34	273	33
35	Lakshmi Vilas Bank	13,301	35	269	34
36	Catholic Syrian Bank	9,829	36	360	32
37	Nainital Bank	3,292	37	101	37
38	Ratnakar Bank	3,230	38	100	38
Total		5,348,783		64,725	

Source: ST 2010–11, pp. 122–151.

Table 5.8 GDP Growth and Inflation Rates (1991-92–2010-11): Five-year Periods

Five-year Periods	GDP Growth Rate (%)		Inflation Rate (%)	
	Minimum	Maximum	Minimum	Maximum
1991-92–1995-96	1.4	7.3	8.0	13.7
1996-97–2000-01	4.1	8.0	3.3	7.2
2001-02–2005-06	3.9	9.5	3.4	6.5
2006-07–2010-11	6.7	9.6	3.8	9.6
20-year Average	6.7		6.7	

Source: RBI, *Handbook of Statistics on Indian Economy*, 2015–16.

Notes: GDP (at factor cost, base year 2004–05, at constant prices), Table 230; rates of inflation (all commodities), Wholesale Price Index, Table 238.

five-yearly minima and maxima of inflation rates broadly declined over this period.

GDP growth recorded the highest average of 8.2 per cent from 2003–04 to 2010–11, the last eight years of this period. Real GDP growth during the Tenth Plan Period (2002–03 to 2006–07) averaged 7.6 per cent, the highest average rate of growth during any plan period so far. Thus, the movements of growth rate and inflation rate both were generally positive for the economy and the banking system.

Research is needed to be undertaken on the hypothesis that periods of decline in GDP growth rates and of rise in inflation rates coincide with years of drought.

'After going through a heavy downturn as bank reforms stepped in, SCBs recorded robust performance' (as per published data) over the current period. India successfully managed the challenge of the global financial crisis during the last four years of this period, viz., 2007–08 to 2010–11 and reached the pre-crisis levels of economic growth. New challenges would arise with new opportunities and threats. Global competition could soon be a matter of fact. In the foreseeable future, Indian banks, particularly the PSBs, will have to manage with constraints of capital, competence and governance.

5.13.1. Policy Reversals

During the 20-year period, particularly the first half, the banking system went through significant reforms which strengthened its structure and systems. Several policy reversals were recorded:

1. *Deregulation and liberalization of the banking system*: Deregulation liberated the banking system from severe controls of the State and RBI. Most policy announcements flowed from deregulation of the economy and the banking system.

2. *Partial privatization of public sector banks*: Compulsions of the GOI forced it to allow PSBs to make public issues of equity in order to augment their capital to meet CA requirements.

3. *Entry of new private sector banks*: New PrSBs were allowed to be established after a gap of more than two decades. It has promoted induction of new technology and competition in banking.

4. *Entry of more foreign banks and opening of more branches*: The rationale which allowed entry of new PrSBs also allowed entry of new foreign banks.

5. *Distinct shift in the credit and monetary policy framework*: There was a distinct shift in the credit and monetary policy framework and operating procedures from direct instruments of monetary control to market-based indirect instruments.

6. *Deregulation of the interest rate structure*: Deregulation of the interest rate structure was a key component of financial sector reforms. This has not only helped in improving the competitiveness and resource allocation process in the financial system but has also facilitated the monetary transmission mechanism. All interest rates, barring select rates—savings deposits, non-resident Indian (NRI) deposits, small loans up to ₹2 lakhs and export credit, were deregulated.

5.13.2. Technological and Financial Upgrades

At the same time, technological and financial upgrades and innovations, taking place globally, arrived in India too. The traditional face of banking had begun to change fast. New products and services, never part of traditional banking, soon became important segments of the business of banking in India. The distinctions among various segments of the financial services industry had begun to blur. 'Globalisation, financial deregulation and improvements in technology have had a profound effect on the financial landscape in recent years. These developments have intensified competition. There was greater scope to diversify risk and manage it efficiently.'[55]

Computerisation as well as the adoption of core banking solutions was one of the major steps in improving the efficiency of banking services. The new private sector banks and most of the foreign banks were the front-runners in adopting technology. For old private sector banks and PSBs, adoption of technology was an arduous task because of historical records and practices. However, by end of 2010–11, almost 98% of the branches of PSBs were fully computerised, within which almost 90% of the branches were on core banking platform.[56]

Further, introduction of ATMs had enabled customers to do banking without visiting the bank branch. Total number of ATMs of SCBs at end-March 2010–11 was 74,505, of which over 45 per cent were off-site ATMs.[57]

5.13.3. Public Sector Banks: Dominance in Decline

Continuing from Chapters 3 and 4, Table 5.9 presents market share of PSBs in the Indian banking sector as it moved from 1991–92 to 1992–93 to 2010–11.

Table 5.9 *Market Share of Public Sector Banks: Dominance in Decline 1991–92, 1992–93 and 2010–11*

		1991–92		1992–93		2010–11	
Serial No. (A)	Parameters	Indian Banking Sector (52) (₹ in crore)	Public Sector (28) (% Share)	Indian Banking Sector (52) (₹ in crore)	Public Sector (28) (% Share)	Indian Banking Sector (47) (₹ in crore)	Public Sector (26) (% Share)
1	TA	313,845	95	351,369	93	6,691,991	79
2	Deposits	246,053	95	278,689	94	5,375,743	81
3	Advances	149,483	96	161,908	95	4,103,165	81
4	Branches	48,196	92	48,824	92	75,764	84

Source: Parameters: STs of various years.

Compare the 1991–92 size of the PSBs with their corresponding size of 1990–91 (Table 4.9). Their size and deposits had dropped, albeit by 1 per cent. By the end of 1992–93, their share declined further. It may be noted that the number of banks in the banking system, the PSBs and the private sector remained the same, both in 1991–92 and 1992–93. But by the end of 2010–11, as the new PrSBs had stormed into the system and the number of foreign banks too had gone up, the market shares of PSBs in the cited four parameters had declined by large percentages of 8 to 14.

As the reforms were introduced in 1991–92 and 1992–93, and CA of PSBs declined, GOI entered to contribute to the capitals of its banks. Hence the leverage of PSBs was a little higher than the banking system. But the year 2010–11 was different. The leverage of PSBs was much lower than that of the system. The ROA of PSBs was lower than that of the Indian banking system. The GOI was now not able to stem the decline of PSBs in the evolving competitive environment. One of the reasons obviously was the crunch of financial resources PSBs were then facing. Partial privatization had helped but a little. Higher levels of privatization should be expected. Going by their status at the end of 2010–11, the dominance of PSBs is on the path of decline.

5.13.4. Closing Comments

As a measure of financial development of the economy, it is to be noted that aggregate deposits of the banking system had risen to 71.9 per cent of the national income at the end of 2010–11. It had declined from 78.0 per cent at the end of 2008–09.[58]

India successfully managed the challenge of the global financial crisis during the last four years of this period, viz., 2007–08 to 2010–11 and reached the pre-crisis levels of economic growth. New challenges would arise with new opportunities and threats. Global competition could soon be a matter of fact. In the foreseeable future, Indian banks, particularly the PSBs, will have to manage with constraints of capital, competence and governance.

We began this chapter with the declaration, 'the windows begin to open'. At the end of the chapter that question remained: Did the windows open? Yes, several windows did open wide; some windows opened only partially; those are the windows of transparency and of corporate governance; but those very windows of PSBs remain mostly shut. 'Secret reserves' may remain secret; but for provisions for loan losses to remain hidden is a big opacity. We are not sure whether all the provisions have been disclosed to the regulatory authority and provided for. 'Corporate governance for the PrSBs is being rigorously enforced, but that for the PSBs, the question mark still stands.'

'The financial review and analysis that has been attempted with some serious effort, therefore, may not reflect the real state of the banking system's health. Applying sophisticated tools of analysis to data of questionable quality yields questionable results'. C-FAB, in its report, had observed 'that in Indian conditions the time is not yet opportune for practising full disclosure in respect of secret reserves and loan loss provisioning. The issue, however, may be reviewed in due course'. 'C-FAB's Report was submitted in 1985. Twenty-five years later, the time may be ripe for the RBI and the GOI to review this significant issue.'

5.A. Annexure

Statement 5.1. Main Heads of SCBs' BS: 1991–92–2010–11

Statement 5.2. Main heads of SCBs' PLA: 1991–92–2010–11

Statement 5.1 *Main Heads of SCBs' BS: 1991-92–2010-11 (Continued)*

(₹ in crore)

Particulars/Years	1991–92	1992–93	1993–94	1994–95	1995–96	1996–97	1997–98	1998–99	1999–2000	2000–01
Liabilities										
1 Own funds (Capital + reserves)	8,838	10,927	22,315	30,956	36,695	43,314	53,543	54,994	62,445	67,741
2 Deposits	261,907	294,854	349,364	402,433	457,607	536,387	644,117	770,820	900,307	1,055,234
3 Borrowings	22,439	28,677	14,762	25,234	42,267	22,759	25,859	40,248	45,360	55,421
4 Bills payable	10,624	11,301	12,927	13,854	17,154	20,283	21,453	24,615	24,406	28,547
5 Other liabilities	33,393	30,326	35,849	34,314	45,188	47,360	50,563	59,871	77,850	88,031
Total Liabilities/TA	**337,211**	**376,131**	**435,217**	**506,792**	**598,910**	**670,104**	**795,535**	**950,548**	**1,110,368**	**1,294,974**
Assets										
6 Cash and bank balances	42,910	46,879	59,835	72,937	86,586	83,439	102,972	125,460	130,349	145,614
7 Money at call and short notice	5,237	5,291	4,485	5,221	13,730	23,981	28,813	44,740	36,042	44,789
8 Investments	97,533	113,738	154,024	171,524	186,162	222,852	272,074	339,496	413,871	491,908
9 Advances	158,003	170,334	168,250	206,512	251,968	274,841	324,642	369,570	443,469	525,683
10 Fixed assets	1,962	3,510	5,009	6,967	9,515	10,748	12,608	14,500	15,480	16,209
11 Other assets (Non-banking assets + other assets)	31,566	36,379	43,590	43,630	50,949	54,244	54,425	56,781	71,158	70,771

Statement 5.1 Main Heads of SCBs' BS: 1991-92–2010-11 (Concluded)

(₹ in crore)

Particulars/Years	2001-02	2002-03	2003-04	2004-05	2005-06	2006-07	2007-08	2008-09	2009-10	2010-11
Liabilities										
1 Own Funds (Capital + reserves)	84,160	97,330	116,569	149,610	183,181	219,175	315,558	367,949	430,124	509,892
2 Deposits	1,202,699	1,355,623	1,575,530	1,837,559	2,164,682	2,696,980	3,320,054	4,063,202	4,752,454	5,616,432
3 Borrowings	107,180	86,535	96,104	168,352	203,148	242,870	297,351	473,597	524,763	673,925
4 Bills payable	32,399	34,428	42,614	36,765	49,593	55,096	59,344	52,525	62,816	62,113
5 Other liabilities	109,075	122,830	144,203	163,223	185,260	249,285	334,180	281,373	254,981	321,161
Total Liabilities/TAs	**1,535,513**	**1,696,746**	**1,975,019**	**2,355,509**	**2,785,863**	**3,463,406**	**4,326,489**	**5,238,645**	**6,025,138**	**7,183,523**
Assets										
6 Cash and bank balances	150,854	125,555	161,049	176,165	218,275	294,998	393,359	426,372	484,891	586,518
7 Money at call and short notice	53,425	35,040	34,158	37,267	42,644	58,789	39,965	67,411	64,376	63,471
8 Investments	588,058	693,085	802,755	869,737	866,508	950,769	1,176,156	1,449,550	1,719,188	1,916,050
9 Advances	645,743	739,233	863,632	1,150,836	1,516,811	1,981,216	2,477,040	2,999,925	3,497,054	4,298,705
10 Fixed assets	20,083	20,198	21,403	23,051	25,082	31,363	42,394	48,362	49,565	54,095
11 Other assets (Non-banking assets + other assets)	77,350	83,635	92,023	98,453	116,543	146,272	197,575	247,023	210,070	264,683

Source: Various STs.

Statement 5.2 Main heads of SCBs' PLA: 1991-92–2010-11 (Continued)

(₹ in crore)

Particulars/Years	1991–92	1992–93	1993–94	1994–95	1995–96	1996–97	1997–98	1998–99	1999–00	2000–01
Income										
1 Interest earned	35,067	37,486	37,866	44,529	56,137	66,494	73,732	87,319	99,507	114,951
2 Non-interest income	4,686	4,489	5,828	6,523	8,930	9,742	12,112	12,705	15,879	17,127
3 Total income	39,753	41,975	43,693	51,052	65,068	76,236	85,844	100,024	115,386	132,078
Expenditure										
4 Interest expended	23,783	27,838	26,826	29,042	37,273	44,856	50,292	60,882	69,317	78,152
5 Operatingexpenses	8,879	10,249	11,487	14,226	17,592	19,141	20,928	25,167	27,579	34,179
6 Total expenditure	32,663	38,086	38,313	43,269	54,865	63,997	71,219	86,049	96,896	112,331
Profit										
7 OP (Before provisions andcontingencies)	7,091	3,889	5,381	7,784	10,203	12,239	14,625	13,975	18,490	19,747
8 Provisions and contingencies	5,811	8,039	9,024	5,561	9,282	7,770	8,174	9,315	11,117	13,248
9 OP	1,280	(4,150)	(3,643)	2,223	921	4,470	6,451	4,660	7,373	6,499
10 Provision for tax	0	0	0	0	0	0	0	0	0	0
11 PAT	1,280	(4,150)	(3,643)	2,223	921	4,470	6,451	4,660	7,373	6,499

Statement 5.2 Main heads of SCBs' PLA: 1991-92–2010-11 (Concluded)

(₹ in crore)

Particulars/Years	2001-02	2002-03	2003-04	2004-05	2005-06	2006-07	2007-08	2008-09	2009-10	2010-11
Income										
1 Interest earned	126,973	140,545	144,028	155,801	185,388	264,104	308,481	388,822	415,754	491,667
2 Non-interest income	24,056	31,575	39,724	34,426	35,368	43,766	60,391	74,930	78,518	79,564
3 Total income	151,030	172,120	183,753	190,227	220,756	307,869	368,872	463,752	494,272	571,230
Expenditure										
4 Interest expended	87,516	93,520	87,567	89,079	107,161	162,387	208,001	263,221	272,084	298,891
5 Operating expenses	33,696	38,007	43,515	50,136	59,201	72,309	77,282	89,268	99,770	123,129
6 Total expenditure	121,212	131,527	131,082	139,215	166,362	234,697	285,283	352,489	371,854	422,020
Profit										
7 OP(Before provisions and contingencies)	29,818	40,593	52,671	51,012	54,394	73,173	83,589	111,263	122,418	149,210
8 Provisions and contingencies	18,242	23,567	30,400	30,065	29,812	34,714	40,863	58,495	65,309	78,879
9 OP	11,576	17,026	22,271	20,947	24,582	38,459	42,726	52,768	57,109	70,331
10 Provision for tax	0	0	0	0	0	0	0	0	0	0
11 Profit after tax	11,576	17,026	22,271	20,947	24,582	38,459	42,726	52,768	57,109	70,331

Source: Various STs.

Notes

1. RBI, *Report of Committee to Consider Final Accounts*, 113–117.
2. *Report of the Committee on the Financial System*, 145–146 (CFS, hereinafter).
3. Also see C&F-1, 112, 115, paragraph 3.145.
4. TP *1991–92*; C&F-1, 113–114, 116.
5. C&F-1, 118.
6. CFS, 88–89.
7. C&F-1, 133.
8. CFS, 73–74.
9. C&F-1, 116.
10. TP *1997–98*, 1.
11. *Report of the Committee on Banking Sector Reforms*, 1–13; RBI, C&F-1, 120–121; TP *1997–98*, 2–4. (C-BSR, hereinafter).
12. Most structural and regulatory measures taken by the RBI in this regard in this period were communicated through the medium of its regular annual and mid-term monetary and credit policy statements.
13. TP *1990–91*, 79–80.
14. TP *1998–99*, 28.
15. TP *1999–2000*, 23–25.
16. Ibid.
17. *1998–99*, 71, 74.
18. *2010–11*, Table IV.15, 76.
19. C&F-1, 111–112.
20. Chapter 4, B.5.
21. TP *1999–00*, Chapter 2, Box II.2.
22. C&F-1, 111.
23. C&F-1, 111; TP *1995–96*, 96–97.
24. TP *2010–11*, 87.
25. Ibid., 88.
26. TP *1995–96*, 96–97.
27. TP *1998–99*, 14.
28. TP *1999–2000*, 6.
29. TP *2000–01*, 26.
30. TP *1998–99*, 14.
31. TP *2010–11*, 88.
32. RBI, *Financial Stability Report,* June 2011, 39.
33. This paragraph is based on TP *1999–2000*, 7.
34. TP *2005–06*, 17.
35. RBI, *Financial Stability Report,* June 2011, 37.
36. TP *2008–09*, 56.
37. TP *2005–06*, 102.
38. TP *2008–09*, 56, 59, 63.

39. TP *2010–11*, 95.
40. TP *1991–92*, 9.
41. C&F-1, 115.
42. CFS, 72.
43. Facts including data about the new PrSBs in this section were collected from TPs 1992–93 to 2010–11.
44. C&F-1, 123.
45. Ibid.
46. Ibid., 124.
47. CFS, 145–146.
48. *The Economic Times*, Interview given by Manu Shroff, 18 December 1991, Mumbai.
49. For fuller details on the subject, refer to C&F-1, 125–126.
50. RBI, *Mid-term Review of Monetary and Credit Policy*, 2000–01.
51. C&F-1, 123.
52. The two paragraphs within quotes are either substantially based on, or summarized from, C&F-1, 133–134
53. Information within quotes from, and other summarized from C&F-1, 124.
54. TP *2003–04*, 192.
55. Paraphrased from TP *2005–06*, 10.
56. TP *2010–11*, 90.
57. TP, *2010–11*, 90–91.
58. ST, *2010–11*, 11.

6

A Century of Banking in India

Rooted to National Purpose

I. THE KALEIDOSCOPE OF INDIAN BANKING

The Indian banking system has undergone several major transformations over the last 100 years. These transformations were founded on different operating backgrounds and, hence, different policy frameworks. In the pre-1950 period, the Indian economy was undeveloped and weak; the banking system was undeveloped and weak. Both operated on the 'laissez-faire' doctrine. The RBI had just reached adolescence by the end of this period. It could not have moved the banking system much under the British Raj and the 'imperialism' of Imperial Bank of India. Banking in the period 1950–1968 was promoter-owned, and controlled and run by them. It was soon subjected to a system of direct and rigid monetary and credit controls by the now nationalized RBI, but it could not affect their ownership and control. The banking system in the period 1969–1991 saw a paradigm change from the ownership-control of capitalist-promoter to government ownership, and bureaucratic control and direction in which the RBI was mostly eclipsed by the GOI, especially in the first half of this period. The period of 1991–2011 saw another paradigm shift—to a deregulated and liberal banking system. By the early 1990s, the banking system and a large number of its constituents had grown large. The policy instruments of indirect control of the economy and banking came into play and began to influence the management of the banking system. Partial privatization, partly under fiscal compulsions and partly by intent, began to erode government ownership, but not control. The banking system got clearly divided into public, Indian private and foreign private sectors. Main Landmarks:

Broadly, it is in the above multiple contexts that the canvas of Indian banking system could be said to have undergone revolutionary changes in ownership, organization and direction while continuing to grow and diversify over the 20th century and beyond. Taking a long-term historical perspective, the main landmarks of the Indian banking odyssey were three:

1. The banking system's path of evolution and development from the beginnings of an unorganized and uncontrolled system to the present organized and fairly liberal system.
2. In that 100-year path of history, nationalization of the major segment of the banking industry stood out tall in terms of purpose and impact; hence, it is sliced out as a separate landmark. It is important to view the history of the working of PSBs from 1955 to 2011 and subject them to an assessment.
3. The defining and final goal of the banking system as advocated vehemently by the Indian national leadership, before and after Independence, inside and outside the legislature, was the achievement of the 'national purpose', that is, to secure to the rural and urban poor of the country economic security by directing banks to deploy their funds for them. Banks were earlier not into finance of agriculture and other rural activities for the poor; they were made to 'soil' their hands with entry into villages.

The three landmarks are the subjects of narration in the following three sections II–IV.

II. EVOLUTION AND DEVELOPMENT OF THE BANKING SYSTEM

The detailed story of the path of evolution and development of the banking system as described in the preceding five chapters is summarized below in terms of its most important stages of transformation.

6.1. Indian Banking in the Pre-Independence Period

At the beginning of the 20th century, Indian commercial banking existed mainly as an unorganized sector. But there were also two IJSBS, Allahabad Bank and PNB, which shone as the members of a tiny organized sector. Three Presidency banks also existed then that merged in 1921 to become Imperial Bank of India. The launch of the Swadeshi movement in 1906 saw the establishment of seven more Indian-owned banks one after another.

The failure of a large number of small banks during 1913–1914 drew the attention of the then GOI to widespread ignorance of the existence of the banking industry. It resulted in the launch of a countrywide survey to collect data on bank failures, apart from basic data on banks. Collection of bank data from the banks in the form of STs, thereafter, became an annual feature. From then on, the government and its legislature became more involved in the working of the banking system. This growing interest by the State during the 34 years beginning from 1913 manifested itself in: (a) bringing of banks under the jurisdiction of the Companies Act, 1913, (b) national legislature's increasing involvement in debating banks' role in dispensing rural credit, and advocating social control and nationalization of banks, (c) debates for setting up a central bank for the country and later about its ownership, and (d) a protracted yet unsuccessful journey to enact a separate law for banking companies.

In the 1940s, the banking system grew at a hectic and uncontrolled pace. Non-scheduled banks remained outside the purview of RBI; even their exact number was not known. Ever since some records became available in 1913, not a single year had passed without bank failures. In fact, the number of bank failures had increased since mid-1930s into the 1940s. It had been said then that the Indian banking system 'was freer than the free banking that prevailed in the US around the civil war'. Although RBI was already in existence for more than 12 years, it hardly had any powers to supervise and regulate the banking system; those powers lay with the GOI. RBI's repeated efforts since 1939 to get a banking company law passed had not succeeded, often due to the opposition of Imperial Bank. At the end of this period, it was a fast growing, unorganized and weak banking system, built on inadequate capital base, unhealthy bank practices and unskilled professionals.

At the beginning of the 20th century, there were three Presidency banks with deposits of less than ₹16 crore, nine IJSBs with deposits of ₹8 crore and eight exchange banks with more than ₹10 crore as deposits, totalling 20 banks with deposits of over ₹34 crore. At the end of 1946, the Indian banking system consisted of 690 IJSBs (scheduled and non-scheduled), the Imperial Bank of India and 15 exchange banks, having total branches numbering 5,373 and total deposits of ₹1,187 crore.

The efforts of the Indian polity to promote the institutionalization of banking system by enacting a banking law and to nationalize RBI, in order to facilitate harmonization of the fiscal policy of GOI and monetary policy of RBI, had failed owing to the intransigence of RBI and Imperial Bank, acting as they were the instruments of the British Raj.

6.2. Post-Independence Transformations

The transition of the unorganized and inefficient banking system into an organized and efficient banking system began almost immediately after Independence. The law nationalizing RBI came into force on 1 January 1949. The BCA was passed in 1949. The 1947–1949 period remains marked for attaining these two cherished objectives of the Indian polity. Both these changes hugely strengthened the regulatory and supervisory structure of the banking system. Despite these positive developments, bank failures continued and even increased due to the impact of disruptions in the banking system caused by the Partition, decline in the state of the economy, and the enforcement of the BCA itself. By the end of 1949, GOI seemed to have found its feet, and so had RBI. RBI could begin to oversee the working of the banking system more intensely and the banking system was beginning to look a little stable. The 1950–2011 years can be noted for the journey of the banking system to become an organized and efficient system for growth and development and, then, to a destination at which it would have become the desired instrument of national transformation. That journey is traversed below:

6.2.1. An Organized and Efficient Banking System in the Making: 1950–2011

Three major policy actions were taken by RBI during this 60-year period. One was the process of consolidation of banks which began in 1950 and lasted almost till March 1991. The second was to begin using direct instruments of monetary policy vis-à-vis the then unorganized state of the banking system and non-existence of the money and securities markets. Use of direct instruments as a policy covered the period 1950–1981. The third major policy action was the deregulation and liberalization of the economy including banking. It began without any fanfare around the year 1981, gained national momentum in 1991 and was continuing in 2011. Brief description of the three follows:

6.2.1.1. Consolidation of Banks: 1950–1991

The RBI had decided in the 1950s that, to protect public savings, it would be advisable to wind up weak, non-viable banks or merge them into stronger ones. The axe began to fall immediately on the weak and the wicked; and the number of non-scheduled banks began to fall fast. The substantive change in India's geography due to Partition and the integration of 538 princely states into the Indian Union led to the banks in the princely states being brought into the fold of the regulatory control of the RBI. This added to the running story of weak banks and bank failures. Reinforced by the enactment of the BCA, RBI took upon the task of consolidating the commercial banking structure through liquidation and amalgamation of weak banks. The number of Indian SCBs and non-SCBs declined substantially between January 1950 and March 1991, by which date RBI had almost completed the task of pruning weak scheduled and non-scheduled banks. The following statement sums up the results:

Pruning of Banks: 1950–1991		
Year	No. of Scheduled Banks	No. of Non-scheduled Banks
1950	78	521
(Jan.)		
1968	58	17
1980	62	3
1991	53	3
(March)		

6.2.1.2. Shift to Direct Instruments of Credit and Monetary Policy: 1950–1981

Shortages of agricultural commodities and inflationary conditions prevailed almost throughout this period. This impelled RBI to tighten its monetary policy by making use of instruments of blunt direct credit controls on the banking system. The bank rate, which had stayed at 3 per cent constantly since November 1935, was raised in instalments to 6 per cent in 1965. It was lowered to 5 per cent in March 1968.

An administered interest rate structure was imposed on banks to prevent application of low rates on speculative activities, high rates on productive activities and diversion of large credit to big business. It resulted in a complex structure. Selective credit controls on agricultural activities from 1956 and a credit authorization scheme for large borrowers from 1965, possibly unavoidable in prevailing circumstances, added to the complexities of the interest rate structure. Many of these provisions remained operative till 1980 and after. In pursuance of promoting RB and PSL, several structural and schematic changes were introduced. Targets for expansion of branch network in rural areas and for lending to weaker sections of the society had been set and were being pursued.

'One of the outcomes of huge plan expenditure during the 1970s and 1980s was that the GOI's budget expanded and the banking sector was used to finance the fiscal deficits.' (Repeated from Chapter 4.4.2) Fiscal policy then completely dominated monetary policy; in fact, there was total dominance of the central government over RBI. RBI's autonomy had been severely dented. In order to counter the impact of deficit financing, RBI raised CRR from 5 per cent in 1973 to 15 per cent over the years 1973–1989. Besides, an additional CRR of 10 per cent was introduced in 1983. The banks also became a captive source of funds when GOI asked RBI to raise SLR. Between 1970 and 1990, SLR was raised from 26 per cent to 38.5 per cent. Thus, the two ratios combined amounted to 63.5 per cent of the bank funds, the highest ever, for several years.

6.2.1.3. Policy Reversals: Deregulation and Liberalization: 1981–2011

The sub-period '1981–1991' was the era of deregulation without a pre-planned framework. The proliferation of different lending institutions and schemes under directed credit programmes plus the operation of commercial banks including RRBs and cooperative banks had led to a complex set of interest rate structures. It was found that about 200 rates of interest were in effect by the middle of 1980s. It was then that the structure of interest rates at the short end began to be rationalized.

The vast 'banking system shift' from urban areas to rural and semi-urban areas had resulted in huge expansion of banking transactions over a much larger geography. Banks' lines of command and control got stretched to breaking point and smaller bank branches were now manned by untrained, junior personnel. The potential consequences of this serious organizational problem came to be realized in the early 1980s. RBI took up the task to consolidate the banking system and to build on the gains of the 1970s. Key elements: slowdown in branch expansion, drawing up of comprehensive action plans by banks to re-write their systems and procedures, actions to relieve policy-related constraints on bank profitability by raising coupon rates of government bonds and interest on cash balances held with RBI, allowing greater flexibility in bank service charges and strengthening the capital base of banks.

In the beginning of the 1980s, most of the financial markets were still characterized by controls, mispricing of financial products, restrictions on the flow of transactions, barriers to entry, low liquidity and high transaction costs, many of them are the characteristics of less-developed financial markets. These features severely inhibited the growth of the financial markets and reduced the allocative efficiency of the resources channelled through them.

The proliferation of directed credit programmes, the administered interest rate structure, fast (non-viable) branch expansion, substantial increases in statutory pre-emptions had an adverse impact on profitability. Monetary policy was not yet attuned to the use of market-based 'indirect' instruments.

Relaxation of controls on the financial markets including the banking system began in 1981. Several actions were initiated throughout the 1980s, particularly from the mid-1980s, which essentially started the process of liberalization of the banking system. Major policy changes were the introduction of treasury bills, recreating the money market, and rationalization and partial deregulation of interest rates. BRA was amended in 1984 to address the decline in the role of banks due to disintermediation; banks were allowed to undertake merchant banking activities through the setting up of subsidiaries. Widespread diversification into new instruments of deposits and credit was permitted. Banks were permitted to open new subsidiaries to run new financial services such as mutual funds, equipment leasing, housing finance, venture capital, factoring and portfolio management. By the end of June 1991, banks had set up 25 subsidiaries for these diverse activities. Banks were allowed to open overseas branches. Selective credit controls were dismantled. Credit Authorisation Scheme was abolished in 1989.

In contrast, the sub-period (1991–2011) was a period of wide-ranging deregulation and liberalization on a planned basis. A committee appointed by RBI in 1982 to examine the desirability of greater or full disclosure in the published accounts of banks submitted its report in 1985 and was acted upon in 1991. Two committees appointed in 1991 and 1997 to review the financial and banking systems to improve efficiency and competition in banks made sweeping recommendations to transform bank policies and systems, and the regulator's prescriptions. Most recommendations relating to income recognition and asset classification, provisioning for NPAs and investment portfolios,

CA, removing monetary authority-imposed constraints on bank performance, deregulation of interest rates, lending limits and methods, branch licensing policy, allowing new banks into the private sector and others were accepted and implemented. Meanwhile, it seemed that targeting of RB and PSL had been relaxed.

> In this period, technology had broadened the horizon of banking business and, in the context of deregulation, it contributed to the emergence of a more open, competitive and globalised financial market. While it has contributed to improvement in efficiency of banking operations, it has also necessitated the need for increased prudence in managing those operations.[1]

At end-March 2011, the banking sector continued to be stable. It was 'adequately capitalized'.[2] But tomorrow is another day.

III. NATIONALIZATION OF BANKS

Nationalization of banks has three aspects to consider. One is a summary of the stories leading up to each nationalization. It is part A of this section. Second is the bringing together of the comparative performance of PSBs vis-à-vis PrSBs. It is measured, in major part, in terms of comparative market shares of the PrSBs and PSBs over the full period. This is analysed in part B of this section. Third is the operation of PSBs in achieving the national purpose—the defining goal of nationalization. This concept is taken up in Section IV.

6.3. Stories behind the Four Nationalizations

6.3.1. Nationalization of Reserve Bank of India: 1948

The demand for nationalization of banks reportedly began to be made in the 1920s. The first RBI Bill was introduced in the legislature several years later. But the idea floundered as while the Congress Party in the legislature championed State ownership, the government wanted it to be set up in the private sector. Finally, RBI was set up in 1935 as a private sector unit.

When a revised Bank Bill (Bill for a Banking Companies law) was introduced in the Legislative Assembly in November 1944, one of the suggestions made in the debate was that banking should be nationalized.

After the installation of the interim government in September 1946, there was a strong demand again in the Legislative Assembly and a section of the media that the government should nationalize industries, public utilities, banks and civil aviation.

The Banking Companies Bill was then on the anvil. In the meantime, in a minute of dissent, five members of the Select Committee on the Bill observed that all banks should be nationalized at an early date and that, as a first step, Reserve bank and Imperial bank may be made State banks.

In January 1947, a member of the legislature sent notice of a resolution to the government recommending that necessary steps be taken to nationalize Reserve Bank and Imperial Bank as a prelude to nationalization of banking and insurance in India.

In February 1947, another member of the legislature moved a resolution to the effect that the RBI be taken over by the government and converted into a State bank. The member had written that the monetary organization of the country should be of national concern and should not be confined to a limited number of shareholders 'who are none but capitalists'.

On 28 February 1947, Finance Minister, Liaquat Ali Khan, announced the decision to nationalize RBI. Funnily, even after the announcement of this decision and its rationale, the first finance minister of independent India, R. K. Shanmukham Chetty, wrote to RBI Governor, C. D. Deshmukh, in early 1948 requesting the latter's opinion about the nationalization of RBI. Both, between them, indulged in 'flip-flops' on the subject.

The British Government did not allow RBI to be nationalized, although Bank of England had been nationalized in March 1946. RBI was finally nationalized in 1948, effective 1 January 1949.

6.3.2. Nationalization of Imperial Bank and Associates: 1955 and 1960

Before the State take over of RBI, the demand for nationalization of RBI and Imperial was frequently made together. Even the exchanges between the GOI and RBI often linked the nationalization of the two banks together.

On 3 March 1948, Prime Minister, Jawaharlal Nehru, wrote that decision has already been taken to nationalize Reserve Bank and Imperial Bank. The Imperial Bank discussed the issue in April and resolved that the government's proposal to nationalize the Bank was regarded as totally unjustified and unnecessary. It forwarded its views to RBI for transmission to the government. While forwarding the resolution to the government, the governor added that the nationalization would be a serious mistake.

The government considered the whole matter and in February 1949, Dr John Mathai, the new finance minister, announced that the government did not consider it feasible to proceed with the nationalization of Imperial Bank. In a Note to the bank's central board, the managing director reported a 'realistic' statement of Vallabhbhai, deputy prime minister, that the government had neither the capacity nor the means to undertake nationalization of any industry at present. The managing director of Imperial wrote post this statement that the danger of the bank being sacrificed on the altar of socialistic ideologies has receded. The reader would have noticed the flip-flops again.

The demand for nationalization of Imperial, however, continued and eventually led to the appointment of the RBEC by the GOI in November 1949 to suggest measures for extending banking facilities to rural areas. This was followed by the appointment of the Committee of Direction of AIRCSC in 1954. This latter Committee recommended the nationalization of Imperial Bank and entrusting this Bank with the responsibility for spreading banking facilities to the remote regions of the country. This Bank to be called SBI would be formed by amalgamating into it eight state-associated banks in the former princely states as its, eventually seven, subsidiaries on 10 September 1959. GOI accepted this recommendation. SBI was formed on 1 July 1955 and SBI Group in 1960.

6.3.3. The Short-lived Social Control over Banks: 1967–1968

Although the issue of resolving neglect of rural and other backward areas by banks began to be addressed after Independence, there was another issue which had not been addressed. There was apprehension that big business houses in the country might acquire control over a significant proportion of the country's banking assets and misallocating bank credit in favour of their conglomerates and consequently upset the socio-political structure of the country.

Hence, the concept of social control over banking was born in 1967. Its main object was to achieve a balanced spread of the precious resource of bank credit, especially to the poor in rural and other backward parts. But soon enough, it was concluded by the government authorities that this concept would not be allowed to operate and 14 largest PrSBs were nationalized.

6.3.4. Nationalization of 14 Banks: 1969

Contrary to the stories behind other nationalizations narrated above and below, there was no story to tell in this case. The decision to take over the 14 banks was quick and decisive. Indira Gandhi, the then prime minister, took the decision on a socio-economic rationale, and, within 24 hours, on 19 July 1969, broadcast it to the nation on 19 July 1969. The defining event of Indian banking, the single most important economic decision taken by any government since 1947, had been announced without any debate.

6.3.5. Nationalization of six Banks: 1980

Six more banks were nationalized on 15 April 1980 on administrative grounds, on the advice of the RBI.

Thus, the saga of bank nationalizations was complete. Each of them had a different reason to be nationalized. But, in the end, all these nationalizations ended up serving the national purpose. It is dealt with in the Section IV.

6.4. Public Sector Banks vis-à-vis Private Sector Banks: A Contrast by Financials: 1955–2011

In this part, the market share in significant financial parameters of PSBs is compared against those of Indian PrSBs and foreign banks for the years when the ownership of the GOI in banks changed and other relevant years so that the picture is complete up to 2011. This is shown through four Tables—6.1–6.4, for 10 select years.

Table 6.1 shows that, in 1955, the market share of public sector (SBI) in TA and branches was 25 per cent and 17 per cent respectively. This share of SBI Group in 1960 grew to 38 per cent and 34 per cent

Table 6.1 Market Share of Public Sector Banks: The Beginnings: 1955, 1960 and 1968

Serial No. (A)	Parameters	1955		1960		1968	
		Indian SCBs* (72) (₹ in crore)	PSBs (SBI) (1) (% Share)	Indian SCBs (77) (₹ in crore)	PSBs (SBI Group) (8) (% Share)	Indian SCBs (58) (₹ in crore)	PSBs (SBI Group) (8) (% Share)
1	TA	1,030	25	1,937	38	4,839	32
2	Deposits	894	25	1,732	39	4,393	31
3	Advances	497	21	1,005	29	2,870	33
4	Branches (no.)	2,772	17	4,081	34	7,321	32
(B)	Ratios	Private Sector	Public Sector	Private Sector	Public Sector	Private Sector	Public Sector
5	Leverage (equity: TA)	6.46	4.79	4.27	2.83	2.09**	2.09
6	ROA (%)	0.61	0.38	0.57	0.32	0.51	0.51

Source: Tables in previous chapters.

Notes: *Excludes foreign banks in Table 6.1 and Tables 6.2 and 6.3; figures in parenthesis are number of banks; Indian SCBs includes PSBs.

** Bifurcation between PrSBs and PSBs was not available in 1968 for items 5 and 6.

Table 6.2 Market Share of Public Sector Banks: Complete Dominance: 1969, 1980 and 1990–91

Serial No. (A)	Parameters	1969		1980		1990–91	
		Indian SCBs* (58) (₹ In crore)	PSBs (22) (% Share)	Indian SCBs (62) (₹ In crore)	PSBs (28) (% Share)	Indian SCBs (53) (₹ In crore)	PSBs (28) (% Share)
1	TA	5,532	93	47,577	95	270,152	96
2	Deposits	5,008	93	42,477	95	220,244	96
3	Advances	3,398	94	26,105	95	136,572	96
4	Branches (no.)	8,736	83	31,233	87	47,825	92
		Private Sector	Public Sector	Private Sector	Public Sector	Private Sector	Public Sector
5	Leverage (equity: TA)	3.24	1.98	1.01	1.04	1.90	2.31
6	ROA (%)	NA	NA	0.08	0.10	0.38	0.17

Source: Tables in previous chapters

Table 6.3 Market Share of Public Sector Banks: Dominance in Decline: 1991–92, 1992–93 and 2010–11

Serial No. (A)	Parameters	1991–92		1992–93		2010–11	
		Indian SCBs (52) (₹ In crore)	PSBs (28) (% Share)	Indian SCBs (52) (₹ In crore)	PSBs (28) (% Share)	Indian SCBs (47) (₹ In crore)	PSBs (26) (% Share)
1	TA	313,845	95	351,369	93	6,691,991	79
2	Deposits	246,053	95	278,689	94	5,375,743	81
3	Advances	149,483	96	161,908	95	4,103,165	81
4	Branches	48,196	92	48,824	92	75,764	84
(B)	Ratios	Private Sector	Public Sector	Private Sector	Public Sector	Private Sector	Public Sector
5	Leverage (equity: TA)	2.54	2.56	2.52	2.71	9.91	5.48
6	ROA (%)	0.31	0.30	0.38	(1.06)	1.39	0.92

Source: Tables in previous chapters.

Table 6.4 Public, Private and Foreign Sector Banks: Changing Fortunes: Market Shares: 1950, 1968, 1990–91 and 2010–11

Serial No.	Years	Foreign Banks			PrSBs			PSBs			Banking System (SCBs) (including foreign banks)		
		Number of Banks	TA (%)	Total Branches % (Number)	Number of Banks	TA (%)	Total Branches % (Number)	Number of Banks	TA (%)	Total Branches (%) (Number)	Number of Banks	TA (₹ in crore)	Total Branches
1	1950*	16	19	2.4 (66)	75	81	97.6 (2,713)	–	–	–	91	1,067	2,779
2	1968	15	10	1.7 (125)	50	61	66.4 (4,946)	8	29	31.9 (2,375)	73	5,396	7,446
3	1990–91	23	5.74	0.31 (151)	25	3.74	8.36 (4,010)	28	90.54	91.33 (43,815)	76	286,556	47,976
4	2010–11	34	7	0.42 (319)	21	19	15.77 (12,001)	26	74	83.81 (63,763)	81	7,183,523	76,083

Source: STs, Tables in previous chapters

Note: *Earliest year for which data for all the three parameters for all the bank groups is available.

respectively, but had already declined in 1968. Deposits had shown a similar trend, but advances had increased in 1968 too. In respect of two available measures of financial strength for 1955 and 1960, the PrSBs' shares were better that those of PSBs.

Table 6.2 shows that on addition of 14 banks in 1969, the PSBs attained domination; their market share in TA, deposits and advances shot up to 93–94 per cent, while, in terms of branches, their market share grew to 83 per cent. In terms of leverage, PSBs fared worse in 1969 but were better in 1980 and 1990–91. ROA had declined for the banking sector, but was better for PSBs in 1980 and worse in 1990–91. 'The year 1990–91 was the peak year for PSBs'.

Table 6.3 shows that the decline in dominance of PSBs' market share began from 1991–92/1992–93, except in branches. Their leverage had improved further but was less than the banking sector as a whole. Leverage had increased due to the impact of reforms from 1991–92; but ROA had declined for the same reason. The decline in dominance of PSBs in 2010–11 was starkly visible, as new PrSBs turned out with strong growth, financial position and financial results. PSBs are known to have better results in 2010–11, but obviously, their share had still declined.

Table 6.4 shows that in 1950, there were no PSBs. Foreign banks appear separately for the first time in the study. Foreign banks commanded 19 per cent of the TA and 2.4 per cent of the branches in the banking system. In 1968, PSBs (SBI Group) commanded 29 per cent of the TA and 31.9 per cent of the branches of the system. In 1990–91, PSBs (28) commanded 90.54 per cent of the TA in the banking system. That was the peak year for the PSBs. In 2010–11, the market share of PSBs had declined to 74 per cent of the BS size and 83.81 per cent of the branches of the banking system.

It may be noted that foreign banks had a few distinguishing features which made them different from Indian banks. Their leverage is quite often too low or too high. In the earlier years of his study, it often was nil or far too low. Their C–D ratios were usually higher than those of Indian banks. Many of them were one-office banks, all of these features yielding high ROA.

Number of foreign banks in India used to fluctuate wide from year to year. Their number was 16 in 1947. Their number remained between 13 and 17 for 20 years. It was 15 in 1968. It rose to 21 by the end of 1980s. The number rose faster in the 1990s, particularly after 1995–96. It was 29 in 1995–96, 37 in 1996–97 and 44 in 1999–2000. It began to decline from the year 2000–01 (42) to 29 in 2007–08. The number closed at 34 in 2010–11. The causes of different rates of movement in numbers were either banks' decisions or RBI's policies or both.

IV. THE NATIONAL PURPOSE

6.5. Evolution of the Idea

After 1920, the Congress Party became the principal leader of the Indian Independence movement under the leadership of Mahatma Gandhi. Its social policy was based on the idea of lifting up of all the sections of society which particularly involved improvement of the lives of economically underprivileged and socially marginalized people. It became a broad-based secular political party, with members from all religions, castes, creeds, ideologies and with political leanings from the right, left and centre. As time passed, it had become a party of members with hybrid socio-economic-political backgrounds, all joined together in the common fight for the independence of the country.

In terms of the 1934 Act, RBI was accorded a special responsibility to take steps to promote agricultural credit through the banking system. The Act provided for the establishment of an Agricultural

Credit Department in the Bank with the object of advising the governments and lending institutions on matters pertaining to agricultural credit. The above translated into predominantly an advisory and developmental role for RBI to support existing lending institutions, in enlarging the quantum of agricultural finance and improving its delivery to farmers.

It had been observed, though, that only modest beginnings had been made in the early years of the Bank, and that the activities of RBI in this sphere did not blossom till about the 50s. Even till several years later, the progress made had been negligible.

'The first demand for nationalization of banks' by the Congress Party before Independence was for the nationalization of RBI and Imperial Bank of India, very often together. The common denominator of this demand was that both the banks were symbols of the British Raj. However, status of these banks remained untouched until Independence, as the British rulers will not accept otherwise. After Independence, RBI was nationalized effective 1949, as it was intended to serve the essential economic purpose of securing coordination of the monetary and fiscal policies of the country.

The country adopted its 'constitution' for the country on 26 January 1950. The constitution resolved to constitute India into a sovereign socialist republic and to secure to all the citizens equality of status and of opportunity. This was a clear statement of the path the nation had resolved to tread. This statement gave the people of the country their 'national socio-economic purpose'.

The clamour for nationalization of banks and injection of bank credit into the rural economy since before Independence took concrete shape in the 1950s. As the era of five-year plans to achieve a socialistic pattern of society kicked-in in 1951, steps to make bank policies align with the national socio-economic goals began in right earnest.

'Imperial Bank' became SBI on 1 July 1955. The purpose was that this Bank should deploy its large resources for rural development, as had been recommended by a national committee. It was the first major step to make rural development the national socio-economic purpose of nationalization. But nothing significant had been achieved by the SBI Group by 1968.

'We conceptualize the idea of "national purpose" as the purpose to secure economic security and well-being of the extremely poor of this nation by assisting them with affordable bank finance to run their vocations'.

At the ground level, this meant broadening the geography and extending the profile of the bank customer for balanced development of the country. It was understood that the function of finance can best be managed by banks. Banks in India, before nationalization, for all practical purposes, were not into rural, tribal and other poor areas for loaning for agricultural finance and allied rural activities.

In the 1960s, the hybrid set of socio-economic-political leanings existent in the Congress Party had begun to surface on the Party landscape; opposition to nationalization of banking had sprouted within the party. A compromise called 'social control' over the banking system followed in 1967 in order to hasten the resolution of neglect of agriculture and allied rural activities. Concluding this to be a non-starter, Prime Minister, Indira Gandhi, took a bold decision to 'nationalize the 14 largest PrSBs of the country' on 19 July 1969. This action immediately achieved two goals. First, the path for spread of RB and PSL for the poor was rendered clear. Second, the nexus of 'big business' and banking industry, and, flowing there from, concentration of economic power among certain wealthy and powerful groups of people was broken. This second strategic action had prevailed until 2010–11 and seemed to have been ingrained in the national purpose of the country for the future.

This action was followed by the 'nationalization of another six banks in 1980'.

6.6. Translation of National Purpose into Achievements

The measly growth of RB and PSL from 1951–1952 to 1967 (even after the nationalization of Imperial (SBI) and its subsidiaries) is given below. Pursuit of RB and PSL, as already dealt with in Chapters 3, 4 and 5, is summed up below, first for years 1951, 1952 and 1967.

Summary Data on Bank Credit to Agriculture/Industry and Branches

	At the end of ₹ crore	Agricultural Credit %*	Credit to Industry %*
March 1951	12	2.1	34
March 1967	57	2.2	64
	Rural Branches (No.)	Per cent of Total Branches	
Dec. 1952	540	13	
Dec. 1967	1247	18	

*Note:** = Per cent of total bank credit.

In contrast, growth of these parameters from 1969 to 2011 (select years), in a vigorous pursuit of national purpose, is shown in Tables 6.5 and 6.6.

Looking at Table 6.5 for the growth of RB comprising rural branches, rural credit and rural deposits, it can be seen how their rates of change increased upwards after nationalization of the 20 banks. The upward rates began to decline during the process of deregulation and other reforms. Also, the pressure to expand into rural and other poor and non-viable geographies was eased. Branch network was pruned and consolidated. Rates of growth of credit and deposits declined and

Table 6.5 Growth of RB (1969–2011): Select Years

As at the End of	No. of Bank Offices		Credit Outstanding		Deposits		C–D Ratio (%)	
	Rural	% of Total	Rural (₹ crore)	% of Total	Rural (₹ crore)	% of Total	Rural	All-India
June 1969	1,443	18	115	3.3	306	6.3	37.6	71.9
June 1975	6,807	36	534	6.0	1,026	9.0	52.0	71.4
June 1980	15,105	47	2,643	10.7	4,644	12.5	56.9	66.1
June 1985	30,185	59	7,278	13.8	10,411	13.4	69.9	66.1
Mar. 1991	35,206	58	18,599	14.9	31,010	15.4	59.9	60.0
1991/1969 = 24 times								
Mar. 1992	35,269	58	20,692	15.1	35,750	15.0	55.4	57.9
Mar. 1996	32,981	51	29,012	11.4	61,313	14.4	58.6	47.3
Mar. 2001	32,640	48	54,431	10.3	139,431	14.7	53.5	39.0
Mar. 2006	30,610	43	126,078	8.3	226,061	10.8	55.8	71.5
Mar. 2011	33,367	36	295,814	7.3	493,266	9.2	59.9	75.7
2011/1991 = 0.95 times								

Source: Year 1969: C&F – 1, Table 3.27, p. 102; rest of the years: RBI, BSR, various years.

Note: % in Table 6.5 is the percentage of the total (all population groups) of the specific parameter.

Table 6.6 *Growth of PSL (1969–2011): Select Years*

As at the End of	Priority Sector Advances (₹ in crore)	Growth % **	Priority Sector Advances In Total Advances (%)
June 1969	504		14.9
June 1970	838	66	21.2
June 1975	2,292	173	27.5*
June 1980	7,278	218	37.0*
June 1985	19,829	172	44.9*
Mar. 1991	44,572 1991/1969=88 times	125	37.7
Mar.1992	47,318	6	37.1
Mar. 1996	80,831	71	32.8
Mar. 2001	182,255	125	35.5
Mar. 2006	548,774	201	37.2
Mar. 2011	1,337,333 2011/1991=30 times	144	33.9

Source: RBI, BSR, various years.
Notes: * Percentage is of non-food credit; ** Each growth percentage is over the preceding figure.

C–D ratio also began to stagnate. Although, we do not have any data to that effect, possibly the scope for continuous expansion in increasingly far-flung and poorer rural and other areas were narrowing.

Looking at the trend of growth of PSL in Table 6.6, these advances increased rapidly at more than 100 per cent for several years; they had grown about 88 times in 22 years of 1969–1991. But in the next 20 years of 1991–2011, they had grown 30 times. Priority sector advances as a percentage of total advances of the banking sector (SCBs) peaked at about 45 per cent, after which the percentage had declined to the 30s zone.

6.7. Financial Inclusion

When RBI introduced 'financial inclusion' in its monetary policy statement of 2005–06, it had advised banks to make available a basic banking 'no-frills' account with low or nil balances and nil charges, and to expand the outreach of such accounts to vast sections of the population in the country. Since then, the GOI and RBI had pursued the spread of this concept by the addition of new schemes and instruments of inclusion. These included the introduction of BC/BF model, promotion of financial literacy-cum-counselling, and adoption of information and communication technology (ICT) solutions for achieving greater outreach. These instruments of expansion may have a lot of scope. Future in this area may be limitless, as these methods may reduce costs, be economical to deploy and may displace brick-and-mortar branches.

At end-March 2011, the number of rural bank accounts with credit outstanding was about 4 crore; the number of rural bank deposit accounts was about 25 crore. Fuller details of achievements of financial inclusion were provided in Chapter 5 (Table 5.3). It was stated by RBI that, at end-March 2010, out of every 1,000 persons, only 99 had a credit account and 600 had a deposit account. It was stated then by RBI that the extent of financial exclusion was staggering.

Significantly high RB and PSL targets have already been achieved. It may be understood that RB and PSL shall continue to grow, although at declining rates; the rate of branch expansion in rural and semi-urban areas would also decline. But, post-2011, potential of growth of rural depositors and borrowers is still regarded to be high. Given the fact that current levels of economic development in the economically weaker regions of the country and among the very poor are still low, even small rates of growth may yield high levels of income for many. This would point to further expansion of volumes of expansion of bank business in these areas.

As already pointed out, new avenues of banking growth will open up with the innovation of financial inclusion which will be supported by the introduction of new low-cost methods. Deployment of business correspondents and new low-cost technology will largely reduce the costs of providing banking services. What may need to be done, therefore, is to ensure that access to banking services is provided to all potential borrowers and depositors. Full costs, financial as well as non-financial, of implementing the national purpose have perhaps never been ascertained. It was well known, though, that the costs of achieving this goal have been high which had made banks hesitant to spread into the rural and poor areas of the country. Financial inclusion, the new instrumentality of banking growth, will now optimize the cost-benefit of banking growth. It would be expected that growth of banking among the poor will now accelerate.

V. THE FINANCIALS: 1949–2011

Financials of the banking system (SCBs) have been analysed in preceding five chapters covering 1946/1947–1949 in Chapters 1–2, and 1950–2011 in Chapters 3–5. We may now cast a look at select financials to view an aggregate picture of their growth in the complete period.

6.8. Composition of Balance Sheet: 1950–2011

The BS of a bank, like that of any other business firm, is a living organism whose composition (structure) would change every day as new transactions take place all the time. The mix of assets and liabilities would also change with the change of management policies and strategies in the context of the changing environment of business. All asset and liability items are inter-related. Change in one would affect some others.

Changing our focus from an individual bank to the consolidated BS of the banking system (SCBs) spread over 60 odd years, it should be clear that changes in the BS of individual banks would either get aggregated or cancelled out in a consolidated BS of a group of those banks. More so, when we are looking at the consolidated BS of several banks over several years. In such cases, only macro, long-term changes would be visible. If any significant changes have occurred in the composition of the BS of the Indian banking system, it may be viewed by us from the eight main heads of assets and liabilities at the end of 1950, 1968, 1990–91 and 2010–11. The year 1950 represented a still unorganized banking system composed of a large number of strong and weak banks. The year 1968 was a slowly consolidating banking system, engaged in eliminating weak banks and working under direct controls of the regulator. The year 1990–91 saw the banking system dominated by PSBs, and, therefore, expecting even more of a homogenous BS. Finally, the year 2010–11, which was experiencing a relatively deregulated, liberal and diversified banking environment, when seven new PrSBs had joined the system, several new foreign banks had entered the system, would show a composition of a consolidated BS different from the preceding one. Furthermore, could changes, if any, be thrown up when every bank has to present a BS in a uniform format? This means that there are huge limitations on the study of the comparisons we are visualizing. Nevertheless, having recognized the limitations, we may view the comparative picture. The instrument used for comparisons is the common size balance sheet (CSBS) as represented in Table 6.7.

The BS has been divided into eight items. Some items, that is, (a) borrowings and bills payable (BP), (b) cash and bank, call money and CRR, (c) fixed assets and other assets, have been combined for their small sizes and uniform nature. Taking up 'Equity' first, it had declined to 2 per cent by 1968 and 1990–91, meaning a highly leveraged BS. The year 1950–1968 and, even more specially, 1990–91 were under close supervision and even control of RBI and GOI. A closed system

Table 6.7 SCBs' Common Size BS: 1950, 1968, 1990–91 *and* 2010–11

Assets/Liabilities Years (No. of Banks)	1950 (91)	1968 (73)	1990–91 (76)	2010–11 (81)
1. Equity	6	2	2	7
2. Deposits	87	90	81	78
3. Borrowings & BP	5	5	13	10
4. Other liabilities	3	3	4	4
Total Liabilities/Assets	100	100	100	100
5. Cash and bank (includes call money and CRR)	14	11	15	9
6. Investments (includes SLR)	38	26	28	27
7. Advances	45	60	50	60
8. Fixed and other assets	3	3	8	5

Source: Annexures to Chapters 2–5, Statements on BS.

without competition could work with a leveraged system under a government-run regime. Indian banking system has been and still is a 'deposits-oriented system'. From 87 per cent share in 1950, it had increased to 90 per cent in 1968, as equity declined. In 1991, deposits recorded a big dip to 81 per cent (in a public sector dominated system) as borrowings jumped from 5 per cent to 13 per cent, and fixed and other assets increased from 3 to 4 per cent. In 2011, share of deposits declined further to 78 per cent as equity rose to 7 per cent in the reforms era. Looking at the assets side, the dominant relationship is always between advances and investment portfolios, as these are two parameters competing for funds. Their relationship can be clearly observed from their figures. Not only that, as deposits is by far the major source of funds for banks, advances and investments are the main users of those funds. Also, as net demand and time liabilities of banks change and the prescribed rates of CRR and SLR are changed, the quantum of cash and investments would have changed. In the 1969–1990-91 period, fixed assets increased sharply to 8 per cent, as possibly due to the fast expansion of branch network and investment in computer infrastructure.

It has been observed that each BS was different in composition from others. Also that not only items on the liabilities side have inter-relationships among themselves, they have relationships with items on the assets side too, and vice versa.

It should also be noted that more and larger changes would have happened among the items within each portfolio. More changes would have happened from year to year too. For example, changes in size between shot-term and long-term deposits would have occurred frequently due to several factors, including changes in interest rates on different categories of deposits. The type of loans available to borrowers and the requirements of borrowers itself would have changed frequently too. Thus, it can be observed that an analysis of comparative BS can be a useful educative exercise.

6.9. Main Financials

Table 6.8 brings together the data on principal financials of the banking system measured on six parameters for three periods of about 20 years, each comprised in 1950–2011, on a comparative basis.

Among the six parameters, five are financial parameters. The sixth is number of branches. 'The financials of the years 1969–1990-91' were the best on five parameters. This period showed the highest CAGR in all parameters except PAT. Post nationalization, while the parameters of TA, branches, deposits and advances expanded fast due to the spread of banking into wider geography as per targets, profits were affected adversely due to higher administrative costs and lower revenues. The period of 1950–1968 was the last of the three periods in

Table 6.8 Main Financials: 1950–2011

Parameters	1949 Absolutes (₹ in crore)	1950–1968 CAGR (Base = 1949)	1969–1990-91 CAGR (Base = 1968)	1991-92–2010-11 CAGR (Base = 1990–1991)	1950–2010-11 CAGR (Base = 1949)	2010–11 Absolutes (₹ in crore)	Growth 2010–11/1949 (No. of Times)
TA	1,073	9	20	17	15.54	7,183,523	6,695
Total Branches (no.)	2,788	5	9	2	05.6	76,083	27
Total Income	37	13	21	17	17.15	571,230	15,466
Deposits	927	9	19	17	15.35	5,616,432	6,059
Credit	452	11	19	19	16.20	4,298,705	9,510
PAT	5.24	5	20	27	16.86	70,331	13,422

Source: Author.

performance. Over the full period of 61 years (1950–2010-11), CAGR on all parameters ranged between 15.35 and 17.15. 'BS of the banking system had grown 6,695 times in this period'. Branches, by their very nature and measured in numbers, had to grow by a different criterion.

6.10. Leverage Ratio: 1950–2011

6.10.1. Declining Leverage: 1950–1991

Declining leverage for 45 years, 1950–1993-94, was a special feature of the banking system. 'Its leverage ratio was 5.87 in 1949'. A decline began from 1950. It had fallen to 2.09 at the end of the period 1950–1968. The decline continued in the next period 1969–1990-91. It declined to 1.87 in 1969 and continued at below 2 until 1989–90. Contribution of additional capital in the next year raised leverage to 2.24 in 1990–91.

6.10.2 Rising Leverage: 1992–2011

Reconstruction of the BS began from 1991–92 and leverage ratio rose to 2.62 and 2.91 in 1991–92 and 1992–93 respectively as contributions to bank capital began to meet CA requirements. Leverage ratios of foreign banks were usually high. CA requirements for PSBs and old PrSBs, coupled with high leverage ratios of new PrSBs and foreign banks, added up to push average leverage ratios up. In 1993–94, leverage rose to 5.13. 'In 1994–95, it rose to 6.11, crossing 5.87 of 1949 for the first time'. Leverage fluctuated below and above 6.0, before it went up to 7.29, the highest in the period of our study. It was 7.10 at the end of 2010–11.

6.10.2.1. A Leverage Ratio under Basel III

In an attempt to increase the systemic resilience by strengthening capital standards at individual bank level, Basel III's regulatory capital framework had proposed a non-risk-based leverage ratio as a backstop to the risk-based capital requirement. It was proposed to test a minimum Tier I leverage ratio of 3% beginning 2013 capturing both on-and-off balance sheet exposures. (Repeated from Chapter 5.5.4.5)

VI. THE 21ST-CENTURY BANKS: 1946–2011 (SEVENTH AND LAST IN THE SERIES)

This section attempts a review of 42 banks whose comparative status in terms of their sizes was compiled in six tables in Chapters 1–5. This review is made in Tables 6.9–6.13 from those six tables in the series.

The oldest bank in this list is SBI whose first ancestor was the Bank of Bengal which was established in 1806. 'SBI is thus 204 years old. The youngest centurion is Bank of Baroda'—102 years old. The youngest bank in this list of 42 is 'State Bank of Travancore', which is 65 years old.

(a) Table 6.9 ranks banks by the size of their BS (TA at the end of the five select years). SBI, as expected, had retained rank 1 throughout. Ranks of other banks had changed over the years. PNB was at number 2 in 1946. Partition in 1947 costs it branches, property and cash. Its rank had fallen. But at the end of 2010–2011, it had regained its second rank. Canara Bank, Union Bank, Syndicate Bank, Oriental Bank of Commerce, Vijaya Bank, Corporation Bank and Federal Bank had improved their ranks by more than 10 positions. State Bank of Mysore had seen a decline in its rank by 16 positions.

(b) Table 6.10 ranks the banks by number of branches. SBI retained its first rank by this criterion also. Branches were opened by banks mainly according to targets fixed by RBI. Hence, not much movement in ranks is noticed. Only Union Bank of India and Federal Bank improved their ranks by 26 and 17 positions. Ranks

Table 6.9 Ranks of 42 Banks: 1946, 1949, 1968, 1991 and 2011 (According to TA)

Serial No.	Bank	1946	1949	1968	1991	2011	Serial No.	Bank	1946	1949	1968	1991	2011
1	SBI	1	1	1	1	1	23	Andhra Bank	23	20	19	14	15
2	PNB	2	5	4	3	2	24	Punjab & Sind Bank	24	27	35	21	23
3	Bank of India	3	4	3	2	4	25	Corporation Bank	25	25	24	25	13
4	Central Bank of India	4	2	2	6	7	26	Jammu & Kashmir Bank	26	30	31	29	27
5	UCO Bank	5	3	6	7	9	27	Bank of Maharashtra	27	26	15	15	20
6	Bank of Baroda	6	7	5	4	3	28	Oriental Bank of Commerce	28	34	26	20	10
7	Allahabad Bank	7	8	12	12	12	29	South Indian Bank	29	29	29	34	29
8	Indian Bank	8	9	14	8	14	30	Catholic Syrian Bank	30	32	34	35	36
9	State Bank of Mysore	9	11	20	26	25	31	Bank of Rajasthan *(figure for 1947)	31*	28	27	32	–
10	State Bank of Hyderabad	10	10	17	19	16	32	ING Vysya Bank	32	33	33	30	28
11	United Bank of India	11	6	8	13	17	33	Karur Vysya Bank	33	31	32	37	31
12	Dena Bank	12	15	9	16	22	34	Karnataka Bank	34	35	30	33	30

No.	Bank					
13	State Bank of Bikaner & Jaipur (Bank of Jaipur)	13	17	-	-	-
14	Indian Overseas Bank	14	12	13	9	8
15	New Bank of India	15	24	25	24	-
16	Canara Bank	16	16	7	5	5
17	State Bank of Bikaner & Jaipur (Bank of Bikaner)	17	14	16	22	24
18	Union Bank of India	18	19	10	11	6
19	State Bank of Travancore	19	23	18	23	21
20	State Bank of Patiala	20	18	21	17	19
21	State Bank of Indore	20	21	23	27	-
22	Syndicate Bank	22	22	11	10	11
35	Nainital Bank **(figure for Sept. 1946)	35**	36	42	41	37
36	City Union Bank	36	39	39	39	33
37	Lakshmi Vilas Bank	37	41	36	38	35
38	Ratnakar Bank	38	37	41	42	38
39	Tamilnad Mercantile Bank	38	38	40	36	32
40	Vijaya Bank	40	40	28	18	18
41	Dhanlaxmi Bank	41	42	38	40	34
42	Federal Bank	42	43	37	31	26
43	State Bank of Saurashtra	-	12	22	28	-

Source: Author.

Note: ---=merger.

Table 6.10 Ranks of 42 Banks: 1946, 1949, 1968, 1991 and 2011 (According to No. of Branches)

Serial No.	Bank	1946	1949	1968	1991	2011	Serial No.	Bank	1946	1949	1968	1991	2011
1	SBI	1	1	1	1	1	24	Bank of Maharashtra	24	21	16	14	16
2	Central Bank of India	2	2	3	3	3	25	ING Vysya Bank	25	23	34	32	28
3	PNB	3	3	2	2	2	26	Karur Vysya Bank	26	25	30	36	31
4	Syndicate Bank	4	5	7	10	7	27	South Indian Bank	27	25	24	30	27
5	Allahabad Bank	5	7	17	9	8	28	Vijaya Bank	28	28	21	18	20
6	UCO Bank	6	6	4	7	9	29	Jammu & Kashmir Bank	29	37	39	NA	29
7	Indian Bank	7	8	9	11	11	30	Catholic Syrian Bank	29	24	31	34	32
8	Canara Bank	8	14	6	6	6	31	City Union Bank	31	32	36	39	35
9	Dena Bank	8	9	10	15	19	32	Punjab & Sind Bank	31	35	38	19	22
10	Indian Overseas Bank	10	14	13	13	10	33	State Bank of Travancore	31	25	18	21	24
11	Andhra Bank	11	11	19	16	13	34	Lakshmi Vilas Bank	31	31	29	35	34
12	New Bank of India	11	28	32	22	–	35	Bank of Rajasthan (Figures for 1947)	35	21	27	31	-

No.	Bank					
13	State Bank of Bikaner & Jaipur (Bank of Jaipur)	13	10	–	–	–
14	Bank of Baroda	14	12	4	4	4
15	Bank of India	15	18	8	5	5
16	State Bank of Hyderabad	15	17	15	20	18
17	Corporation Bank	17	19	25	26	17
18	State Bank of Mysore	17	19	20	24	26
19	United Bank of India	17	4	14	12	14
20	Oriental Bank of Commerce	20	37	35	25	12
21	State Bank of Patiala	21	14	23	23	21
22	Tamilnad Mercantile Bank	21	40	40	38	36
23	State Bank of Bikaner & Jaipur (Bank of Bikaner)	23	12	12	17	23
36	Karnataka Bank	36	32	26	33	30
37	State Bank of Indore	37	30	28	28	–
38	Nainital Bank (Figures for Sept. 1946)	38	35	41	41	37
39	Ratnakar Bank	38	40	41	40	38
40	Union Bank of India	40	37	11	8	14
41	Dhanlaxmi Bank	41	43	37	37	33
42	Federal Bank	42	42	33	27	25
43	State Bank of Saurashtra	NF	32	22	29	–

Source: Author.

Notes: –=merger; NA=Not Available; NF=Not Formed.

of Dena Bank and Tamilnad Mercantile Bank declined by more than 10 positions.

(c) Table 6.11 is different. It shows the CAGR of TA of 38 banks in the four periods of our study.

(d) Table 6.12 classifies CAGRs shown in Table 6.11 into four classes.

(e) Table 6.13 lays out the movement of market share of SBI in TA and total branches of 42 banks (these 42 banks being the market) among which it has throughout been the largest bank.

Main features from Tables 6.11 and 6.12 are described below:

(a) 17 banks had recorded negative CAGR during 1947–1949, the only period in which it occurred. The list includes five banks such as PNB and SBI which were directly affected by the Partition. Out of six banks in the then princely states, three banks recorded negative CAGR. But there were another eight banks also which had shown negative growth. Two reasons may be adduced to the cases of negative growth. One, it was not only the Partition of the country; it was a particularly disturbed period of the country's history and the economy. Second, a three-year period was probably too short to recover from adverse developments. At the other extreme were Central Bank of India and United Bank of India which had recorded a CAGR of 48.5 and 42.3 respectively, the highest rates in the whole period of 1947–2011.

(b) In the '1950–1968 period', three banks recorded a CAGR of more than 20, the highest being 27.4. Those three banks were relatively small. Nainital Bank's CAGR was the lowest at 2.8.

(c) The '1969–1990-91' period recorded the highest levels of CAGR. 20 banks had recorded a CAGR of above 20. The highest was of Punjab & Sind Bank (31.50) and the lowest was of Dena Bank at 15.3.

(d) The last 'period of 1991-92–2010-11' had recorded the highest CAGR of 25.9 by Dhanlaxmi Bank; the lowest CAGR was 12.6 clocked by the Indian Bank. Eight banks had achieved a CAGR of above 20.

Table 6.11 Growth of 42 Banks by TA (1946–2011): Select Periods

Serial No.	Bank	1946 TA (₹ in crore)	1949/1946 CAGR	1968/1949 CAGR	1991/1968 CAGR	2011/1991 CAGR	2011/1946 CAGR	2011 TA (₹ in crore)
	PSBs							
1	SBI	294.39	(3.0)	8.6	20.4	13.8	13.7	1,223,736
2	State Bank of Hyderabad	12.94	15.0	6.7	18.9	18.4	14.9	106,698
3	State Bank of Travancore	5.35	(4.2)	13.7	19.0	17.2	15.7	70,977
4	State Bank of Mysore	14.41	(9.2)	8.4	17.4	17.7	13.4	52,032
5	State Bank of Indore	5.23	(1.4)	9.3	20.1	–	–	–
6	State Bank of Saurashtra	–	–	7.8	17.7	–	–	–
7	State Bank of Bikaner & Jaipur	6.37	12.8	11.4	17.9	16.2	15.2	62,954
8	State Bank of Patiala	5.23	11.1	10.6	20.6	16.8	16.0	81,286
9	Central Bank of India	42.54	48.5	7.2	15.8	14.0	14.0	209,757
10	PNB	77.81	(12.5)	12.1	17.5	16.2	14.0	378,325
11	Bank of India	69.82	(2.2)	10.9	18.4	14.7	14.0	351,173
12	Bank of Baroda	35.44	(1.0)	13.5	18.4	16.0	15.2	358,397
13	UCO Bank	41.97	29.9	6.6	17.1	14.1	13.6	163,398

(Continued)

Table 6.11 (Continued)

Serial No.	Bank	1946 TA (₹ in crore)	1949/1946 CAGR	1968/1949 CAGR	1991/1968 CAGR	2011/1991 CAGR	2011/1946 CAGR	2011 TA (₹ in crore)
14	Allahabad Bank	30.76	0.9	7.9	19.4	15.9	14.0	151,286
15	Dena Bank	10.46	(7.4)	16.4	15.3	15.6	14.5	70,838
16	Indian Bank	24.73	(2.8)	8.6	22.4	12.6	14.0	121,718
17	United Bank of India	12.82	42.3	8.4	17.2	14.0	14.6	90,041
18	Canara Bank	6.45	8.4	17.9	21.8	15.9	18.2	336,079
19	Union Bank of India	6.19	(0.4)	18.0	19.5	18.1	17.6	235,984
20	Syndicate Bank	4.26	4.5	19.3	19.6	15.7	17.6	156,539
21	Bank of Maharashtra	2.07	5.6	21.0	18.4	15.4	17.6	76,442
22	Indian Overseas Bank	8.67	5.4	14.1	20.7	15.9	16.5	178,784
23	Andhra Bank	4.07	11.9	12.6	20.9	17.6	17.0	108,901
24	Corporation Bank	3.00	0.3	11.5	22.0	22.9	18.0	143,509
25	New Bank of India	8.31	(22.4)	9.3	22.8	–	–	–
26	Oriental Bank of Commerce	1.70	(24.9)	19.1	25.3	21.0	19.3	161,343
27	Punjab & Sind Bank	3.56	(16.0)	5.7	31.5	16.4	16.4	68,550
28	Vijaya Bank	0.33	10.1	20.4	27.6	16.2	21.1	81,691

	PrSBs							
29	Bank of Rajasthan	0.77	28.4	13.1	19.8	–	–	–
30	South Indian Bank	1.55	(4.5)	13.5	17.8	21.7	16.6	32,820
31	Jammu & Kashmir Bank	2.89	(25.8)	11.3	25.2	18.9	16.2	50,508
32	Karur Vysya Bank	0.69	11.2	11.9	19.0	23.2	17.7	28,225
33	Catholic Syrian Bank	0.93	(0.7)	11.3	20.7	15.7	15.3	9,829
34	Vysya Bank	0.73	2.2	13.0	25.2	18.1	18.2	39,014
35	Karnataka Bank	0.60	2.2	16.1	20.3	20.4	18.2	31,693
36	Nainital Bank	0.53	3.6	2.8	23.7	17.4	14.4	3,292
37	Ratnakar Bank	0.38	8.1	7.8	18.5	19.0	14.9	3,230
38	Tamilnad Mercantile Bank	0.38	6.6	8.0	26.5	19.7	17.8	16,117
39	City Union Bank	0.49	(2.8)	8.2	22.1	24.0	17.2	14,592
40	Lakshmi Vilas Bank	0.39	0.0	15.5	19.8	19.4	17.4	13,301
41	Dhanlaxmi Bank	0.28	8.7	11.8	18.3	25.9	18.1	14,268
42	Federal Bank	0.03	18.6	27.4	26.2	21.5	24.7	51,456

Source: Author.

Table 6.12 CAGR of Total Assets of 42* Banks: Four Periods (1947–1949, 1950–1968, 1969–1990-91 and 1991-92–2010-11)

Ranges of CAGR (below) Period (across)	1947–1949 (No. of Banks)	1950–1968 (No. of Banks)	1969–1990-91 (No. of Banks)	1991-92–2010-11 (No. of Banks)
Negative	17	00	00	00
0–10	13	16	00	00
>10–20	07	23	22	36
>20	04	03	20	02
Actual no. of Banks*	41	42	42	38

Source: Author.

Table 6.13 Market Share of SBI among 42 Top Banks: 1946, 1949, 1968, 1990–1991 and 2010–2011

	Market Share of SBI					
	TA (₹ in crore)			Total branches (number)		
Market Share Years	SBI	42 Banks	Market Share of SBI (%)	SBI	42 Banks	Market Share of SBI (%)
1946	294	759	39	443	2,115	21
1949	269	884	30	377	2,056	18
1968	1,279	5,263	24	1,544	6,930	22
1990–91	91,511	304,189	30	7,937	41,545	19
2010–11	1,223,736	5,348,783	23	13,284	64,725	21

Source: Author.

(e) It may be concluded from a comparison of the four periods that 'the 1969–1990-91 period had shown the highest CAGRs overall'.

(f) We may also look at the 2011/1946 column of Table 6.12 which shows each bank's CAGR of the BS for the whole period of 64 years, 1946–2010-11:

    (i) No bank had recorded a CAGR of less than 13

    (ii) 13 banks had achieved a CAGR between 13 and less than 15

    (iii) 23 banks had achieved a CAGR between 15 and less than 20

    (iv) Only two banks had achieved a CAGR of more than 20; Vijaya Bank of 21.1 and Federal Bank of 24.7.

(g) Finally, we may note an interesting fact in Table 6.12: In 1946, the 'largest bank' of the top 42 banks, Imperial Bank, had TA of ₹294.39 crore. In 2011, the 'smallest bank' of the top 38 banks, Ratnakar Bank, had TA of 3,230 crore.

The reader may locate many more such interesting comparative facts in the same Table.

Table 6.13 produces the market share of SBI (Imperial in 1946), (the number 1 bank throughout), among the 42 (38 in 2011) top Indian SCBs continuously in existence since 1946 in terms of two measures of size, viz., TA and total branches. In terms of TA, the market share of SBI continued to decline from the peak of 39 per cent in 1946. It fluctuated and ended at 23 per cent in 2010–11. In terms of branches, SBI's share had increased beyond its 1946 share of 21 per cent to 22 per cent in 1968; but it ended in the year 2010–11 at 21 per cent. (It may be pointed out that the market shares of Imperial were also compared for the years 1946 and 1949 in Chapters 1 and 2, but the parameters of comparison and the groups of banks with which comparisons were made were different, hence not comparable with data in Table 6.13.)

VII. CONCLUDING THOUGHTS

In this chapter, an attempt has been made to bring together the essence of significant long-term developments in the banking system narrated in the preceding chapters. Final thoughts to wind up this study remain:

1. Significance of the much-maligned 1969 bank nationalization
2. Role of PSBs in achieving the national purpose
3. Role of transparency
4. Time for further privatization of PSBs

6.11. Significance of the Much-Maligned 1969 Bank Nationalization

Nationalization of 14 banks in 1969 was termed by some as the defining event of Indian banking. Some others termed it as unconstitutional and noted it with scepticism. Despite its achievements, some intellectuals still term it as a populist measure; some others term this step as lunatic. We term it as the 'national purpose' whose intent was to redirect resources of the banking system to the rural and other undeveloped parts of the country for equitable socio-economic development. In the then prevailing social, economic and political ethos of the country, the modus operandi of hoisting nationalization was, in retrospect, unavoidable. The achievements of nationalization have been significant. If allowed to peep into the future, more enduring benefits will be reaped in the future:

1. The CAGRs of TA (BS size) and total income of the banking system during 1969–1990-91 were the highest in the period 1950–2010-11; this gave a big push for faster growth of RB. More banks recorded higher CAGRs in this period than in any other.
2. The growth of RB and PSL had grown fast from end-June 1969 to end-March 1991. Between the two dates:

Rural branches of SCBs had grown from 1,443 (18 per cent of the total) to 35,206 (58 per cent of the total);

Rural deposits had grown from ₹306 crore (6.3 per cent of the total) to ₹31,010 crore (15.4 per cent of the total);

Rural credit outstanding had grown from ₹115 crore (3.3 per cent of the total) to ₹18,599 crore (14.9 per cent of the total);

Rural C–D ratio had grown from 37.6 per cent to 59.9 per cent; and

PSL had grown from ₹504 crore (14.9 per cent of the total) to ₹44,572 crore (about 40 per cent of the total).

'Perhaps the 1969–1990-91 period has been, and shall remain, the peak period for the development of banking infrastructure in rural, northeast and other undeveloped parts of India.' It has been noted that the growth of all the above parameters had slowed after 1991.

6.12. Performance of Public Sector Banks in Achieving the National Purpose

It is known that the burden of the huge effort to spread banking to the undeveloped parts of India fell mostly on the PSBs. They were nationalized to accomplish that. It is also known by now that these banks were made to bear huge financial cost. Soon, that cost ballooned as the priority sector loans began to fall in the irrecoverable category of advances. The tangible cost of that effort impacted the banks' financials immediately. Banks are run on public confidence. The GOI and RBI decided to hide much of the impact from banks' income statements and BS; otherwise banks would soon lose their credibility in the eyes of the public, and their customers will soon run away from them. The intangible moral cost of opacity of accounts too has been high.

'The contribution of the banking system, particularly of the public sector banking system, to achievement of the national purpose has been really huge. The contribution needed to be measured not by commercial profit–loss alone, but by social cost-benefit analysis too.' Look not at the 'net profit' alone but at the 'national purpose' also.

6.13. Restore Transparency

It would have become apparent from the remarks above that keeping negative financials hidden has a cost. Banks are known to transfer profits to secret reserves for use in times of adversity. But keeping losses as hidden is not an acceptable proposition. If doing this was unavoidable in the 1970s and 1980s, the argument is no longer valid in 2011. C-FAB considered this matter. It was appointed in 1982 and had reported in 1985. It had considered the matter of disclosure and observed in its recommendations that '[I]n Indian conditions the time is not yet opportune for practising full disclosure in respect of.... loan loss provisioning.... . The issue, however, may be reviewed in due course.' The above has been repeated from Chapter 5. We also need to repeat what we observed then (the last sentence of Chapter 5): 'Twenty-five years later, the time may be ripe for the RBI and the GOI to review this significant issue.'

6.14. Time for Further Reduction of Ownership of Public Sector Banks to below 51 Per cent

The citadel of nationalization was breached in December 1993 when a small public issue of equity was made by a PSB. This process of privatization continued thereafter, bits by small bits. It was unavoidable, perhaps; GOI needed funds to contribute to the capitals of banks it owned, to meet the prescribed CA requirements. PSBs were already being run on low leverage. Making public issues was one method to raise capital which was hardly possible then because of the weak financials of those banks. Instead, rights issues and private placements were periodically resorted to over the years 1993 to 2011. At the end of 2010–11, government shareholding in PSBs ranged roughly between 57 per cent and 85 per cent, though the laid-down minimum statutory requirement is 51 per cent. This minimum could be reduced to at a level at which the government could still be the largest owner of these banks; banks would be run by professional management.

Notes

1. TP *2001–02*, p. 2.
2. RBI, *Financial Stability Report, June 2011, Foreword.*

Decline of PSBs and Strategies for a Turnaround (2011-12–2016-17)

I. DECLINE OF PSBs

The banking system has undergone another transformation since the beginning of the 21st-century. It seems that the decline of PSBs had begun sometime in the 1980s. It was difficult for an external analyst to pinpoint the beginning of this phenomenon as the financial statements had by then entered into a period of opacity. But soon external analysts could read this trend from the published bank statements and began to publish the fact of non-disclosure of 'true and fair' positions of banks. But as the banks entered into the period of deregulation and liberalization after the implementation of the report of the CFS (1991) commenced, its recommendations regarding CA, provisioning for NPAs and transparency requirements were enforced. Banks' capital ratios improved to Basel requirements and ratios of provisions against

NPAs improved. Consequently, the published financial strength and profitability of PSBs seemingly improved.

But this nice-looking financial state of PSBs began to wane around the beginning of the second decade of this century. Since then, this decline has been seen to be worsening. The three tables, E.1–E.3, provide a snapshot of the financial state of Indian SCBs, with particular focus on PSBs.

Table E.1 details a few major macrofinancials for the year, 2010–11 (as the reference year) and three select years, 2011–12, 2015–16 and 2016–17 to provide the trend of the developments since 2010–11.

It can be seen from Table E.1 that it took the first three major parameters six years (2016–17/2010–11) to nearly double. Branches increased by about 1.5 times in the same period. One can also notice a decline of CAGR of all the five parameters YOY in 2015–16 and 2016–17 over 2011–12. Overall, CAGR over the six years was 11–12 per cent for TA, deposits and advances; that of branches was 7 per cent, while that of net profit had declined by 11 per cent.

Conclusion: A decline in the growth and performance of Indian SCBs on account of all the five parameters had been recorded by 2015–16.

Table E.2 makes for a depressing reading. It provides yearly movement of 'net profit' of four bank groups, two PSB groups and two PrSB groups, for the years 2010-11–2016-17.

Following conclusions can be drawn:

- All banks had shown profit in the year 2010–11.
- Year 2011–12 showed that one old PrSB had made a loss, which was not uncommon for old PrSBs even in earlier years.

Table E.1 *Indian SCBs' Major Macrofinancials: 2010–11, 2011–12, 2015–16 and 2016–17*

₹ in billion

Serial No.	Parameters	2010–11	2011–12	2015–16	2016–17	2016–17/ 2010–11 (Times)	CAGR 2010–11/ 2016–17
1	TA	66,920	77,327	123,148	133,491	1.99	–
	CAGR		16	12	8		12
2	Deposits	53,757	61,766	96,339	106,484	1.98	
	CAGR		15	12	11		12
3	Advances	41,032	48,438	75,329	77,839	1.90	
	CAGR		18	12	3		11
4	Tot al branches (No.)	75,764	102,377	112,252	116,106	1.53	
	CAGR		35	2	3		7
5	Net profit	626	722	233	308	0.49	
	CAGR		15	(25)	32		(11)

Sources: Items at 1, 2 and 3: TP 2010–11, 2012–13 and 2016–17; items at 4 and 5: ST 2016–17.

- Year 2012–13 did not show any loss-making bank.
- Adverse results began to spread over more than one group of banks from 2013–14. In that year, two nationalized banks and one 'old' PrSB showed losses.
- Similarly, one nationalized bank and two old PrSBs made losses in 2014–15.
- Years 2015–16 and 2016–17 were really damaging. Year 2015–16 showed 16 banks making losses: 1 SBI associate bank, 13 nationalized banks and 2 old PrSBs. RBI had become really severe in identifying NPAs in banks through an asset quality review (AQR) in 2015. It brought out high levels of underprovisioning by banks; consequently, banks had to make an increased provisioning for

Table E.2 Indian SCBs' Net Profits of Bank Groups: 2010-11–2016-17

₹ in billion

S. No.	Banks/Bank Groups	2010–11 Amt.	2010–11 No. of Banks	2011–12 Amt.	2011–12 No. of Banks	2012–13 Amt.	2012–13 No. of Banks	2013–14 Amt.	2013–14 No. of Banks	2014–15 Amt.	2014–15 No. of Banks	2015–16 Amt.	2015–16 No. of Banks	2016–17 Amt.	2016–17 No. of Banks
1	SBI Group	119	6	153	6	178	6	137	6	163	6	116	5	(14)	6
	SBI	83	1	117	1	141	1	109	1	131	1	100	1	105	1
	SBI associates profit making	36	5	36	5	37	5	28	5	32	5	26	3	–	–
	Loss making	–	–	–	–	–	–	–	–	–	–	(10)	1	(119)	5
2	Nationalized banks	330	20	342	21	328	21	233	21	208	21	(296)	21	(100)	21
	Profit making	330	20	342	21	328	21	258	19	212	20	34	8	81	12
	Loss making	–	–	–	–	–	–	(25)	2	(5)	1	(330)	13	(181)	9
3	New PrSBs	146	7	188	7	241	7	292	7	346	7	381	7	400	9
	Profit making	146	7	188	7	241	7	292	7	346	7	381	7	400	9
	Loss making	–	–	–	–	–	–	–	–	–	–	–	–	–	–
4	Old PrSBs	31	14	39	13	49	13	46	13	41	13	32	12	22	12
	Profit making	31	14	40	12	49	13	48	12	44	11	36	10	39	11
	Loss making	–	–	(1)	1	–	–	(3)	1	(3)	2	(4)	2	(16)	1
5	Total Indian SCBs	626	47	722	47	796	47	708	47	763	47	233	47	308	48
	Profit making	626	47	723	46	796	47	735	44	761	44	576	31	624	33
	Loss making	–	–	(1)	1	–	–	(27)	3	2	3	(343)	16	(32)	15

Source: ST 2016–17, Table 8.

NPAs thereafter. Banks had been made conscious to make true disclosures.

- Year 2016–17 showed 15 banks making losses: five SBI associates, nine nationalized banks and one old PrSB.
- Results of 2015–16 and 2016–17 starkly bring out the fact that, in 2015–16, 14 out of 16 banks, and in 2016–17, 14 out of 15 banks were PSBs.
- None of the 'new' PrSBs had shown a loss in any of these years.

Table E.3 shows the market share of PSBs among Indian SCBs on five major bank parameters in 2010–11, 2011–12, 2015–16 and 2016–17.

Comparisons of market shares of PSBs in 2010–11, 1991–92 and years prior to that, summarized in Table 6.3 had recorded their declining market shares. The years 2015–16 and 2016–17 in Table E.3 show further declines in all the four major parameters of the banking system. ROA showed a negative return of 0.07 per cent and 0.10 per cent in these two years.

To conclude: While the performance of Indian SCBs had declined in the two years 2015–16 and 2016–17, that of PSBs had declined comparatively sharply.

II. PERSISTENCE OF NPAS

The major cause of low performance of most PSBs that is highlighted in all the analyses is the occurrence of unusually large NPAs in the PSBs. It is intended to go into this subject below by looking at the latest available figures.

Table E.3 Market Share of PSBs: 2010–11, 2011–12, 2015–16 and 2016–17

Serial No. (A)	Parameters	2010–11		2011–12		2015–16		2016–17	
		Indian SCBs (47) (₹ in billion)	PSBs (26) (% Share)	Indian SCBs (47) (₹ in billion)	PSBs (26) (% Share)	Indian SCBs (48) (₹ in billion)	PSBs (27) (% Share)	Indian SCBs (48) (₹ in billion)	PSBs (27) (% Share)
1	TA	66,920	79	77,158	78	123,148	74	133,491	73
2	Deposits	53,757	81	61,766	81	96,339	78	106,484	76
3	Advances	41,032	81	48,448	80	75,329	74	77,839	71
4	Branches (no.)	75,764	84	80,918	83	112,252	78	116,106	78
(B)	Ratios	Private Sector	Public Sector	Private Sector	Public Sector	Private Sector	Public Sector	Private Sector	Public Sector
5	ROA (%)	1.39	0.92	1.53	0.88	1.50	(0.07)	1.30	(0.10)

Sources: 2010–11: Chapter 6, Table 6.3; 2011–12: TP 2011–12, Table IV.1, Table IV.10; 2015–16 and 2016–17: TP 2016–17, Table V.2.

E.1. Non-performing Advances Since the 1980s

It may be noted that even before 2011–12, the picture of NPAs of Indian SCBs, particularly PSBs, was not exactly rosy. The subject of NPAs of Indian SCBs had been a serious problem facing the banking industry since before 2011. Two Narasimham Committees (1991 and 1997) had made major recommendations to resolve this issue for PSBs. Action taken by the GOI on the recommendations was to repeatedly shore up the PSBs' capital by its contributions to banks' capital. Fresh capital issues and rights issues by banks were sanctioned. Partial privatization of some PSBs was also allowed. As a result, GNPAs of PSBs had declined from 23.2 per cent at end-March 1993 to 14.4 per cent of gross advances by end-March 1998. At March-end 2011, NPAs of SCBs stood at the following levels: GNPAs/Gross advances were at 2.25 per cent, and NNPAs/Net advances were at 0.97 per cent. These ratios were an improvement over those of the previous three years. Thus, a major contribution to this improvement was brought about by the GOI contributions to the capitals of PSBs and consequent increased write-offs of NPAs, and, possibly, not because of declining NPAs.[1]

E.1.1. Non-performing Advances Since 2010–11

Tables E.4 to E.6 reinforce the fact of increasing NPAs by drawing up the picture of NPAs by the subgroups of banks for the years 2010–11 to 2016–17. Table E.4 shows the GNPAs and NNPAs ratios of Indian SCBs for the seven-year period (It may be noted that GNPAs at the end of a year are arrived at by adding fresh NPAs arisen during that year to their opening balance, deducting NPAs, probably recovered, during that year and write-offs of some NPAs during that year. GNPAs and NNPAs may be regarded as the 'subjective' amounts that involve figures arrived at by estimates and judgement; these amounts are the result of additions, deductions

Table E.4 Indian SCBs' Movement of GNPAs and NNPAs: 2010-11–2016-17

					₹ in billion
Serial No.	March Ended	GNPAs Amount Outstanding	NNPAs Amount Outstanding	GNPA Ratio	NNPA Ratio
1	2010–11	979	417	2.5	1.1
2	2011–12	1,423	649	3.1	1.4
3	2012–13	1,941	987	3.2	1.7
4	2013–14	2,644	1,426	3.8	2.1
5	2014–15	3,233	1,754	4.3	2.4
6	2015–16	6,119	3,498	7.5	4.4
7	2016–17	7,918	4,331	9.3	5.3

PSBs

Serial No.	March Ended	GNPAs Amount Outstanding	NNPAs Amount Outstanding	GNPA Ratio	NNPA Ratio
					₹ in billion
1	2010–11	746	360	2.4	1.2
2	2011–12	1,172	591	3.3	1.7

Sources: ST 2016–17, Table 1: Indian banking sector at a glance; TP 2011–12, Trends in NPAs, Bank group-wise, p. 67.

and write-offs). GNPA ratios of Indian SCBs had risen every year from 2.5 per cent in 2010–11 to 9.3 per cent in 2016–17; similarly, NNPA ratios had risen every year from 1.1 per cent to 5.3 per cent. These figures for PSBs are available for years 2010–11 and 2011–12 only in STs; their GNPA ratios were 2.4 per cent and 3.3 per cent respectively, and NNPA ratios were 1.2 per cent and 1.7 per cent respectively for those years.

Table E.5 compares GNPAs of PSBs with those of PrSBs from 2010–11 to 2016–17. It can be seen that GNPAs of both PSBs and

Table E.5 Bank Group-wise GNPAs and GNPAs to Gross Advances of Indian SCBs: 2010-11–2016-17

					₹ in billion
Serial No.	March Ended	GNPAs		GNPAs to Gross Advances (%)	
		PSBs	PrSBs	PSBs	PrSBs
1	2010–11	710	179	2.3	2.5
2	2011–12	1,125	182	3.2	2.5
3	2012–13	1,645	204	3.6	2.1
4	2013–14	2,272	242	4.4	1.8
5	2014–15	2,785	337	5.0	1.8
6	2015–16	5,400	559	9.3	2.1
7	2016–17	6,847	919	11.7	2.8

Source: ST 2016–17, Table 18 under 'Other Tables'.

PrSBs rose steadily every year of this period. GNPAs as percent of gross advances of PSBs rose from 2.3 per cent in 2010–11 to 11.7 per cent in 2016–17, while those of Private Sector Banks Group (PrSBG) declined from 2.5 per cent to 1.8 per cent in 2013–14 and 2014–15, and then rose to 2.1 per cent and finally to 2.8 per cent in 2016–17. Thus, the GNPAs of Public Sector Bank Group (PSBG) had risen much faster in sharp contrast to those of PrSBG.

Table E.6 compares priority sector NPAs with those of the non-priority sector for PSBs, PrSBs and total Indian SCBs for years 2015–16 and 2016–17. Priority sector NPAs for PSBs was 25.5 per cent in 2015–16 and had declined to 24.1 per cent in 2016–17. Those for PrSBs were 21 per cent in 2015–16 and had declined to 18 per cent of the total NPAs. But non-priority sector NPAs had risen for all groups of banks, those of PrSBs being at higher percentages.

Table E.6 Indian SCBs' Sector-wise NPAs (As on 31 March 2016 and 2017)

							₹ *in billion*
		Priority Sector NPAs		*Non-priority Sector NPAs*		*Total NPAs*	
Serial No.	*Bank Group*	*Amt.*	*Per cent*	*Amt.*	*Per cent*	*Amt.*	*Per cent*
1	**PSBs**						
	2016	1,281	25.5	3,740	74.5	5,021	100.0
	2017	1,543	24.1	4,868	75.9	6,411	100.0
2	**PrSBs**						
	2016	101	21.0	382	79.0	483	100.0
	2017	133	18.0	605	82.0	738	100.0
3	**Total Indian SCBs**						
	2016	1,382	25.1	4,122	74.9	5,504	100.0
	2017	1,676	23.4	5,473	76.6	7,149	100.0

Source: TP 2016–17, p. 77 (modified).

The signs of rising stress in the banking system had become increasingly evident in the years beginning 2011–12. Stressed assets (non-performing, and restructured and/or written-off assets) of the banking system which stood at 9.8 per cent at the end of March 2012 had moved up sharply to 14.5 per cent at the end of December 2015. For PSBs, stressed assets for the same period had spiked from 11.0 per cent to 17.7 per cent.

It can be observed from the preceding analyses that ever since the two Narasimham Committees highlighted the problem of NPAs in the 1990s and prescribed their solution, the movement of NPAs had recorded fluctuating rates of change during 1992–93 to 2016–17. As noted before, GNPAs of PSBs had declined during end-March 1993–end-March 1998. At end-March 2011, GNPAs/Gross advances of

SCBs stood at 2.25 per cent and their NNPAs/Net advances were at 0.97 per cent. But a perusal of above three Tables tells us how GNPAs and NNPAs of Indian SCBs had moved up again, particularly of PSBs.

III. NPA MANAGEMENT: NEW LAWS AND STRATEGIES

Banks had been regularly making efforts with their defaulting borrowers to resolve the problem of non-repayment or delays in repayments, particularly since the 1990s. The GOI, in consultation with RBI, had resorted to legislation to get the overdues repaid. Debt Recovery Tribunals (DRTs) were set up under Recovery of Debts Due to Banks and Financial Institutions Act, 1993. But large and influential borrowers had been able to stall the progress in the DRTs. This had led to the enactment of Securitisation and Reconstruction of Financial Assets and Enforcement of Security Interest Act (SARFAESI) in 2002. It allowed banks to auction residential or commercial properties to recover loans. Several asset reconstruction companies (ARCs) were set up under SARFAESI to help reconstruction of bad loans without the intervention of courts. But NPAs went on accumulating due to administrative and/or bureaucratic and even political reasons.

RBI seemed to have finally concluded that the PSBs needed deeper analysis and new strategies and methods to recover NPAs.

E.2. Asset Quality Review

The first major step was to undertake a special RBI inspection of advances portfolios of banks called AQR on a large sample size in August 2015. AQR was a critical step in ascertaining the actual aggregate quantum of NPAs across the banking system. It covered most of the larger bank borrowers. By this, about 200 borrower accounts were identified to be classified as NPAs. As a result of this exercise, NPAs of five banks alone were estimated to be ₹126,816 crore. It meant an addition of ₹73,485 crore to the stated NPAs (GNPAs) of those banks. As a consequence of AQR, huge annual understatement of NPAs by banks was identified. In the following year, that is, 2016–17, NPAs of banks shot up to an astonishing figure of ₹252,371 crore.

E.3. Insolvency and Bankruptcy Code: Main Features

The second major step was for RBI to get Insolvency and Bankruptcy Code (IBC) enacted into a law. IBC was passed in May 2016. Its main features were spelt succinctly in an address by governor, RBI in 2017.

Addressing the inaugural session of the National Conference on Insolvency and Bankruptcy: Changing Paradigm, on 19 August 2017, Urjit R. Patel, governor, RBI, spoke at length on *Resolution of Stressed Assets: Towards the Endgame*.[2] He had encompassed the essential elements of stressed assets and the IBC. It is best to summarize those elements below.

1. The GNPA ratio of the banking system at 9.6 per cent and the stressed advances ratio at 12 per cent as of 31 March 2017, on the back of persistently high ratios in the past few years, was indeed a matter of concern. It was, indeed, a matter of concern that 86.5 per cent of the GNPAs were accounted for by large borrowers (each with an exposure of ₹5 crore and above). The challenge in dealing with the issue gets accentuated when observed against the capital position of some of the banks, particularly public sector ones.

2. Time-bound resolution or liquidation of stressed assets would be critical for declogging the bank BS. The government,

Insolvency and Bankruptcy Board of India (IBBI), the regulator under IBC Code and the RBI had been working together to comprehensively address the challenge. Specific measures had been taken to strengthen the legal, regulatory, supervisory and institutional framework aimed at the ultimate objective of facilitating quick resolution of stressed assets in a time-bound manner.

3. Recent measures addressed two key lacunae in the earlier framework: one, the absence of a hard-coded, time-bound period for resolution; and two, agency and coordination failures at banks and Joint Lenders Forums (JLFs) in pushing through viable restructuring plans.

4. The enactment of the IBC Code was a watershed towards improving the credit culture in our country. Prior to the IBC, India had seen multiple laws that governed various facets of a corporate rescue and/or insolvency process, without having a comprehensive legal framework that envisaged a holistic process applicable to troubled or defaulting companies. The IBC provided for a single window, time-bound process for resolution of the issues.

5. It was found that while 'the IBC was in place... the required action in respect of the large stressed accounts was not forthcoming on the part of the banks and JLFs. (Because) part of *the inertia was the typical (and severe) agency and moral hazard problems of not resolving NPAs when the banking sector was majorly government-owned.'* (Emphasis ours)

6. It was to address this market failure that the need for statutory backing to the RBI to direct reference of cases under IBC was considered necessary. The Banking Regulation (Amendment) Ordinance 2017, empowers the RBI to issue directions to banking companies to initiate an insolvency resolution process in respect of a default, under the provisions of the IBC, the governor had concluded. The Ordinance was later passed into an Act.

E.4. Attempts to Dilute Insolvency and Bankruptcy Code and Connected Regulations

Soon after the enactment of IBC, attempts began to dilute its main features.

1. Attempts to chip away at the landmark IBC Code had begun months after it was written into law. IBC had abolished the previous alphabet soup of regulatory forbearance. It was then provided for lenders to consider even those with one day of missed interest payments as defaulters and take all companies in default for over 180 days to National Company Law Tribunal (NCLT) (set up under IBC). RBI came under pressure to dilute this essential feature.

2. Lenders had identified around 20 out of 32 stressed assets to be referred to NCLT. But some of the defaulting power companies resorted to the courts to delay the resolution of the matters concerning NPAs. On 27 August 2018, Allahabad High Court denied relief to these power companies. On 11 September 2018, however, the Supreme Court granted interim relief to these companies, directing lenders to maintain status quo on the RBI circular (for banks to resolve these cases within 180 days). The Supreme Court was to hear the matter on 11 November 2018.

3. It was found that while 'the IBC was in place... the required action in respect of the large stressed accounts was not forthcoming on the part of banks and Joint Lenders Forums.' Part of the inertia was the 'typical (and severe) agency and moral hazard problems of not resolving NPAs when the banking sector is majorly government-owned'.[3]

Raghuram Rajan, former governor of RBI, met the Parliamentary Estimates Committee recently and submitted a Note. The Note[4] made it abundantly clear how many corporate borrowers have gamed the system, both in obtaining loans and in the resolution process. He also observed that too many loans were made to well-connected promoters who had a history of defaulting on their loans. Rajan also highlighted how numerous Indian promoters have systematically undermined the debt recovery process, whether under the earlier process of DRTs or the SARFAESI Act. 'Unfortunately, he observed, the same malaise seemed to have infected even the IBC', which was hailed as the best solution for quick resolution of NPAs. Indian businessmen had found ways to either destabilize the process or to take back their companies at steep discounts.

4. A serious issue had been raised by the GOI, recently, with the RBI for relaxation in the prompt corrective action (PCA) framework, so as to enhance the lending capacity of weak banks (PCA is a policy action guideline which comes into effect when a bank's financial condition worsens below certain limits, termed as 'trigger points'. The limits set are in the form of three financial indicators, viz. CRAR, NNPA and ROA. This means that RBI puts certain restrictions on these banks on matters such as branch expansion, provisioning levels and management compensation. The objective is to bring weak banks back to health by closely overseeing their working. Thus, the PCA framework compliments IBC to resolve the NPA problem of banks over time).

It so happens that 11 of the 12 banks, currently under PCA, are PSBs. While these banks are showing signs of improvement in their financial condition, GOI is anxious to get relaxation of PCA trigger points so that those weak banks can begin to lend. According to GOI, certain segments of bank borrowers like non-banking financial company (NBFCs) require bank funds urgently from banks. The opposite argument is that loosening the trigger points would result in accentuation of bad loans. Because of these conflicting arguments, this issue has become a bone of contention between GOI and RBI.

IV. OWNERSHIP + MANAGEMENT: NOT A GOOD GOVERNANCE PRACTICE

It is commonly accepted that NPAs have been 'the basic cause' of the decline of banks, particularly the PSBs. However, 'the root cause' of their big decline is now recognized as the ownership and control-management of PSBs by the government. Ownership and control-management of an entity are not regarded as 'best governance practice'. Lack of transparency of banks' books accentuates this problem. Several committees appointed by GOI and RBI have reported on governance issues which affect Indian banks adversely. Relevant views and recommendations of a number of such committees and experts are summarized below.

1. In their Note to the Report of the Committee on the Financial System, 1991, two members of the Committee, M. Datta Chaudhuri and M. R. Shroff, had added, 'We believe that ensuring the integrity and autonomy of operations of banks and DFIs is by far the more relevant issue at present than the question of their ownership'.[5] The Note continued:

   [I]n line with the above and the concept of self-denial by the Government of its ownership rights, which the Committee has rightly advocated, we think that the Government should not appoint its officials on the boards of public sector banks and financial institutions. The Banking Division of the Ministry of Finance, as at present constituted, should consequently be abolished,[6]'

   Later, Shroff, in an interview, had observed, 'As Prof Chaudhuri pointed out, the government representative on a bank board is not a mere joint secretary; he has the majesty of the power of the state behind him.'[7] The GOI did not take any action on this Note of Dissent.

2. A committee, chaired by P. J. Nayak, was appointed by RBI in January 2014 to review the governance of Board of Directors of Banks in India. It reported in May 2014.[8] The report deals extensively with governance issues which affected PSBs adversely. The committee's recommendations are meant to separate ownership from management by the government. Some of these recommendations are summarized from the report[9] below:

   (a) There are several external constraints imposed upon PSBs which are inapplicable to their private sector competitors. These encompass dual regulation, by the Finance Ministry and by the RBI, which goes beyond the discharge of a principal shareholder function, the manner of appointment of directors to boards, the short average tenures of chairmen and executive directors of PSBs, etc. (Recommendation 2.2)

   (b) The government needs to move towards establishing fully empowered boards in PSBs, solely entrusted with the governance and oversight of the management of the banks. (Recommendation 4.1)

   (c) All non-ownership functions, whether of a regulatory or development nature, should be transferred from the government to RBI. (Recommendation 4.7(d))

   (d) The government should consider reducing its holding in banks to less than 50 per cent, in order to restore a level playing field to PSBs in the matter of vigilance enforcement, employee compensation and the applicability of the Right to Information Act. (Recommendation 4.7.o)

3. **L. K. Jha Memorial Lecture 2017**

   Professor Vijay Joshi, delivering the 15th L. K. Jha Memorial lecture[10] had observed that 'Poor performance in PSBs is the result of the way in which they are governed.... And poor governance, in turn, stems from the disempowerment of bank boards by the government, which has proved to be impossible to alter in India's political culture.' After referring to the passage of IBC, the Banking Resolution Ordinance in 2017, and the proposed actions on recapitalization of banks, thereafter, Joshi went on to observe,

'But the basic problem of poor governance in PSBs will remain after recapitalisation, with a high chance of a return to square one in future. Radical reform of bank governance is thus imperative....' After describing what he calls a triple-track approach to solve the governance problems, Joshi observes again, 'All previous attempts to put real distance between the government and the PSBs have run into the sand.'

4. The C-FAB had concluded that '[I]n Indian conditions the time is not yet opportune for practising full disclosure in respect of secret reserves and loan loss provisioning. The issue, however, may be reviewed in due course'.[11]

V. BRINGING ABOUT A TURNAROUND

In a thought-provoking Professor D. T. Lakdawala Memorial Lecture in November 2017[12] on 'Future of Public Sector Banking', Y. V. Reddy, former governor, RBI, observed, 'I submit that the origin of public sector banking was political; it was through an ordinance; its evolution has been political and its future will, perhaps, be determined on political economy considerations.'[13] While discussing the future of public sector banking, Reddy had again observed, 'I feel that a minimum share of public sector banking in our system should be maintained for several reasons.' We summarize some of these here. 'First, large sections of people still feel more at ease with PSBs .... Second, government needs some presence ... for implementing its programmes that need to penetrate into vast sections of population in remote areas.' Third, having experienced the excess of private finance, there is a need for countervailing forces to the private finance.'..... Reddy also suggested that there should be a minimum share of public sector banking that is essential for strategic reasons.[14]

The sum and substance of the recommendations made in expert committee reports and expert lectures in Section IV, above, is that corporate ownership at above 50 per cent of each PSB coupled with management of those PSBs leads to a triad of politician-bureaucrat-business nexus in practice. It leads to misgovernance and misperformance of PSBs. The solution may lie in reducing ownership to below 50 per cent, may be a minimum of 25–30 per cent (to keep ownership at a level of healthy participation in PSBs management by government representatives), at the same time to induct professional skilled management to run the PSBs. This will help bring about a turnaround in the PSBs' performance and, at the same time, allow the government-stakeholder to keep a tab on the operations of PSBs. If implemented, these suggestions should hopefully transform into an era of positive performance for PSBs.

Notes

1. Based on Chapter 5, 183–184.
2. Patel, *Resolution of Stressed Assets.*
3. Ibid., (Underlined by us).
4. Rajan, Raghuram. *Live Mint*, 16 September 2018.
5. *Report of the Committee on the Financial System*, 145.
6. Ibid., 145–146.
7. *The Economic Times*; also see Chapter II, F.
8. Nayak, *Report of The Committee to Review Governance.*
9. Ibid., 4–5.
10. Joshi, *India's Economic Reforms.*
11. RBI, *Report of Committee to Consider Final Accounts of Banks*, Chapter 5.A.1.
12. Professor D.T. Lakdawala Memorial Lecture on 'Future of Public Sector Banking', Institute of Economic and Social Research, 17 November 2017, Ahmedabad.
13. ibid., 4.
14. ibid., 28–29.

Statistical Tables Relating to Banks in India since 1913
A Critique

I. INTRODUCTION TO STATISTICAL TABLES

Statistical Tables Relating to Banks in India (ST) was brought out for the first time by the department of statistics of the Government of India (GOI) in 1915 for the years 1913–1914. The opening statement of its Introductory Memorandum read: 'The object of the statistical tables appended to this memorandum is to show in detail the latest available statistics relating to banking, and the results of a statistical enquiry into bank failures in India in 1913 and 1914.' It was an important landmark in the history of Indian banking, as the official gathering and disseminating of banking data became an annual feature thereafter. After publishing it for 25 years, the GOI entrusted this task to the Reserve Bank of India (RBI) in 1939, being the 'appropriate authority' to collect and publish banking statistics in the country.

It is significant that this essential data bank continues to be published for the last 100 years or so and remains as the only official source of Indian banking statistics. This publication and the *Report on Trend and Progress of Banking in India*, another annual publication of RBI, are the twins which serve the important role of pre-eminent sources of annual data and developments in the Indian banking system.

II. CHANGING CONTENTS OF STATISTICAL TABLES

A.1. Statistical Tables Contents: 1913–1948

The first Companies Act in India was passed in 1913, the same year for which first Statistical Tables data became available. There were no special provisions applicable to banks in the Companies Act, 1913. The government sought data from banks and banks, not all of them necessarily, submitted partial data at their will. Bank data was also collected from bank statements published, if any, in the media. Contents of the first ST, that is, ST 1913, comprised the balance sheet items of capital, reserves, deposits and cash balances of a few bank groups, with no income and expenditure data. This practice continued, more or less on a uniform basis, until 1936 when an amendment to the Companies Act, 1913, was passed to incorporate a chapter on banking companies. This enabled the GOI to collect, and the annual STs to publish information on advances and investments of banks also. Subsequently, RBI, on taking over the task of publishing STs from 1939, began to ask banks for some additional information under the Reserve Bank of India Act, 1934. In 1946, ST included the profit and loss account of banks also, but only in aggregate for all SCBs. The BS details, though incomplete, were available for Imperial Bank, other

Indian SCBs in aggregate and all SCBs together. This was the status at the time of Independence and lasted till 1948.

A.2. Statistical Tables Contents: 1949–1988-89

The passing of the Banking Companies Act (BCA), 1949, transformed the scenario. Since then, this Act, and regulations and rules framed thereunder have prescribed the contents of published financial statements. By far the major content of STs since 1949 has consisted of the two financial statements of all SCBs and a few sub-groups of SCBs, aggregated together. As stated elsewhere, it was a practice (until 1991–92) to show the two contingent items, 'bills for collection' and 'acceptances, endorsements and other obligations' as per *contra*, that is, on both sides of the BS. But interestingly, it was found for the year 1949, as published in ST 1950, that some bank groups' BS totals included figures for these contingent items, while for some others, BS totals excluded these two items. This would have caused confusion to the readers.

As for bank-wise financial statements, these were not published in STs between 1947 and 1970, although some statistics about some banks or the other were published annually. SBI (Imperial Bank until 1954) was the one exception to this, perhaps because it had enjoyed a special status since its inception as Presidency banks, and it was by far the largest bank of the country and was regularly providing its financial statements to RBI. Bank-wise PLA details of PSBs began to be published from 1971 and continued until 1988–89. But individual PrSBs' PLA details were not published. BS details of individual SCBs (except SBI) were not published. This ST inconsistency was resolved from the year 1991–92 when bank-wise PLA and BS details of all SCBs began to be published; these continue to be published to date.

A.3. Statistical Tables Contents: 1989-90–2010-11

In March 1982, RBI appointed a Committee 'to Consider Final Accounts of Banks' (called Ghosh Committee) to review the published financial statements of banks with a view to their better presentation and greater disclosure. The Committee's report was submitted in 1985, but was implemented from 1991–92. Henceforth, bank financial statements were to be presented in a vertical format. The formats were to be summarized statements of significant items of assets and liabilities and income and expenditure; details were to be provided by way of schedules to those statements. The format apart, the significant matter was that the contents of some items in both the BS and PLA were changed. These changes are described below.

The published BS data had followed a single format, as prescribed by law over the period 1949–1990-91. This format allowed actual details of assets and liabilities, which had changed from time to time, to be incorporated into it. The BS format was overhauled by law from 1992, as stated *supra*.

The PLA format was changed from time to time, five times mainly, during the entire period. The BCA, 1949, had prescribed a PLA format since it came into effect, until 1992, when the format under the law was completely revised which remained in effect till 2010–2011. But the contents of PLA were changed in STs frequently by RBI, sometimes drastically, so that a single format could not accommodate all the changes; hence, the formats underwent changes.

A.4. Bank Groups

While the contents of both the BS and PLA described above could be viewed vertically as items of assets and liabilities and of income and expenditure, another type of change had to be shown in additional columns. This was the change in the number of bank groups which appeared in different years.

A.5. Changes in the Contents of Balance Sheet and Profit and Loss Account

Changes in the contents of BS and PLA need to be described in some detail.

A.6. Contents of the Balance Sheet

BS content had changed little over the period 1949–1990-91. Substantial changes were, however, made effective in the accounting year 1991–92, as stated supra. Apart from the change in the manner of its presentation, already mentioned, two major changes were made in the BS content:

1. Two items, viz., acceptances, endorsements, and other obligations, and bills for collection, were, hitherto, being shown as contra items on the BS. These were contingent liabilities and contingent assets simultaneously. These were removed from the BS and shifted to be shown in notes to the BS.

2. Treatment and placement of provisions in the BS were revised to improve its presentation without improving BS transparency. As a result, the contents of major items of investments and advances on the assets side, and deposits and provisions and contingencies on the liabilities side underwent changes. As a result, the BS till 1990–91 became non-comparable with the BS from 1991–92.

A.7. Contents of Profit and Loss Account

As noted supra, PLA content in STs has been changed five times over the period 1946–2010-11:

1. 1947–1948. The first format of PLA from the year 1946 included a long list of items of income and expenditure, as published by banks. There was no law or regulations prescribing a format.

2. 1949–1965. The changes made under the BCA reduced and reorganized the items of income and expenditure. This format prevailed up to the year 1965, although a slight change in PLA contents was made from 1951.
3. 1966–1969. ST decided to discontinue publication of income and expenditure details as per the legal format to replace it with a different set of items culled from Form A2 from the year 1966. This form was secured by RBI as a special return from banks and contained a different classification of items of income and expenditure. The rationale for this change was provided in the paragraph eight of the Introduction to ST 1967. Briefly, it said that the previous published PLA (of the year 1965 and earlier) showed net profit of banks after making several undisclosed provisions and, perhaps, creating secret reserves. Hence, the disclosed net profit was not the true figure of a year's profit. This was a fact. But the new format gave rise to three new issues: (a) The new PLA format had deviated from the legally prescribed format; (b) The new format condensed the bank group details to Indian SCBs, foreign SCBs and the aggregate of the two, that is, TSCBs, only, thus even eliminating details of SBI, which had been published since 1947; (c) But the most important issue was that it created a major anomaly: the duration of the new PLA would be from the last Friday of year-1 to the last Friday of year-2, which would not be a consistent period of 12 months, but a period of less or more than 12 months from year to year. The issues made the PLA data non-comparable from year to year.

Realization of these mistakes perhaps made RBI to discard this format from the year 1970.

1970–1990-91. The new format from the year 1970 created another issue. It was condensed and combined into only three heads of income and three heads of expenditure, almost totally shorn of detail. This continued till the year 1978.

1991-92–2010-11. Like the BS change from 1991–92, the changes in the PLA effective 1991–92 in the manner of showing provisions and contingencies changed its contents hugely. These changes were implemented as a result of recommendations of Ghosh Committee.

III. ERRORS OF OMISSION AND COMMISSION

During the 26 years, 1913–1938, that the GOI published ST, 25 volumes were actually published, as the years 1915–1916 were combined to produce a single volume.

During the 72 years (1939–2010-11) of publishing by RBI, ST had passed through several vicissitudes:

1. During 1939–1945, RBI combined two years' ST into single volumes three times, twice due to, as stated by RBI, the shortage of paper in the WWII years.
2. During 1946–1987, ST was published every year with a usual time-lag of about two years, sometimes three years; but the volume for the year 1987 was out in 1991.
3. The accounting year for banks was changed from the calendar year to the financial year, that is, from 01 April of a year to 31 March of the year following, in 1988. Therefore, the first volume after 1987 was produced for the 15-month period of January 1988–March 1989.
4. Between the 5 years, 1989-90–1993-94, ST was not published for three years, viz., 1989–90, 1991–92 and 1993–94 (and never acknowledged). This had not happened before and has not happened since.
5. Between 1992–93 and 1998–99, ST volumes were incorrectly numbered in all the six years of its publication.

6. The three volumes for 1992–93, 1994–95 and 1995–96 were all published in 1998, and the three volumes for 1996–97, 1997–98 and 1998–99 were all published in 1999. This acceleration made up the past delays in publication and brought ST up to date.

7. Prior to official implementation of the recommendations of Ghosh Committee in 1991–92, it seems ST attempted incorporation of some of the Committee recommendations into its BS format in ST 1990–91. It made a mess of it. It could not handle the implementation of contra items and some other details.

8. Thus, the years 1989–90 to 1998–99 were the 10-year period of turmoil for STs. Their publication was delayed, misnumbered and even missed.

9. It seems that the change in the accounting year from the year 1988–89, the major change in contents and formats of financial statements from 1991–92, possibly the big change from manual data entry to computerization of bank data in the 90 s caused the preparation of ST volumes to go higgledy-piggledy.

Regularity was restored from the year 1999–2000. The 1999–2000 volume was numbered correctly and published well in time—in November 2000, that is, in eight months from the end of the year—and since then every subsequent volume has been produced within 8–9 months of the expiry of the relevant accounting year.

Thus, out of the maximum possible number of 98 volumes from 1913 to 2011, eight years were combined into four two-year volumes and three volumes were not published. In all, 91 volumes of ST had been published up to 2010–11.

IV. CONCLUDING REMARKS

The first ST published by RBI in 1941 had observed in its Prefatory Note that 'special care, however, has been taken to see that statistical continuity is maintained as far as possible with the previous ....' issues of the ST. But it had often failed to maintain that statistical continuity in producing this important publication during its history so far. Going often against the legal contents, RBI broke this essential attribute for ensuring inter-year consistency and comparability of financial data for analysis and policymaking.

The changes brought about from 1991–92 were a major positive contribution to improvement in content and presentation of, but not better disclosure in, financial statements of banks.

This piece of research overcomes most, if not whole, of the weaknesses of data quality by deciding to restrict the study to the main, significant heads of income and expenditure, and assets and liabilities of the two financial statements. This has enabled us to harmonize the data on a common pedestal.

Bibliography

A. Publications of Reserve Bank of India

RBI. *Statistical Tables Relating to Banks in India (1939–2017)*. Mumbai: RBI.

GOI. *Statistical Tables Relating to Banks in India (1915–1938)*. Calcutta: GOI.

RBI. *Report on Trend and Progress of Banking in India (1949–2017)*. Mumbai: RBI.

RBI. *Report on Currency and Finance (2006–2008)*. Vol. 1. Mumbai: RBI, 2008.

RBI. *History of the Reserve Bank of India (1935–1951)*. Vol. 1. Bombay: RBI, 1970.

RBI. *History of the Reserve Bank of India (1951–1967)*. Vol. 2. New Delhi: RBI, 1998.

RBI. *History of the Reserve Bank of India (1967–1981)*. Vol. 3. Mumbai: RBI, 2005.

RBI. *History of the Reserve Bank of India (1981–1987)*. Vol. 4. New Delhi: RBI, 2013.

Other Publications-

RBI. *Annual Report (1947–1950)*. New Delhi: RBI.

RBI. *Basic Statistical Returns of SCBs in India (various years)*. Mumbai: RBI.

Handbook of Statistics on the Indian Economy, Annual

RBI. *Mid-term Reviews of Monetary and Credit Policy* (periodic, every year). Mumbai: RBI.

RBI. *Financial Stability Report (semi-annual)*. Mumbai: RBI.

RBI. *Report of Committee to Consider Final Accounts of Banks*. Mumbai: RBI, 1985

The Reserve Bank of India Act, 1934.

RBI. STs, 'Statistics at a Glance', 1967–2010-11.

B. Reports, Books and Articles

Chawla, O. P. 'Financial Statements of Public Sector Banks: Law, Facts & Fiction'. *The Economic Times*, April 26, 1990.

——'Bank Annual Reports: Non-disclosure and Distortion of Profits: 1979–1984'. *Financial Express*, July 12, 1990.

——'Turnaround in Nationalised Banks: Looking beyond Illusions'. *Business Standard*, The Money Manager, 26 October 1995.

——'Window-Dressing: Opening up the Windows'. *The Economic Times*, August 8, 1996.

GOI. *Report of the Indian Central Banking Enquiry Committee*, 1931.

Joshi, Vijay. India's Economic Reforms Reflections on the Unfinished Agenda (Fifteenth L K Jha Memorial lecture). Reserve Bank of India, 11 December 2017.

Krishnan, R. *History and Scope of Banking Legislation in India* (Technical Studies prepared for the Banking Commission). Vol. II, 374–382. Bombay: Reserve Bank of India, 1972.

M. Narasimham. *Report of the Committee on the Financial System* (mimeo). Government of India, Ministry of Finance, 1991.

M. Narasimham. *Report of the Committee on Banking Sector Reforms*, Government of India, Ministry of Finance, 1997.

Nayak, P. J. *Report of The Committee to Review Governance of Boards of Banks in India*. Mumbai: RBI, 2004.

Ninan, T. N. '1974—The Invisible Turning Point'. *Business Standard*, 27 October 2014.

Patel, I. G. *Glimpses of Indian Economic Policy: An Insider's View*. New Delhi: Oxford University Press, 2002.

Professor D T Lakdawala Memorial Lecture, Sardar Patel Institute of Economic and Social Research, 17 November 2017, Ahmedabad.

Rajan, Raghuram. *Live Mint*, 16 September 2018.

SBI. *The Evolution of the State Bank of India: The Era of the Imperial Bank of India (1921–1955)*. Vol. 3. Mumbai: State Bank of India & SAGE Publications, 2003.

Shahi, Ujjawala. *Banking in India, Past, Present and Future*. New Delhi: New Century Publications, 2013.

Tandon, Prakash. *Banking Century: A Short History of Banking in India and the Pioneer—Punjab National Bank*. New Delhi: Viking, 1988.

Tannan, M. L. *Tannan's Banker's Manual*. Vol. 2, 24th ed. Gurgaon: Lexis Nexis, 2011.

The Economic Times, interview of Manu Shroff by Ms Sucheta Dalal, 18 December 1991, Mumbai.

Index

About the Author

Om Prakash Chawla, MCom, PhD, is a former director and professor of NIBM, Pune. He was the director, NIBM, during 1991–1994 and professor at NIBM during 1980–1994.

Dr Chawla had a brilliant academic career at Birla College at Pilani, from where he topped in the BCom and MCom degree examinations of the University of Rajasthan. He remained a teacher in his entire career from 1955 to 1994. Much of his academic career from 1955 to 1975 was spent in the Universities of Rajasthan and Udaipur, first as a lecturer and then as a reader in the Faculties of Commerce and Management. He secured his PhD degree on personal taxation in India. It was published as a book in 1972. He moved from Rajasthan to Bombay (later, Mumbai) to join the NIBM in 1975 in the disciplines of bank finance, credit management and allied academics. In this tenure, he pioneered studies in bank treasury management and bank balance sheet management. Dr Chawla conducted several professional training programmes, seminars and conferences for top managements of banks. He has participated in several conferences and seminars abroad.

He was the founder-president, Bankers' Investment Dealers Club, an association of money and securities market dealers of banks, established to activate the dormant treasuries of banks. He was a member of several RBI and Indian Banks Association Committees.

Dr Chawla has authored/edited 10 books, most of which were published by NIBM. He has published many papers in journals, Indian and foreign, and in financial newspapers.

He spent two years, 1979–1980, abroad as a consultant in financial systems and public finance, Commonwealth Secretariat, London. In this capacity, he taught at the Eastern and Southern African Management Institute, Arusha, Tanzania. He went back to that Institute as a consultant for tenures of two to six weeks during 1981–1983.